· THE SHELL GUIDE TO ·
THE ISLANDS OF BRITAIN

• THE SHELL GUIDE TO •
THE ISLANDS OF BRITAIN

NORMAN NEWTON

Islands are bits of the land
that prefer their own company,
recluses that sea and wind
address in peculiar accents.

ANGUS MARTIN

David & Charles

(Page 2) Lobster pots and the inter-island ferry at
Gutcher, on the Shetland island of Yell (*Sue Anderson*)

British Library Cataloguing in Publication Data
Newton, Norman
    The Shell guide to the islands of Britain.
    I. Title
    914.104

    ISBN 0-7153-9883-0

Typeset by Ace Filmsetting Ltd, Frome, Somerset
and printed in Great Britain
by Butler & Tanner Ltd
for David & Charles
Brunel House Newton Abbot Devon

Contents

Introduction   6

Part I The Island Context
1   The Archaeology of Islands   20
2   Holy Islands   32
3   Island Folklore   43
4   Island Communications and Tourism   52
5   Dispersal and Emigration   64
6   Island Government   74
7   Living on an Island   82

Part II Island Groups
8   The Northern Isles   96
9   The Western Isles: the Outer Hebrides   108
10 The Western Isles: the Inner Hebrides   129
11 The Clyde Islands   169
12 The Irish Sea Islands   182
13 The English Islands   196
14 The Channel Islands   207
15 Concluding Thoughts   220

Acknowledgements   221
Index   222

Introduction

THIS book is a celebration of the islands of Britain in all their variety and diversity. To visit them all involves travelling throughout the length and breadth of the British Isles, for islands, large and small, are found all around our coasts.

THE SELECTION PROCESS

The literature of islands is vast, although only a relatively small number of books about islands is in print at any one time. In order to prevent this book from growing into a multi-volume encyclopaedia, the hundreds of small uninhabited islets, some no more than overgrown rocks, which surround the British coastline, have been omitted. Also omitted, for the most part, are islands that are inhabited, usually seasonally, by naturalists and bird wardens. Nor have I included all the islands, mainly along the south coast of England and in the Thames estuary, which are connected by road to the mainland. Part of the charm of islands is getting there, preferably by ferry. Of course, many islands have airports, which are a great boon for people with weak stomachs or a shortage of time, but to approach an island by sea has the great advantage of giving you time to relax, unwind, leave your troubles behind, and generally whet your appetite for the island experience to come.

There are three exceptions to the 'no connecting roads' rule: Anglesey and its Holy Island, because they are so interesting, historically important and unmistakably insular, and Seil Island off the west coast of Scotland, which is connected to the mainland by its eighteenth-century 'Bridge over the Atlantic' – a gift to the local tourist board. And *if* the long-planned bridge over the sea to Skye is ever built, then the misty Isle of Skye – to many people the epitome of a Scottish island – will become an exception too.

This selection procedure still leaves nearly one hundred islands, which are inhabited by about 500,000 people. Of these, 400,000 live in the Channel Islands, the Isle of Wight, Anglesey and its Holy Island, and the Isle of Man. Thus, 20 per cent of the islanders of Britain live in sparsely populated, often remote places, and there is no doubt that these 100,000 people are a special breed, with special characteristics which other Britons find appealing.

So this is not an encyclopaedia of island Britain, nor a gazetteer of the hundreds of islands, large, small and tiny, which lie off Britain's coasts. Islands appeal to different people for different reasons and some of the commoner themes are explored in the first part of this book. For people who are interested in the natural environment of Britain – the rocks, flora and fauna – islands offer the chance to study and enjoy an ecology which usually has changed little since the end of the last Ice Age. For archaeologists and students of the early history of the islands around Britain, there are many places where prehistoric or monastic sites, castles and crofting villages survive better than at most mainland sites of the same period.

THE ATTRACTION OF ISLANDS

Islands were often a focus of religious activity, not only in early Christian times, but in the even earlier, prehistoric period. Whatever it was that led the Druids to Anglesey and the early Christian saints to places like Iona and Lindisfarne, part of that attraction survives today, as proved by the hundreds of thousands of visitors to those places. One perceptive line of analysis even sees the flocking of day-trippers to these locations as an instinctive secular pilgrimage.

Island folklore preserves something of the magical environment in which even the mainland population of the British Isles once lived. Many of the tales and legends, customs, rituals and even relatively modern ceremonials are a fascinating subject for study. The discovery of Britain's offshore islands as interesting places to visit dates to the late eighteenth century and became a major industry in the Victorian period. Some of the history of island tourism, with some of the issues raised, are discussed in Chapter 4. The dispersal and emigra-

Calmac's *Lord of the Isles* at Castlebay, Barra, sharing the pier with some of the local fishing fleet

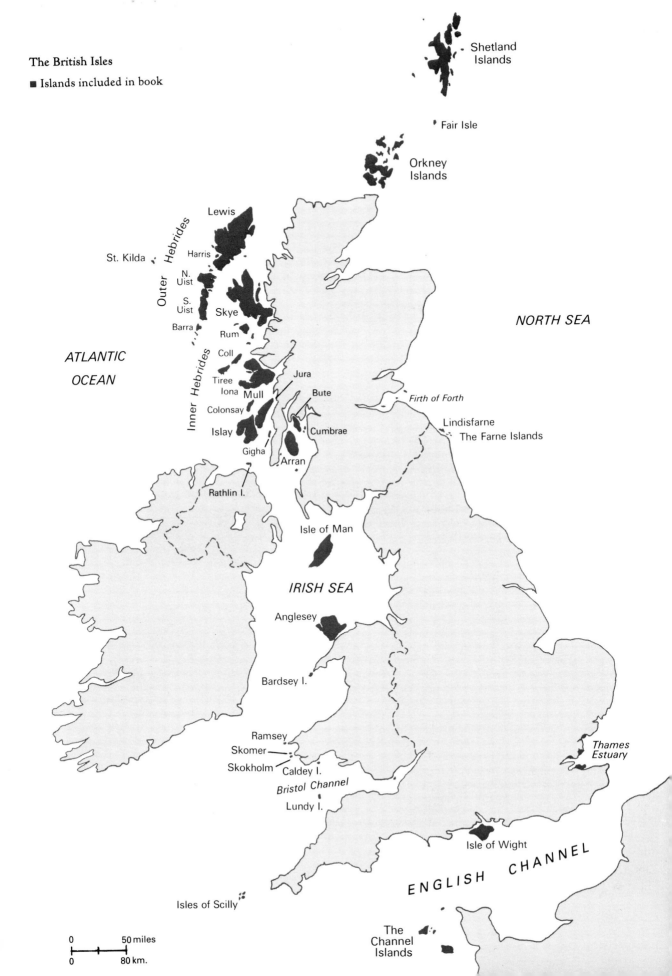

The British Isles

■ Islands included in book

Shetland Islands

Fair Isle

Orkney Islands

NORTH SEA

Lewis

Outer Hebrides

Harris

St. Kilda

N. Uist

S. Uist

Barra

Skye

Rum

Coll

ATLANTIC OCEAN

Inner Hebrides

Tiree

Iona

Mull

Colonsay

Islay

Gigha

Jura

Bute

Cumbrae

Arran

Firth of Forth

Lindisfarne

The Farne Islands

Rathlin I.

Isle of Man

IRISH SEA

Anglesey

Bardsey I.

Ramsey

Skomer

Skokholm

Caldey I.

Bristol Channel

Lundy I.

Thames Estuary

Isle of Wight

ENGLISH CHANNEL

Isles of Scilly

The Channel Islands

0   50 miles

0   80 km.

tion of island populations, especially in the middle of the nineteenth century and especially from Scottish islands, is also a theme which reverberates strongly today. In this historical and social context, some of the problems affecting life in the islands around Britain today are also examined in some depth.

The government of the various islands off the British coasts is often grounded in centuries of history and tradition and is an interesting study in its own right. The Channel Islands and the Isle of Man are not part of the United Kingdom, do not send representatives to the Westminster parliament and have their own systems of government. They are, however, Crown possessions, owing allegiance to the monarch who occupies the British throne. With the entry of Britain into the European community, several areas of life have become more complex and no doubt further adjustments and 'harmonisation' will be required. But the Brussels Commission, which has been very supportive of cultural minorities throughout the community, can surely accommodate some of the anomalies which make life difficult for its bureaucrats and Eurocrats. Most islanders, especially where they are vulnerable to day-trippers, will have wished sometimes that special passports and regulations could be used to control the hordes of visitors, but in fact UK citizens do not require documents of any kind to visit any of Britain's offshore islands. The Scottish Tourist Board, exploiting this idea, has an 'Island Passport' scheme under which tourists are invited to take a 'passport' to island post offices for stamping, with the possibility of entering a draw for prizes when enough stamps have been collected. It is a popular scheme with tourists but not with island post office staff.

There is no doubt that islands have a universal appeal, particularly to children and holidaymakers, and many people have written and speculated about their attraction and influence. An excessively psychoanalytic explanation would have it that the experience of being surrounded by water, preferably sea-water, in some way re-creates the universal experience of being in the womb. Others see islands as excessively romantic places, conditioned, perhaps, by some childhood experience or by television holiday programmes. Apparently, almost everybody is attracted by islands, would like to visit them, spend their holidays there and, in some cases, actually to make their home on one.

ISLAND LIVING

The influence of these ideas and feelings about islands in our culture is considerable, especially on islands and islanders, who have to bear the brunt of fulfilling tourists' emotional needs, if that is what they are. But what do islanders think of all this? How does living on an island affect *them*? Some answers are perhaps to be found in two classes of people. The first, which is much more numerous, consists of islanders who have had to move to the adjacent mainland, or perhaps much further afield, for strictly practical reasons involving housing, employment, further education, marriage and career opportunity. They are often bitter when they leave, have no desire to return home and are scathing about the mainlander's rose-tinted view of what islands are all about.

The second class of people who can speak from personal experience about island living and what it means for them, are the minority who uproot themselves and their families from secure mainland jobs, sell up their houses, cars and possessions, leave their particular rat-race in a glow of self-congratulation and moral superiority, and go to live on the island of their dreams. However, as well as having devastating effects on fragile island societies and economies, such incomers frequently have devastating effects on each other. The few – and

Oban Bay from Pulpit Hill, the gateway to the Hebrides: Calmac's *Isle of Mull* and *Lord of the Isles* are berthed at the South Pier, adjacent to the railway station

they are numerically a very small number – who settle 'permanently' in their new homes, are usually tough, self-reliant, resourceful, flexible, determined, stubborn and lucky. The many who stay for a few years and leave in a state of exhaustion, bewilderment, impoverishment and bitterness, are far more typical of island incomers.

Of course, money helps. Especially, it helps to make it possible to get away from some aspects of island life which incomers find most difficult, which seem to be, in no particular order, the

weather, tourists, other islanders and an occasionally suffocating sense of isolation. If you are very, very wealthy, you can even buy your own island, and this is indeed something which very, very wealthy people seem to like to do. It is not difficult for them to find up-market estate agents who are willing to make it possible to buy, at ridiculous prices, a few acres of useless grazing surrounded by water, which, to the local population, is a barren wasteland with no productive value. More worrying is the fact that from time to time populated islands

developed to cater for these temporary visitors. Modern ferries cross stretches of water that range from a few hundred yards of the sheltered waters of the Solent to the rough waters of the Minch or the Pentland Firth. In one or two cases visitors can drive on to their island over a bridge, as to Anglesey, or to Seil Island in the Firth of Lorne, which is approached by 'the bridge over the Atlantic', but even this accessibility has not ruined the island experience in either of these places, while the causeways that connect tidal islands to the mainland or to other islands seem only to increase their particular appeal. There are even parts of the industrialised islands of the Thames which still have a distinctive charm.

HOLIDAY INFORMATION

The second part of this book is not a comprehensive gazetteer, but considers all the islands off Britain's coasts in groups: the Northern Isles, the Inner

A thatched cottage at Sorisdale on the island of Coll, on the site of a Viking homestead

come on to the market and are purchased, whether for tax purposes or to satisfy some deep psychological need, by wealthy absentee landowners.

Going for a holiday break, whether to the Isle of Wight or to a remote Hebridean island, allows people to participate in these feelings and emotions in a temporary 'safe' way. But returning to the mainland after only a week or two also makes it possible, or even normal, for people to visit islands and never really to see them as they are. A whole industry and infrastructure has been

and Outer Hebrides, the Clyde islands, the Welsh and Irish Sea islands, the English coastal islands, the Isles of Scilly, the Channel Islands and the Isle of Man. Although this is not a guidebook, there is a wealth of information on each of the island groups and a more detailed description or account of one or two 'typical' islands in each group.

No apology is made for the fact that a large amount of space is devoted to the Western Isles of Scotland, since well over 90 per cent of all Britain's islands are to be found in the Inner and Outer Hebrides. If the northern archipelagos of Orkney and Shetland are included, Britain's other coastal islands become a tiny fraction of the total. But the minority have been included, hopefully fairly, partly because so many hundreds of thousands of people visit them and find them fascinating and rewarding, and partly because they assuredly deserve it for their sheer interest and diversity – even in the handful of islands called the Channel Islands there is an island for all tastes.

It is also strongly recommended that visitors who wish to explore islands, especially away from the main roads, should equip themselves with appropriate maps and suitable clothing. Maps are usually available at Tourist Information Centres. The Ordnance Survey 1:25,000 (2½in to 1 mile) green-covered Pathfinder maps are best for hill-walkers, naturalists and archaeologists looking for specific sites. The Ordnance Survey 1:50,000 pink-covered Landranger maps are *not* adequate for these purposes and should be left in your car or be used for general orientation only. For some areas, special leisure maps may be available.

This book gives basic information on how to get to all the islands and describes the main features of interest. However, come prepared to explore the islands yourself. Many people have their own special interests and it is good advice always to enquire locally when you arrive on an island, at the Tourist Information Centre, if there is one, or at your hotel or guest-house. You will find that the locals are prepared to be helpful

Small boats for messing about in, at Corrie on the Isle of Arran (*Highlands & Islands Enterprise*)

when you show interest in some aspect of their surroundings. Whenever possible, buy local leaflets and pamphlets, which are inexpensive and generally excellent value. There you will find details of island history and information on out-of-the-way nooks and crannies that cannot be included here. Every effort has been made to ensure that the information supplied in this book is accurate, but a certain amount of crystal ball gazing has been necessary, especially regarding ferry routes and future developments, and as the author does not have the gift of second sight that some of the people you will meet in the islands have, it would be sensible to confirm travel arrangements as near as possible to your date of travel by telephoning travel operators or the appropriate Tourist Information Centre.

Many islands have their own newspapers or newsletters, some published daily, weekly or fortnightly, others irregularly or seasonally. On Islay, in the Inner Hebrides, the *Ileach*, which is published by the Islay and Jura Council for Voluntary Services, claims the highest saturation coverage of any community newspaper in the country. Organs like this operate as community noticeboards and as such are essential reading for visitors.

Needless to say, national newspapers are also available on the islands, although not always on the day of publication. If it is important to you to keep up with the news, it is better to place an order by telephone in advance; however, the majority of island visitors seem to welcome the opportunity to 'escape' from the news for a week or two.

Seasoned island-hoppers always say that the best time to visit the islands is in the month of May. The machair, the lush, green grazing pasture that backs so many island beaches, becomes a blaze of colour in May and June, when the wild flowers bloom in profusion. May is also a good month for birdwatchers and archaeologists appreciate visiting sites before the bracken and grass make the identification of remains difficult. In June, the long days guarantee extra hours of sightseeing. In the northern isles, it never really gets dark at all. July and August are the months favoured by families, when island accommodation is strained to capacity and the ferries are full of holidaymakers – and their cars. It is also the time of year favoured by that rapacious devourer of tourists, the Highland midge – so come prepared!

Anybody planning to walk on anything but a tarmac road should invest in proper walking boots or at least strongly made walking shoes. Trainers are useless in anything but drought conditions. Wellies are downright dangerous on wet, grassy or rocky slopes. They are not very suitable on dry slopes either. The British Isles experience a frequently changing climate, which is why the weather is a constant topic of conversation. It follows, therefore, that it is prudent to take adequate wet-weather clothing on your island odyssey.

Island weather is, to say the least, variable. Visitors, especially those with young children, will enjoy their holiday all the more if they arrive adequately prepared. Be *prepared* for rain: good waterproof garments and efficient anoraks mean that you can get out and about and enjoy yourself, whatever the weather. Days and days of unrelenting wind and rain *can* happen, especially in winter, but far more typical is showery, squally weather, as wind-assisted Atlantic depressions zoom overhead. Most people find those conditions invigorating and even if you *do* get wet, the chances are that you will have dried out by the time the next squall comes along. And leave your umbrella at home, unless you feel like providing the locals with a little free entertainment!

There is almost always a week of clear, sunny, dry, magical weather in September – but predicting exactly *which* week it will be is, unfortunately, an annual lottery. People who have

It is strongly recommended that anybody thinking of visiting any of the islands described in this book should contact the local Tourist Information Centre for details of accommodation, places to eat and places to visit. Often they sell or give away pamphlets and leaflets of local interest, written by local people. For detailed local knowledge and up-to-date information, these publications are invaluable.

seen the islands in these conditions will agree that it is a chance well worth taking. From October onwards wind and rain can practically be guaranteed, but increasingly visitors are coming to the islands in the 'off' season, as the benefits become more widely known. For bird migrations, mid-October onwards is the best time of the year; for serious archaeologists, the short grass of winter makes ancient sites more visible, and more photogenic; or, for those who find the islands too crowded in the summer months, the autumn or spring months are very appealing. In the dead of winter, the islands are not really a place to be outside for long and in the northern isles darkness descends in mid-afternoon in December. It is, however, a great place to be *inside* in winter, given congenial company and adequate liquid refreshment, as anybody who has ever experienced a Hebridean Hogmanay will testify – if, indeed, they can remember anything at all!

At any time of the year, visitors will find the locals unfailingly courteous and helpful, not to say long-suffering. Given the provocations and strange behaviours to which they are occasionally subjected, the reserves of patience which most islanders have are a source of constant amazement, although not absolute surprise. There are certain basic rules which everybody should follow and which will increase your popularity. Many island roads are single-track affairs, with marked passing places. As well as allowing approaching vehicles to pass safely, these should be used to allow *following* vehicles to overtake. Locals are often in a hurry to meet a ferry, which in many cases is their sole link with the outside world, and do not appreciate dawdling tourists. Don't get upset if a following car honks its horn and flashes its lights – it could be the island doctor on his way to an emergency.

If you should be unlucky enough to become ill while you are on holiday, your first point of contact with the medical services will be the local island general practitioner (GP) or community nurse. Usually, the hotel or guest-house where you are staying will be able to guide you to the nearest doctor. If you are on the move, camping or staying in a caravan, ask at any house, shop, post office or Tourist Information Centre. Don't forget to take medication with you on holiday if it has been prescribed for you and tell the island doctor or nurse if you are allergic or hypersensitive to any drug. If at all possible, try to call the doctor's surgery first or attend only at advertised times. Most island GPs have a large territory to cover and a lot of

visiting to do, so they are not likely to be at home if you just drop in.

Islands are places where everybody helps everybody else – it is appreciated when visitors participate in this philosophy. In the springtime, visitors should avoid fields of sheep altogether, especially at lambing time, and stock should not be disturbed at any time of the year. Leave gates as you find them – it is amazing how many people fail to obey this simple rule. If possible, avoid climbing over fences and stone walls, especially if a gate is within reasonable reach. In areas where sportsmen are shooting deer and game-birds, keep clear. If in doubt, always enquire locally. Scots take seriously their rights to open access in the countryside, but on small islands these rights may conflict with crofters to whom a few lambs more or less can seriously affect their profit margin for that year, if indeed they have one at all. It never hurts to enquire politely if your presence would cause a farmer any problems and you will almost certainly benefit from the local knowledge he is able to impart. Always try to act with consideration for the people who live on islands and respect their way of life. Especially in the Outer Hebrides and Skye, this means respecting the Sabbath. Don't mistake silence for unfriendliness on an island Sabbath.

Traditional tourist activities still must be catered for. Here some youngsters are building coastal fortifications on a Jersey beach (*Jersey Tourism*)

A word for self-catering visitors: there is a great temptation to visit your local supermarket before your island holiday and load up with absolutely everything you could conceivably need. But spare a thought for the local island shops. True, the prices may be a few pence higher than you are used to, but your business, and that of others like you, may in the end make the difference between survival and failure for an island family, and eventually for an island community. Besides, island shops are a great source of news and gossip, where you can find out what is going on, pick up bits and pieces of island folklore and history, and make friends who will last a lifetime. They also sell all manner of leaflets, pamphlets, maps and books which never make it as far as your friendly mainland bookstore. And they can cater for most of your shopping needs.

ISLAND MAGIC

There is no doubt that islands are more expensive to live in, more inconvenient and more demanding. But beyond the plastic detritus left by tourists and the eyesores of metallic rubbish around island dwellings, there really is an almost tangible island magic, which even the most cynical incomer cannot resist. The magic of islands is something which has been known about for a very long time, and is part and parcel of island folklore and island life. The Celtic 'Isles

The peaceful village of
Port Charlotte, Islay,
on the shores of
Lochindaal

of the West' are not just a figment of the imaginations of tourist officers in the Isles of Scilly or the Hebrides. They had a reality to our Celtic ancestors, which unfortunately survives today for many people only in a vague, rose-tinted nostalgic romanticism.

But for native islanders who are in tune with their land and heritage and for the few fortunate incomers who are able to penetrate island reality, there is still magic and wonder all around. It is glimpses of this island magic that make visitors come back again and again. It is living in this dream world of myth and magic which gives islanders the strength to carry on, sometimes against all the odds.

Sometimes islanders fail and succumb to overwhelming social and economic pressures. Many of the Hebrides and some of the smaller islands of the Orkneys, Shetlands and Isles of Scilly once supported large populations but are now deserted. Many Scottish islands support precarious populations, and even the largest islands in the Western Isles and Inner Hebrides are under serious threat to their culture and continuing existence as viable societies.

Most of the islands described in this book are part of the culture province known to tourist officers and Celtic film producers as the Celtic Fringe. But before the Romans invaded Britain the whole of the British Isles was occupied by Celtic people, and before that most of central and northern Europe, too. So, in the island groups off the British coast is a surviving reminder, sometimes no more than a remnant, of a prehistoric culture which once extended from the Shetland Isles to the Channel Islands and over most of the continent of Europe. Perhaps this is why they are so important and why people keep coming to see them.

A final word of encouragement. Many of the islands described in this book are approached from the east. In many cases, the islands do not therefore present their most flattering side to the approaching visitor. But after you have settled into your hotel, cottage, caravan or tent, head for the west coast, where you can usually expect to see miles and miles of empty, unspoiled beaches and spectacular coastal scenery, where the only noises will be the calling of birds and the roaring of the Atlantic surf.

PART I

The Island Context

1
The Archaeology of Islands

BECAUSE of their relative isolation, relatively sparse populations and relatively small-scale agricultural and industrial activities, it is very often the case that archaeological and historical monuments survive better on islands than on the mainland. Of course, this is a generalisation, but it is the case that there are hardly any islands large enough to graze a few sheep which do not show some traces of previous human occupation. Even when islands have been long abandoned, signs of human settlement remain in the landscape, sometimes for thousands of years.

Some islands are nothing short of spectacular in the preservation of their archaeological heritage. Of the British islands, top of the bill surely has to be the Isle of Man, closely followed by the Orkney Islands, which, as a group, must have been more comprehensively dug up and examined by archaeologists than any other portion of the British Isles. All of the islands of the Orkneys have spectacular and well-preserved prehistoric sites, due in large part to the use of

Caithness flagstone as building material. The largest island in the Orkney group, known as the Mainland, has some of the finest archaeology to be found anywhere in Europe, in just a few square miles. The Neolithic village of Skara Brae, the enormous mound of the Neolithic chambered tomb of Maes Howe, the Bronze Age stone circle of the Ring of Brodgar, the Bronze Age standing stones at Stenness, the Iron Age broch at Gurness, the architectural twelfth-century gem of St Magnus Cathedral, Kirkwall, and the marvellous townscapes in Kirkwall and Stromness, are only a few of hundreds of sites. It is no wonder that archaeological field trips keep coming to this very special place.

On the Isle of Man the landscape is more damaged through intensive agriculture and a larger population, but the archaeology is no less spectacular. Megalithic tombs, stone circles and standing stones, cairns, forts and castles form a rich historical backdrop to the complexities of the modern age. Our understanding of Manx archaeology is

(Previous page)
Village Bay, Hirta, where the St Kilda island parliament met. The island was evacuated in the 1930s
(*Sue Anderson*)

20

due in no small measure to World War II. At the outbreak of war, the brilliant German archaeologist Gerhard Bersu was in England – he found Hitler's regime uncongenial – and was interned with his wife on the Isle of Man as an enemy alien. He proceeded to disentangle some of the island's mysteries, as well as paving the way for post-war archaeology with his excavation and research methods. The fruits of his labours, and of others whom he stimulated, can be seen in the island's museum.

But every island has it treasures, some of them unique. The restored abbey of Iona, with its cloisters and stone-flagged sanctuary, the Mesolithic shell mounds of Oronsay, the medieval palace of the Lords of the Isles at Finlaggan in Islay, the Neolithic passage grave at La Hougue Bie in Jersey, the nearly complete broch tower at Mousa, one of the Shetland Isles – and dozens more places to be discovered on an island holiday –

are what make an island visit truly memorable. With the growth of the heritage industry and increased public awareness generally of archaeology and history through radio and television programmes, the past has become a significant element in enjoying the present. On many islands you will find small museums or heritage centres, where you can usually purchase guides to the local attractions. These are also usually available from Tourist Information Centres, which are also increasingly aware of the potential of their islands' history.

Most island holidays involve a fair amount of effort, expenditure and commitment from seasonal visitors, most of whom want to read about the history and archaeology of their holiday island. Because islands are so addictive, visitors will almost certainly have been to other islands and will be in a position to compare and contrast what they see in different places. The time is long gone when it was said sneeringly that an

THE ARCHAEOLOGY OF ISLANDS

Stone furniture in the Neolithic village of Skara Brae, on the Orkney Islands: in the absence of wood, Stone Age carpenters used the local flagstone for their box beds and dressers

(Above) The Neolithic mound at La Hougue Bie, Jersey, which was used as a communal burial place five thousand years ago, with two medieval chapels on top and a German bunker at its base

Bryncelli Ddu, near Brynsiencyn, on the island of Anglesey. Neolithic burial mounds are found throughout the length and breadth of the British Isles
(*MAGMA, Anglesey*)

(Left) A cup-marked
stone at Ballephetrish,
Tiree, dating from the
Bronze Age, around
1500BC; this example
is a hard, dense glacial
erratic which has been
lying on this beach
since the end of the
Ice Age

Details of the cup-
marked stone on
Tiree; experts have no
idea what these
markings mean, but
they are found from
the Northern Isles to
the Channel Islands

23

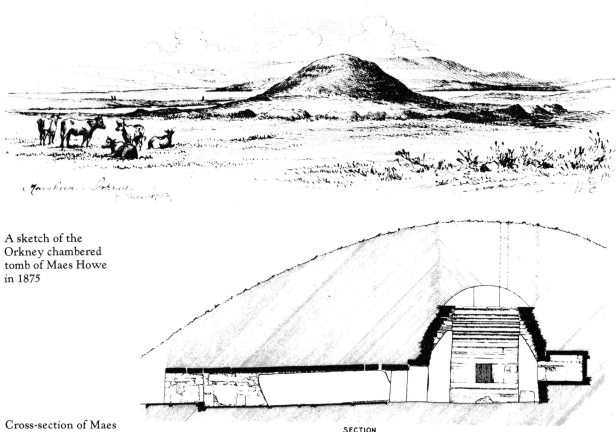

A sketch of the Orkney chambered tomb of Maes Howe in 1875

Cross-section of Maes Howe

SECTION

intelligent tourist is a contradiction in terms. People want to know about the places they visit and are prepared to pay to find out. As well as information booklets and leaflets of all kinds, there has been a rapid growth in recent years in the specialist tour market, even in what used to be called the 'off' season – which, of course, is exactly the time of year when archaeological sites can be seen at their best, when the grass is short and the bracken dead.

HISTORIC SITES OF INTEREST

Possibly the earliest sign of human settlement on any of Britain's islands is in the Channel Islands, on Jersey, where the cave of La Cotte was occupied eighty thousand years ago in St Brelade's Bay, when Jersey was still connected by land to mainland France. However, most of our knowledge of our Paleolithic past is based on mainland sites which, north of the Thames Valley, were destroyed by ice sheets in the last Ice Age.

Jumping quickly forward by seventy thousand years, we are able to trace the progress of our Mesolithic ancestors, as they recolonised what were to become the British Isles after the ice retreated. The thickest and heaviest ice caps in Britain formed over the mountains of Scotland and in fact were so substantial (up to 5,000ft/1,500m thick) that they depressed the land by their sheer weight. When the ice melted, which happened relatively quickly, sea levels around Britain's coasts rose, but with the weight of the ice removed, the land started to rise out of the sea. This 'isostatic recovery' is still going on. The 'raised beaches' that were left high and dry well above present sea level are often the strands on which the Mesolithic folk lived and traces of their activities can sometimes be seen, in the form of shell mounds. These are nothing

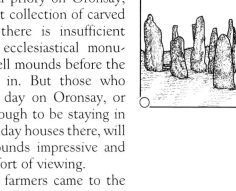

less than the remains of thousands and thousands of sea-food dinners; piles of millions of shells thrown in a heap which over the generations grew to be a substantial mound – some stand up to 16ft (5m) high.

In parts of the British Isles that were far removed from the ice sheets, the edges of the land tilted downwards at the same time as the mainland landmasses were recovering upwards. This process produced not raised beaches – which are seen to such stunning effect throughout Argyll – but flooding. This accounts for the sinuous nature of the Shetland landforms and the flooded landscapes of the Isles of Scilly. On the western coasts of the Outer Hebrides the process continues even today. Extraordinarily low tides sometimes reveal traces of, for example, field dykes under the sea, dating as far back as the Bronze Age. Examples of this in the Scillies perhaps bolstered the legend of Atlantis.

The best place to see prehistoric middens is on the Hebridean island of Oronsay, a tidal island linked to Colonsay, which is reached by ferry from Oban. Few visitors ever make the effort to see them, because there is a very fine medieval priory on Oronsay, with a magnificent collection of carved grave-slabs, but there is insufficient time to see the ecclesiastical monuments and the shell mounds before the tide comes back in. But those who spend the whole day on Oronsay, or who are lucky enough to be staying in one of the few holiday houses there, will find the shell mounds impressive and well worth the effort of viewing.

When the first farmers came to the British Isles around 4000BC, in the period archaeologists call the Neolithic, they were content to cultivate island soils. Indeed, as the mainland was more or less completely covered by forests, island landscapes may have seemed more manageable and so more attractive. Neolithic remains are to be found throughout the length and breadth of the British Isles, but are particularly well preserved in the islands, usually in the form of burial mounds, cairns and chambered tombs. There are regional

Mesolithic shell mound, Oronsay, before excavation at the end of the nineteenth century

(Left) A stone in
South Uist on the
slopes of Beinn
a'Charra, the hill of
the standing stone.

The ruined broch at Carloway, Isle of Lewis. These stone towers stood 40ft (12m) tall and were bell-shaped, with a hollow-walled construction to reduce their weight. They date from the first century BC (*Highlands & Islands Enterprise*)

A stone pillar in the west of Guernsey, in the Channel Islands, known as La Longue Rocque; in 1487 islanders called it La Longue Pierre

variations, but the basic principle of burying the dead, or at least some of them, in communal tombs accessed by passages leading into one or more chambers, is a fairly standard arrangement throughout. Often they will have names that reflect the ignorance of folk about the very existence of ancient cultures – for example, 'Giant's Grave' is commonplace for a chambered tomb. In cases where the stone cairn that originally covered the burial chambers has been removed for dyke-building or for local dwellings, only the enormous 'megalithic' stones of the chambers, capstones and façades remain. There are many examples where this is the case.

The first metalworking peoples – and probably the first Celts – came to the British Isles in the Bronze Age, in general terms dating from 2500 to 1200BC – again, there are regional variations and also a bewildering mix of continuity and innovation at many sites which blurs the distinctions between one 'period' and another. This is the period of round cairns, standing stones and stone circles – the time of Stonehenge. There are island sites which rival Stonehenge in importance and complexity, especially the amazing cruciform stone 'cathedral' at Callanish on the island of Lewis in the Outer Hebrides. The Ring of Brodgar in Orkney is also a truly monumental construction. There are Bronze Age sites on most of the Western Isles of Scotland, on the Isle of Man, Anglesey and the Isles of Scilly. The Channel Islands have their quota, too, and most islands have at least turned up some pottery or metalwork, even if sites are no longer visible. There are also Bronze Age circles and stones in Brittany, which show the remarkable geographical spread of this culture.

Iron Age people would have started to settle in the islands of Britain soon after the beginning of the first millennium BC, and they have left hill-forts and coastal fortifications of various types as their most visible surviving monuments. Some of these fortifications are in spectacular settings, which are highly dangerous, especially to children. Again, there are many regional variations, of which the Hebridean 'dun' and the broch tower of the Western Isles, Skye and Orkney are particularly interesting.

The early Christian period in the history of the islands around Britain is discussed at some length in the next chapter, because of particular reasons which made islands especially attractive to the early Christian saints. In general, remains from this period are found on almost all islands, and in many cases later medieval churches, monasteries, castles and eventually towns developed in places that were first settled by early religious figures. But it is equally the case that many of these early sites, which were chosen because of their remoteness, are now almost inaccessible to the casual visitor. This has the advantage of improving their survivability and enhancing the particular atmosphere to be found in places with a long spiritual history.

As we move into history, as opposed to prehistory, there are many sites of interest to archaeologists. The medieval period is well represented by religious sites and by castles, some of them truly spectacular in their setting. Several islands feature museums of farming life, preserving something of a way of life which in many places lasted up until World War II. The Corrigall Farm Museum in Orkney and the Cregneash Folk Museum in the Isle of Man deserve special mention, but there are many other examples ranging from single thatched cottages to preserved settlements. And because of the universal depopulation of islands in the mid-nineteenth century there are many sad examples of deserted settlements, some dating back into the Norse or even prehistoric period.

Even the field of industrial archaeology is well represented on Britain's islands. Outstanding examples are the ironstone mine of Raasay, in the Inner Hebrides, and the industrial complex around Laxey in the Isle of Man, where the giant Laxey waterwheel of 1854 is preserved, but there are many examples to be found, sometimes in unlikely settings. More recently, the thousands of tons of concrete which make up the fortifications that were constructed during the German occupation of the Channel Islands during World War II are now themselves part of Britain's historical heritage, albeit one which can only be contemplated with sadness.

ARCHAEOLOGICAL ETIQUETTE

It is only common sense to consult landowners about access to ancient monuments, especially where they occur in farming areas. This is not the same thing as asking for permission, which is a touchy subject, especially in Scotland, but where a farmer's stock, crops and livelihood are at stake in an environment which is already economically fragile, it seems only reasonable to make sure that your presence is not disruptive. Usually, you will also learn something.

Particular care should be taken not to disturb stock, especially at lambing time, and dogs should be kept under close control at all times. Gates should always be securely fastened and care should be taken not to damage fencing. With a reasonable amount of common sense and courtesy, there should be no problem. But local folk do not appreciate visitors who behave badly or arrogantly, and who fail to appreciate that making a living in most islands is a highly skilled and difficult undertaking.

Except in areas which are totally devoted to tourism, locals are generally willing to spend a few minutes chatting, giving directions and perhaps some useful advice to visitors. In more remote areas, don't mistake reticence for lack of interest. When islanders are used to only their own company, it is not always easy for them to turn on the social graces.

Many old people who have lived all their lives on islands will have seen a way of life which now survives only in the farming museums mentioned above. They often have a rich store of stories and are well worth spending the time to get to know. One good way to break the ice is to offer to help the locals with some of their chores around the croft or farm.

It is illegal to undertake any form of archaeological excavation, including metal detecting, without a landowner's permission. The most important monuments usually have some form of state protection, which means that landowners cannot touch them either. In Scotland, any object recovered from the ground must be reported to the authorities and can be declared treasure trove by the Queen's and Lord Treasurer's Remembrancer, who is usually referred to in archaeological circles as the Q&LTR. If this is done, financial compensation equal to the market value of the find will be paid to the finder. If it is not wanted for a national or local museum, an object belongs to the finder, not to a landowner, tenant or parent. Failure to report objects found can result in prosecution. Anything found, including fragments of pottery, should not be cleaned up, but should be forwarded as soon as possible to the nearest museum, which will arrange for proper conservation and study. Amateur cleaning invariably detracts from the value of a historical object, as well as limiting research possibilities. Any human remains, of whatever age, must be reported to the police. These rules also apply to rivers and freshwater lochs and lakes, but objects found washed up on the shore or found underwater – for example, on wrecks – should be reported to the Receiver of Wrecks.

THE ARCHAEOLOGY OF ISLANDS

Many archaeological sites are in isolated locations, with access involving rough ground and sometimes with no little danger involved – for example, on precipitous coastal sites. It cannot be stressed too strongly that visitors should exercise due caution in visiting sites mentioned in this book and should make sure that they are properly equipped. Where children are involved, extra precautions should always be taken.

(Above) The standing stones at Callanish, Lewis. Aligned on important points in the lunar cycle, these stones are perhaps one of Britain's most important prehistoric island sites (*Highlands & Islands Enterprise*)

Midsummer sunset over the Paps of Jura in the Inner Hebrides: in 1500BC these stones at Ballochroy, Kintyre, were carefully arranged to work out the exact days of midsummer and midwinter, perhaps for religious and ceremonial reasons

(Above) A typical Hebridean Iron Age fort at Dun Morbhibh on the island of Coll. Pottery decorated with incised animal shapes has been found here

The Bronze Age Ring of Brodgar, Orkney, once had sixty standing stones in a circle, surrounded by a bank and ditch – a northern Stonehenge, over 3,500 years old

2
Holy Islands

THE ROMAN ERA

THE earliest documented instance of a British island being put to a religious use is in the *Annals* of Tacitus, which refers to events in AD61. In that year the Roman Governor of Britannia, Paulinus, was extending the borders of the empire on the island of Anglesey, when his army confronted the local Druids in their stronghold. The description of what happened is graphic indeed:

On the shore stood the opposing army with its dense array of armed warriors, while between the ranks dashed women in black attire like the Furies, with hair dishevelled, waving brands. All round the Druids, lifting up their hands to heaven and pouring forth dreadful imprecations, scared our soldiers by the unfamiliar sight so that, as if their limbs were paralysed, they stood motionless and exposed to wounds. Then, urged by their general's appeal and mutual encouragement not to quail before a troop of frenzied women, the Romans bore the standards onwards, smote down all resistance, and wrapped the foe in the flame of his own brands. A force was set over the conquered, and the sacred groves, devoted to inhuman superstitions, were destroyed. The Druids indeed deemed it a duty to cover their altars with the blood of captives and to consult their deities through human entrails.

It was not often that Roman soldiers would admit to fear, but as usual Roman discipline prevailed. This is the only classical reference to a Druid sanctuary in the British Isles, although there are several accounts of Druids in Celtic tribal societies on the European continent. It was this passage that stimulated the Reverend Henry Rowlands, an Anglesey vicar, to publish one of the first books to tackle the problem of which sites could be connected with the Druids, in his *Mona Antiqua Resaurata: an Archaeological Discourse on the Antiquities*, in 1723. He was not able to come up with any real answers, but he is credited with being the first antiquary to invent Druid stone altars in connection with some of the prehistoric megalithic monuments on Anglesey.

Tacitus' description contains all the

Just as every island has its prehistoric sites, so too it will very likely have remains associated with the earliest history of Christianity in the British Isles. From St Ninian in the Shetland Isles to St Helier in Jersey, almost every island has its saints.

elements most beloved of what we might term the romantic image of this priestly class: ritual cursing, frenzied, dishevelled women, sacred groves, human sacrifice and entrails. That their sanctuaries were often associated with oak groves is implied by Pliny, who gives the only detailed account of a Druid ceremony – cutting mistletoe from an oak tree with a golden sickle and sacrificing bulls.

EARLY CHRISTIANITY

In the period after the demise of the Roman Empire, various early Christian saints established religious communities around the islands of Britain. We know from inscriptions and archaeological evidence that there were adherents of the Christian religion serving in Britannia with the Roman army, but it was not until the late fourth century that the new religion really took hold. Thus St Patrick, who is thought to have grown up in a post-Roman cultural environment near Carlisle, was probably born just before AD400, was captured as a lad by Irish slave raiders, escaped to the Continent, and returned to Ireland as a Christian missionary around 432. He died in 461, having spent most of his life in the Ireland which is now so closely associated with his name. Dedications to this important saint turn up in many islands, as at St Patrick's Isle, Peel, on the west coast of the Isle of Man.

St Ninian came from the same geographical and cultural milieu, and is credited with promoting, if not introducing, Christianity into Scotland. His main religious base was on the Isle of Whithorn, on the north shore of the Solway Firth. Like Patrick, he was essentially a Romanised Briton, whose real name would have been 'Niniavus', or something similar. It is likely that the two men knew each other and may even have been schoolmates. Certainly they were contemporaries. According to Bede, writing in Northumbria in the

A simple Latin cross carved on a rock outcrop at the site of an early Christian monastery at Kirkapol, Tiree. This was done to mark the boundaries of church lands and is found at many early Christian sites

(Above) Another
style of early
Christian carved stone
cross, at Kilnave, in
Islay, in the Inner
Hebrides. The stone
slab is very thin and
although it is very
worn and damaged by
erosion, the elaborate
decoration is still
visible

St Clement's Church,
Rodel, Harris, in the
Outer Hebrides,
which dates from the
twelfth century.
Inside is the finest
medieval tomb in
Scotland, with
intricately carved
decoration (*Highlands
& Islands Enterprise*)

Holy Isle, Arran, seen from the harbour at Lamlash. There are early Christian carvings on the walls of a cave there, the retreat of St Molaise (*Highlands & Islands Enterprise*)

A fine example of an early Christian wheel cross, from Kildalton, Islay, carved from a single piece of epidiorite from the nearby beach. There are similar crosses on Iona and in Ireland, from where the style was introduced into the Hebrides in the 8th century AD

Typical early Christian 'bee-hive' huts: these examples are on the Garvellachs, in the Firth of Lorn. St Cuthbert spent eight years in one of these in the Farne Islands

720s, Ninian built a stone church at Whithorn, called *Candida Casa*. This Latin name survived into the eighth century, because Whithorn is simply the Northumbrian English translation (*hwit aern*, 'white house'). Archaeological excavations at Whithorn have dug through medieval and Norse levels back to Ninian's time, and may even have found the foundations of his white-washed stone church. Ninian is thought to have died relatively young, in the 420s, but he must have been well respected, for his dedications are every-where.

Celtic monasticism grew out of a reli-gious tradition that was quite different, and in many ways quite alien, to the medieval monastic tradition which has left us so many spectacular buildings and ruins throughout mainland Britain – although there are many island examples of medieval monasteries, too. Celtic 'eremetic' monasticism has its roots in the early history of Christianity in Egypt

and the Near East, where under Roman persecution many practitioners of the new religion fled to the desert. By the fourth century, the small communities established by these early ascetics had achieved an international reputation and visitors came from far and wide to see for themselves, at a time when 'established' Christianity throughout Europe was falling prey to worldly temptations. Soon, communal establish-ments started to spring up, especially in Gaul, and it was the introduction of this new style into Ireland which was to prove so influential.

Into this tradition fits the great Celtic religious (and political) figure of St Columba, who in AD563 travelled into exile with some companions and estab-lished a Celtic monastery on the Hebridean island of Iona. The ruins there which so impressed Dr Johnson and are today visited by over half a mil-lion visitors every year, are mostly medi-eval, dating to the period of the Lords of the Isles, who will figure in Chapter 3. Little remains from St Columba's time, apart from one small burial shrine and traces of the surrounding *vallum*, or ditch, which defined and enclosed the ecclesiastical grounds. A couple of artefacts survive from the earliest days of Christianity at Iona, notably the *Brecbennoch*, or Monymusk Reliquary, which was carried in front of King Robert the Bruce's armies at the Battle of Bannockburn (1314), and a beautiful illuminated gospel, intricately decorated, which is thought to be at least partly in Columba's own hand. At the time of the devastating Viking raids soon after 800, the gospel was taken to Ireland for safekeeping, to the monastery at Kells, and is now one of the treasures of Trinity College, Dublin, which has 'hijacked' it and made it known to the world as the *Book of Kells*.

Many traces of early Christian monasteries survive on our offshore islands, which were established by Columba and his contemporaries, for he was only one of many men who were spreading the Christian message. Undoubtedly, he was the most charismatic of the early English saints and, from the point of view of posterity, the most fortunate, because it was one of his successors at Iona, the abbot Adomnan, whose *Life of St Columba*, written in the 680s, is distinguished from all the other lives of early saints by its racy style and fascinating detail of the people and places of Columba's time. Adomnan was supremely skilled in public relations, for he purveyed a heady mixture of fact and the supernatural which is compelling reading even in these sceptical times. But on Caldey Island off the Welsh coast, in Tiree, Lismore, Orkney and Shetland, up and down the Western Isles, on Holy Island in Lamlash Bay, Arran, at Maughold in the Isle of Man and even at Ninian's Whithorn, Irish monks and clerics were founding communities to further their brand of Christianity.

An accident of history brought the religious system of the Irish clergy to the coasts of Northumbria. Oswald, a Northumbrian prince, was exiled among Dalriadic Scots in the Celtic west, where he received a Christian upbringing and learnt the Irish language. It was he who brought Aidan of Iona to the holy isle of Lindisfarne, around 635. This monastic tradition eventually spread to the mainland of Northumbria and further afield to the newly converted English kingdoms.

By contrast, it was just before 600 when Pope Gregory's emissary, Augustine, landed at Thanet and established

Oronsay Cross, carved by an Irish sculptor under the patronage of the Lords of the Isles about 1500

The site of a Celtic
Monastery on Eilean
Naombh, in the
Garvellachs. Early
Irish saints preferred
isolated island
locations

The medieval abbey
on Iona, which was
founded by the Lords
of the Isles on the site
of the early Christian
monastic settlement
established by St
Columba in 563. The
carved stone cross
dates from around
800, just before the
first Viking raids
(*Highlands & Islands
Enterprise*)

THE HOLY ISLANDS

This slab, incised with a simple cross, is traditionally the burial place of Eithne, the mother of St Columba of Iona. In early Christian times, women were not allowed on Iona, even in death

A medieval chapel perched precariously on a rocky outcrop at Kirkapol, Tiree

Christianity in Kent. A different tradition became established and, due to the vigour of its adherents, it soon spread northwards, where inevitably it came into contact, and soon into conflict, with the Celtic traditions of Aidan and his successors. The watershed Synod of Whitby in 664 was held to reconcile the two systems and in particular to decide which branch of Christianity the Northumbrian royal dynasty would follow. Of course, there were technical problems to be sorted out, like the date of Easter or the hairstyle of the monks, but the basic issue was whether the Christians of Northumbria would continue to follow the ways they had learnt from Aidan of Iona who had converted them, or whether they should fall in line with the Christianity of Canterbury, the rest of England, Europe and Rome.

The decision to follow Rome meant that Celtic Christianity became isolated and to some extent marginalised. But within its own cultural area it continued to flourish, until finally it was overcome by the Viking raiders who, by 850, had pillaged and murdered the Celtic church into oblivion. However, Christianity itself was not expunged, but was incorporated into the new regime which established a new system of ecclesiastical polity that was ruled, not through a system of bishops and Celtic monasteries, but by the See of Trondheim, in Norway.

The achievements of Celtic Christianity were many and its influence was far-reaching. In the artistic realm, the skill of the monastic calligraphers, metalworkers and stone-carvers was never surpassed. Little remains of their architecture, but many of the carved stone crosses which stood outside important churches still survive. Many are in the Irish homeland, but there are outstanding examples in the islands, especially on Iona and Islay, both in the Inner Hebrides. The early Christian crosses of Iona are justly famous and much work has been done on their pres-

ervation and presentation. On Islay, the Kildalton Cross, dating from soon after 800, is well preserved for its age and surely ranks, with its counterparts in Iona and Ireland, as one of the most important artistic masterpieces of north-western Europe.

At the opposite end of the artistic spectrum, but dating from the same period, are the simple Latin crosses to be found on burial stones on early Christian sites, or incised on boulders or bedrock to mark the limits of sacred ground.

As well as the communal monastic tradition that was followed by Columba and Aidan, there is a parallel tradition of solitary monasticism, whose practitioners preferred lonely islands. Examples of their 'beehive' cells can be seen in the Garvellachs, in the Firth of Lorn, although perhaps the best survivals are on the rocky pyramid of Skellig Michael, off the south-west coast of Ireland. There are other examples in the Outer Hebrides and in the Northern Isles. Wherever the 'Papay' element occurs in place-names, as in Papa Westray (Orkney), there has almost certainly been an early Christian cell. When the Vikings first visited Iceland around AD1000, they found evidence that monks had even travelled there in search of lonely solitude, to better aid their contemplation, while it has been shown that Brendan's voyages and adventures in the Atlantic Ocean on a similar quest may indeed have resulted in Irish monks discovering America hundreds of years before the first Viking explorers and nearly a millennium before the fifteenth-century Basque adventurer, Christopher Columbus.

These lonely Christians were much admired in the Celtic world and even in a busy monastery like Iona there were facilities for the monks to withdraw to solitary cells for a period. The most extreme practitioners were regarded as having a special gift and were revered for their spirituality. The best documentary sources for an understanding of the spirit of the time are Adomnan's *Life of Columba* and the writings of the Venerable Bede of Jarrow.

Viking raiders virtually wiped out Celtic Christianity in the Scottish islands, on the Isle of Man and in the Channel Islands. The initial massacres and looting were followed by hundreds of years of Norse settlement. In 793 and 794 the Vikings attacked Lindisfarne and Jarrow. By about 820 the monks of Iona had abandoned their monastic settlement and retreated to Ireland, taking with them the beautifully decorated manuscript, at least partly in St Columba's own hand, which became known later as the *Book of Kells*. It is ironic that one of the great historical, literary and artistic treasures of the Scottish nation is now exhibited in a foreign capital, in Trinity College, Dublin. Perhaps Columba would be pleased to see it so well looked after in his own native land.

THE MIDDLE AGES

In the Middle Ages, there was a great period of church-building everywhere, and the islands of Britain are no exception. Although many churches and chapels of the period are now roofless and in ruins, some gems survive. Few people would dispute the claim of St Magnus Cathedral in Kirkwall, the capital of the Orkney Islands, to be the finest medieval island church. St Clement's, Rodel, in Harris, is one of the best parish churches of the period and it survives more or less intact. In the Channel Islands, most of the parish churches of Guernsey and Jersey have medieval cores which often have been much altered. The medieval abbey on Iona has been restored by the Iona community and gives visitors a good idea of what life would have been like there in the Middle Ages. Like Rushen Abbey on the Isle of Man, it came under the diocese of Sodor and Man, and so came under the ecclesiastical jurisdiction of

Trondheim in Norway, sometimes also called Nidaros.

From 1156 to 1493 all of the islands off the west coast of Scotland and the Isle of Man were ruled (or at least claimed) by the MacDonald Lords of the Isles. John of Islay, who ruled from his island palace at Finlaggan in Islay in the early fourteenth century, was responsible for initiating a flourishing period of patronage which resulted in many churches and monasteries, notably Iona Abbey, Ardchattan Priory, Oronsay Priory and Saddell Abbey. Saddell was founded as early as 1160 by the great Somerled himself, but was not completed until early in the next century and was enlarged and developed later. The most notable legacy of this period, apart from the buildings themselves, is the very large number of decoratively carved grave-slabs and stone crosses which are a feature of so many West Highland graveyards.

These slabs and crosses commemorate both secular and religious figures, giving a real insight into island life in the middle ages among the ruling élite.

This drawing of the design on the Oronsay cross-head makes it easier to appreciate its complexity and artistry

A modern roadside shrine on the predominantly Catholic island of South Uist

A sanctuary cross on the tidal Strand between Colonsay and Oronsay, in the Inner Hebrides. Fugitives were supposed to be safe after reaching the boundary of the church lands of Oronsay Priory

3
Island Folklore

MUCH of the surviving folklore of the islands of Britain has its roots in Gaelic or Celtic culture, and in particular the effect of the Norse invaders and settlers who came into the area in the ninth century AD. In the Hebrides and Mann, the MacDonald Lords of the Isles, descendants of Somerled, established a maritime kingdom in the twelfth century, freeing the area from Norse domination. It was very important to their power and prestige that they could establish their credentials, particularly that they were the rightful and authentic inheritors of a Gaelic culture which could be traced back to the 'Golden Age' of Finn MacCoul and Deirdre and all the other heroes and heroines of Irish legends. In the Gaelic-speaking world, they and their exploits were always just under the surface of daily life.

Many of the tales and legends which are recounted as if they were historical events that really happened, are in fact common Indo-European folk stories adapted to local circumstances. Whether this makes them more or less real is a matter for each individual to decide. There is no single objective reality, for reality changes for each person and

Hebridean reality is very different from urban reality. For one thing, the dead are far more 'present' in everyday life in the islands. Indeed, ancestors are part of the living reality of the present. This fact is difficult for visitors and incomers to grasp, but, after a while, it seems obvious.

The Scots writer Neil Munro has written movingly of the dilemma between the real and the unreal, particularly in his intriguing novel *The Well at the World's End*. In this book, questions of reality and illusion, past and present, individual and community, are explored from within the culture. He shows convincingly the depths of cultural conditioning which transcend generations, leaving us in no doubt that there is an underlying reality ever present in the landscape, part of the psychic geography of every native islander. A few incomers have proved that this reality can be penetrated and learnt by those who can read the right cultural maps.

IAIN OG ILE'S TALES

John Francis Campbell of Islay, always known in Celtic circles as Iain Og Ile

Monument to the nineteenth-century folklorist and Gaelic scholar John Francis Campbell, at the head of Lochindaal in his native Islay

(Young John of Islay), was the first to bridge the two cultures, Gaelic and English, and to interpret them to each other. His four volumes of *Popular Tales of the West Highlands*, published from 1860 to 1862, contain the results of years of recording local stories, which were written down in Gaelic and transcribed into English. In almost all cases, when Campbell and his co-workers wrote these stories down, it was the first time in their long history that they had been committed to paper, having been passed down by word of mouth for untold generations.

One of Iain Og Ile's many informants was John MacGilvray, who was described as a 'labourer' from 'Baille Raomainn, Colonsay'. When Campbell recorded his version of *The Knight of the Red Shield* in 1860, John MacGilvray was seventy-two years old. His father was Farquar MacGilvray, a native of Mull, who had learnt the story there in his boyhood. Farquar served in the army in North America for seven years and subsequently settled in Colonsay. He died around 1820, aged about seventy-five. Assuming that he memorised the story in his childhood, as did his son John, this takes the story back to the 1750s and doubtless it was passed on from generation to generation for many

hundreds of years before that. What is remarkable, at least by today's standards, is that the story as written down by Campbell consists of thirteen solid pages of type in *Popular Tales* – an astounding feat of memory repeated many times in the pages of Campbell's tomes.

THE FOLKLORE OF JURA

The island of Jura (Norse: *dyrey*, deer-island) in the Inner Hebrides has some interesting and important folklore attached to it. The main feature of the island is the triangle of high mountains which are located at its southern end. These have been known as the Paps of Jura since at least the sixteenth century. They dominate their immediate landscape and also form part of the seascape for many miles around. From Kintyre, Colonsay, Coll, Tiree and Mull, and from the high tops on the western seaboard of Scotland from Skye to Arran and even from the Isle of Man and Ben Lomond, these distinctive mountains form part of the distant horizon. They are formed of quartzite and their rounded forms and scree slopes are thought to be due to frost shattering at the end of the last Ice Age. Dr John Walker of Edinburgh University carried

out experiments involving atmospheric pressure on the top of Beinn an Oir in 1764. Using a Torricellian barometer he estimated its height as 2,340ft (713m), which was only 231ft (65m) short. On the summit can be seen the remains of an observation point manned during World War II.

Along with the Paps, the most famous feature associated with Jura is the renowned whirlpool of Corrievreckan – *Corrie-Bhreacan*, the cauldron of Breckan. This area of raging tidal turbulence lies at the tip of Jura, between Jura and the uninhabited island of Scarba to the north. According to Gaelic folklore, Breckan was a Viking of some importance who wished to marry a local island princess. Her father was wary of the consequences of such a union, but fearful of offending the Vikings, so he gave his consent to the marriage on condition that Breckan should prove his skill and his manhood by anchoring his longship in the whirlpool for three days and three nights. Breckan agreed to this, but returned to Scandinavia to consult the sages of his native land. He was advised to equip himself with three ropes, one of hemp, one of wool and one woven from the hair of virgins – it was thought that the purity of female innocence would give it the power to resist even the force of the waves. Alas and alack, having anchored in the gulf which now bears his name and having survived the first two nights despite the tearing of first the hemp and then the woollen rope, it appears that one of the contributors to the third rope was less than honest in her proclamation of innocence, for the rope parted and Breckan was drowned.

In *Popular Tales of the West Highlands*, John Francis Campbell repeats the story of the Seven Big Women of Jura, with their magical powers, and the major motifs in the tale will be familiar to folklorists: a horse, a falcon, a sword and a fair lady. Another of his tales, concerning the Old Woman, or Witch, of Jura,

tells of an old woman with magical powers. She lived with a MacPhie of Colonsay, which is the neighbouring island to the north-west. According to the tale, she had a magic ball of thread by means of which she could draw any person or thing towards her. MacPhie was in her clutches and was not allowed to leave Jura. On several occasions he tried to escape to his native Colonsay in his small boat, but always the old woman would spot him, throw the magic ball of thread into his boat and so bring him back to shore.

Eventually, in his old age, MacPhie pretended to be content with his bondage and discovered that the magic of the old woman's magic thread could only be broken if it was cut by an equally magic hatchet. Early one morning MacPhie crept away, with the hatchet, and made his escape from Jura in a small boat. When the old woman noticed his absence, she rushed as usual to the top of Beinn a'Chaolais (the hill of the old woman) and hailed MacPhie:

A Mhic a Phie
A Ghaoils' thasgaidh
An d' fhag thu air a chladach me?

Oh, MacPhie
My love and treasure
Have you left me on the strand? (ie stranded!)

She hurled the magic ball of thread into MacPhie's boat, but he cut it with the old woman's magic hatchet, which he had stolen, and made his escape. She was distraught:

A Mhic a Phie
Charrich, granda
'An d'fhag thu air a chladach me?

Oh, MacPhie
Rough-skinned and foul
Have you left me on the strand?

In despair she slid down the mountain to the sea-shore, pleading with

An Earth Mother statue at St Martin's, Guernsey, known as La Gran'mère du Chimquière. Church authorities often destroyed stones like this as symbols of the old religion – this one was broken in two (*Guernsey Tourist Board*)

speculation. In its longer form it is, in Gaelic, *dub-shide* or *dubh-sithe*, meaning 'the black peace', so MacDuffie can be translated as 'son of the black peace'. As it was a very common name on the islands of Colonsay and Oronsay it has been suggested that it contains a reference to the dark robes worn by the monks of Oronsay Priory, but as the Gaelic word *sithe* (pronounced 'shee') can also mean 'magical' or 'supernatural', the MacDuffie name could equally well have to do with 'black magic'. The word has even found its way into English in 'banshee', from the Gaelic *bean-sithe*, the female fairy whose wailing and shrieking foretold the approaching death of a member of a family. It is by no means beyond the bounds of possibility that the hereditary MacDuffie priors of Oronsay had their ancestral roots in the remote pre-Christian past, as hereditary priests in the Iron Age or earlier. But, of course, this must remain a matter of speculation.

In Islay and Jura the surname Shaw is thought to derive from *sithe* and there are, in fact, many links between Islay, Jura and Colonsay and the MacDuffies and MacPhies.

The kind of mythology recorded by John Francis Campbell (and by other equally skilled folklorists in the other Celtic lands) will be familiar to those who have been brought up on the exploits of Greek and Roman gods, and indeed, Celtic myths share the same Indo-European background. In a pre-scientific age, natural features and natural phenomena were often explained in this way. But since the stories address some of the most basic tribulations of the human condition, who are we to devalue them by asking awkward questions about their reality or historicity? Such questions are irrelevant and miss the point.

In the case of the Witch or the Old Woman of Jura, the story highlights the dilemma of an ageing woman who thinks that she has her man for life, while he has

MacPhie to return. But he would not and the marks left by the old woman's heels as she slid down Beinn a'Chaolais can still be seen. They are called Sgriob na Cailleach – the Slide of the Old Woman. They start near the top of the hill as rocky ravines and end in a trail of boulder scree.

The origin of the name MacPhie is interesting and has given rise to much

An early Christian stone beside a holy well at Kiloran, Colonsay. King Edward VII thought it resembled the chief engineer of the Royal Yacht

A prehistoric Earth Mother statue, defaced and re-erected in the churchyard of Catel, Guernsey

The Paps of Jura as seen from the neighbouring island of Oronsay

secretly been longing for years to escape from the relationship, without knowing how this can be done. Finally, he 'cuts the thread', leaving the relationship, and in this case his long-time mate, literally and symbolically 'washed up' on the shore of the ocean of life – a predicament not unfamiliar in our own age.

Truly, there are many layers to these stories, and how much more meaningful they are when the teller can point to the scars on the mountainside left by the Cailleach's heels.

The Paps of Jura, habitat of women with magical powers, and Corrievreckan, palpable proof of the awesome power of raw nature, with its associated folklore, hint at the possibility of some cult or religious centre in Jura, whose reality is now blurred by the mists of antiquity. A weird piece of circumstantial evidence comes from the classical geographer Strabo who says that Poseidonius mentioned an island near Britain 'where rites are performed like those in Samothrace concerned with Demeter and Kore'. Kore is Persephone, the Greek goddess of fertility, nature and growth. Then Plutarch records a statement by Demetrius of Tarsus that among the Western Isles of Scotland was one 'in which Cronos was held asleep under guard of Briareus'.

Briareus was one of the Uranids, monsters with a hundred arms and fifty heads, who aided Zeus against Cronos and the other Titans. He is often regarded as a sea god and could be seen as a Kraken-like creature inhabiting Corrievreckan, while the profile of the Paps of Jura might be seen as similar to that of a recumbent female goddess or giant.

All of this raises at least the possibility that these waters were visited in classical times and that the two most important features of the area, the mountains of Jura and the great whirlpool, were known to the Greeks and incorporated into their mythology.

ISLAND FESTIVALS AND CEREMONIES

In Guernsey, Sir Edgar MacCulloch, bailiff from 1884 to 1895, was fascinated with the stories and legends told to him by his servant and started to write them down. His work expanded into three closely written manuscript books, which were eventually edited after his death and published. The themes are familiar: ghostly black dogs, witches and wizards, fairies, changelings and magic. They make fascinating reading, and indeed they made fascinating listening when some were read on BBC Radio Guernsey some years ago.

Sadly, we rely for our knowledge of island folklore mainly on the stories that were collected painstakingly by collectors in the nineteenth century. In more recent times a great deal of oral collecting has been done through various recording media, including tape-recording. This has provided a great archive of cultural heritage throughout the Celtic lands, although it also shows just how much has been irretrievably lost. On the Isle of Man, it was done just in time to catch the last native Manx speakers before they died. In the Hebrides, both speech and music has been recorded by the School of Scottish Studies, following the lead of folklorists in the Irish Republic and elsewhere.

Some islands have preserved ancient customs of one kind or another, sometimes in a very watered-down, 'touristy' way. Some islanders persist with superstitions and traditions without really being aware that they are preserving anything – it's just the way things are done. Two of the most spectacular surviving ceremonials are the Shetland fire festival, 'Up Helly Aa', and the Manx Tynwald ceremony.

The constitutional and historical ramifications of Tynwald are explored in Chapter 6, in the discussions of different forms of island government, but here we are concerned with the Tynwald Ceremony, which is held every year on the Manx national day, 5 July. It takes place in the village of St John's, on Tynwald Hill, known in Manx Gaelic as *Cronk Keeill Eoin*, 'the hill of St John's Church'. It is almost certain that the mound where the ceremony takes place is the same mound where the Norse people had their 'Thingvollr' or Law Hill. This tradition of an open-air legislative assembly is common throughout the Viking lands. Tingwall in Shetland and Dingwall in Easter Ross are both names which preserve this idea, although almost every island has its traditional meeting place. There is a famous Thingvollr site in Iceland.

In some places it is possible that the Vikings 'hijacked' an existing ceremonial site and it has been suggested that the Manx Tynwald might be a Bronze Age burial mound. As it stands today, it is 12ft (3.6m) high, rising by four stages or circular platforms, each about 3ft (1m) higher than the one before. The diameter of the base is 76ft (23m). At the Tynwald Ceremony, the lieutenant-governor sits on the summit and arranged around and below him are the members of the legislative council, members of the House of Keys, ministers of religion, and various island and parish officials. There is a tradition that soil and turf from each of the island's twelve parishes are incorporated into the mound.

As part of the ceremony, summaries of laws enacted in the past year are read out, and any Manxman or woman with a grievance can present a petition to the governor. The hill is covered by a canopy, the processional way linking it to St John's Church is flanked by flags and banners and covered with rushes, and thousands of spectators have the privilege of watching an ancient ceremony. In 1979 Tynwald celebrated its one thousandth anniversary.

The Shetland 'Up Helly Aa' festival is the invention of Victorian antiquarians, but it is no less spectacular for that. It started in 1889 and is held annually on the last Tuesday in January. The Shetland islanders march through Lerwick with fiery torches, which eventually are flung dramatically into a full-size replica of a Viking longship, which is sent to a fiery doom in the harbour. An exhibition in Lerwick explains what it is all about.

Early travellers to the islands were fascinated by surviving superstitions and often wrote them down and so preserved them. In 1716 Martin Martin, himself an islander (from Skye), mentions that there was 'a modern crucifix'

ISLAND FOLKLORE

Every island has its own tales and legends and it is interesting that in almost every Tourist Information Centre throughout the length and breadth of the British Isles you will find locally produced publications about island folklore, often in the form of children's books. On the larger islands more ambitious, academic compilations will also be found. But if the Tourist Information Centre is closed or you are unable to find a booklet, there is a remedy which is common to all the islands – head for the nearest pub, buy one of the locals a drink and listen.

on the altar of the church at Oronsay and that the most valuable of several precious stones from this ornamental crucifix was 'in the custody of *Mack-Duffie*, in black *Raimused* Village, and it is us'd as a *Catholicon* for Diseases'. Martin visited Oronsay Priory and recorded the local custom of walking around the church there 'sunwise' – ie clockwise – before entering. While he was staying in Colonsay, at the inn which is now the hotel, his illiterate landlord asked to borrow his book (ie his Bible), which he used to fan the face of a sick member of his family, morning and night. It transpired that there was 'an antient Custom of fanning the Face of the Sick with the Leaves of the Bible'. Martin described the local inhabitants as being 'generally well-proportion'd, and of a black Complexion'. They spoke only Gaelic, were of the Protestant religion and observed the festivals of Christmas, Easter and Good Friday. The women observed the Festival of the Nativity of the Blessed Virgin.

Kilnave Chapel, Islay, where MacDonalds burned Macleans in 1598, a story preserved in oral tradition to the present day by the descendants of one of the survivors

Many traditional stories in the Hebrides date from the medieval Golden Age of the Lords of the Isles. This is Dunivaig, their military stronghold and naval base on the south-east coast of Islay

Fierce faces were often carved on the walls of buildings to scare off evil spirits. This one is in Gorey, Jersey

4

Island Communications and Tourism

EARLY TRAVELLERS

IN the last chapter it was noted that one of the first travellers to some of the more remote islands of Britain was Martin Martin, himself from Skye. In 1703 he published an account of his travels in the 1690s, and in the manner of the time the title page of his book serves as a table of contents and gives a very full account of what is to be found within. Martin's *A Description of the Western Islands of Scotland* covers all of the islands off the northern and western coasts of Scotland, including Orkney and Shetland, and St Kilda. He visited St Kilda in the summer of 1697 and had, in fact, already published a short account of that journey.

Others before Martin Martin had travelled to remote islands and written accounts of their travels, which were often undertaken in connection with their own careers. One such was Sir Donald Monro, High Dean of the Isles, who visited the islands in the course of his work and wrote the first descriptive account, in 1549. Another early travel-ler was Cornelius Ward, a Franciscan missionary, who, with his colleagues, travelled throughout the Hebrides in the 1620s, at great personal risk, in an attempt to bolster the Catholic religion. Documents giving an account of their travels and the names of converts only survived in the Vatican archives because of a dispute over an expenses claim. The papal authorities, and in par-ticular the officials disbursing pay-ments, took a sceptical view of Ward's claims of converts and there was a strong suggestion that he had not, in fact, made all the journeys claimed for, nor converted the numbers stated. The missionaries were supposed to get an annual financial allowance from the Congregation of Propaganda in Rome, but those officials insisted that in order to receive the allowance it was neces-sary for the missionaries to report regu-larly on their work. The Congregation of Propaganda complained that regular reports were not being sent in to head-quarters, and so withheld funds. On the other hand, the missionaries said that they were sending in regular reports, along with pleas for funds. Perhaps some of the reports were lost or intercepted. However, to anybody who has ever tried to extract money from a bureaucracy, it all sounds only too familiar!

Even in 1703, Martin Martin was aware that he was witnessing the end of a way of life, although it is unlikely that he would have thought that the Gaelic language would have come so near to extinction in another three hundred years. In the introduction to his *Description of the Western Isles of Scotland*, he has some interesting comments on island superstitions:

> There are several instances of heathenism and pagan superstition among the inhabitants of the islands related here; but I would not have the reader to think those practices are chargeable upon the generality of the present inhabitants, since only a few of the oldest and most ignorant of the vulgar are guilty of them. These practices are only to be found where the reformed religion has not prevailed; for it is to the progress of that alone that the banishment of evil spirits, as well as of evil customs, is owing, when all other methods proved ineffectual. And for the islanders in general I may truly say that in religion and virtue they excel many thousands of others who have greater advantages of daily improvement.

As well as admiring his observational abilities, it is justifiable to credit Martin with being the first tourist to visit the Scottish islands. Although his prose seems dated, it is no more flowery than many tourist brochures and is surprisingly modern in its attitudes:

> The modern itch after the knowledge of foreign places is so prevalent that the generality of mankind bestow little thought or time upon the place of their nativity. It is become customary in those of quality to travel young into foreign countries, whilst they are absolute strangers at home; and many of them when they return are only loaded with superficial knowledge . . .

Martin's books were published in London and so would have had a reasonable circulation among the reading classes. However, they would have had to compete with a plethora of similar books on every corner of the globe, which was in the process of being opened up to Europeans by voyages of discovery.

The person who really put the islands of Scotland on the map was one of Martin Martin's readers, Dr Samuel Johnson (1709–84). In 1763 he told his young friend James Boswell (1740–95) that 'his father had put Martin's account into his hands when he was very young, and that he was much pleased with it'. Ten years later, the two of them embarked on one of the great travel journeys of all time and one that had a great effect.

However, touring was definitely for the élite at this time and was not cheap. The growth of what might be called middle-class tourism awaited the development of a rail network and above all the invention of the steamboat, which, in terms of speed, comfort and reliability, opened up the islands to mainlanders, not only in the Hebrides but all over the British Isles.

Before long the steamer companies were organising trips to every possible island destination, including St Kilda. Soon accommodation was mushrooming to accommodate visitors; these are the hotels and guest-houses which are being upgraded and modernised at such expense for today's more discriminating visitors.

The explosion of island tourism in the late nineteenth century revolutionised island life in many respects and resulted

ISLAND COMMUNICATIONS AND TOURISM

ISLAND COMMUNICATIONS AND TOURISM

Dun Caan, The distinctively flat-topped hill on Raasay, in the Inner Hebrides, where those early tourists Johnson and Boswell danced a jig in 1773

Specialist holidays are helping to take up the slack left by the decline of mass tourism. Here a lady is enjoying a painting holiday in Guernsey (*Guernsey Tourist Board*)

observations written down fifty or a hundred years ago are relevant today and the superficial differences sometimes do not seem so important.

One particularly intrepid individual was Mrs Frances Murray, who spent her summers on the island of Oronsay in the Inner Hebrides with her family between 1880 and 1887. She has some interesting descriptive passages of life in the Hebrides at that time, which were published in her book *Summer in the Hebrides*. She had been attracted to that particular island 'by the high-sounding advertisement in a well-known time-table' where she read that:

A yacht anchored off Armadale in the Sound of Sleat

in numerous accounts of the adventures of intrepid travellers. The bookshelves of the nation's libraries groan under the weight of the thousands of 'island books', most of which have deservedly sunk without further trace. However, for almost every island there are one or two books which deserve not to be forgotten and which still make entertaining reading. Mostly they are out of print. Interested readers can write to the appropriate reference libraries, usually to the Local History section, and ask for advice as to which of these early accounts are worthy of resurrection. It is a useful way to spend the occasional rainy day on an island holiday – to settle into a Local History room and share one's own impressions of a place with an earlier visitor. Often the insights and

Promenade Douglas, I.o.M.

Edwardian tourists
thronging the streets
of Douglas, Isle of
Man

In late Victorian and
Edwardian times the
number of travellers
grew by leaps and
bounds. Some of the
figures are staggering.
We know, for example,
that 640,000 people
visited the Isle of Man
in 1913.

. . . a run to this island will be the happiest recollection in a man's terrestrial career; for there is the purest atmosphere, and the mildest climate in the west of Scotland. Its scenery is beautiful and varied: its grand gigantic cliffs, in front of which the seagulls, cormorants, and eider ducks, float and scream continually in countless thousands: its pure yellow sandy beaches, some a mile wide, on which the never-ceasing Atlantic swell tumbles in and expends itself in white foam: its endless and extensive caves, are sights that should be seen!

Mrs Murray had to admit that 'fervid as its language was, we were not disappointed in the reality'. It is worth noting in passing that the skills of tourist board publicists have obviously been around for a long time.

In Mrs Murray's day the ferry services were not always very punctual or reliable – 'a boat may advertise to leave at seven in the evening, and yet keep you waiting till seven in the morning, without any manner of apology'. It was particularly inconvenient for the Murray family; as their holiday house was on the tidal island of Oronsay, they often had to set out several hours before the advertised departure time in order to cross the tidal strand safely. Frequently the family had to spend most of the night at the pier at Scalasaig (in Colonsay), in a store-house, although they also spent 'many a pleasant hour in the inn', waiting 'for the hoarse whistle which signalled the ferrymen to hasten to get all aboard the boat'.

The ferry boat was loaded with 'bundles, babies, bales and beasts' and made its way out to the steamer. Often every available inch was occupied by men and boys, and 'barrels and boxes, baskets and bundles of all kinds and sizes tumbled into the boat as she rose and fell in the surge'.

In the 1880s the 'Islay packet' was a boat of 15 tons, heavy enough to ferry cattle, which sailed to Islay once a week to bring over letters and passengers. But Mrs Murray travelled on the SS *Dunara Castle*, which was owned by McCallum, Orme & Co. Ltd. There were deck cabins, staterooms, ladies' cabins and a saloon. The company advertised that 'a Stewardess is always in attendance, and special attention is paid to ladies travelling alone'. From

1881 the *Dunara Castle* alternated with the *Hebrides* in the summer months. These vessels ran circular tours from Glasgow which lasted from seven to eight days, departing from Glasgow every ten days or so. A cabin for the round trip cost £9. There were occasional special cruises to St Kilda and around the Isle of Skye.

These two steamers ran throughout the 1920s and 1930s and are still fondly remembered by many older people in the Hebrides. The *Dunara Castle*, for example, served the Western Isles from 1875 to 1948. They were well-appointed steamers with good accommodation, 'lighted by electricity' and with what the company described in uncharacteristically imaginative language, 'first class *cruisine*'!

Not all Victorian tourists displayed the sympathetic attitudes and interest of Mrs Murray and others. One of the worst was a certain W. A. Smith, whose little book *Off the Chain* at least has the merit of recording much social detail, even if unsympathetically. Published in 1868, it exudes a tone of moral superiority. Most of it is an account of a holiday in Islay in high summer; on one page he describes himself sweltering on the road from Port Ellen to Bowmore with the thermometer showing 90°F (32°C). He was impressed by the male inhabitants of the island, although he was scathing in his criticism of their way of life:

> I always found the men sturdy, intelligent, and hospitable, and ready to give their assistance kindly and good-humouredly; but a total disregard for truth, a 'plentiful lack' of knowledge regarding everything except whisky and potatoes, and the most degrading filth, these are the principal characteristics of the mass of the natives.

Smith's view of the womenfolk was even more extreme:

> . . . not until the women of the island have some higher standard of excellence and cleanliness brought constantly before them; not until the ladies of the lairds visit the cottages of the poor, and exercise the benign influence which ever belongs to a virtuous woman; not until the women are taught by one of their own sex, that a neat wife and a bright clean fireside to welcome him at home are

ISLAND COMMUNICATIONS AND TOURISM

In 1990 Caledonian MacBrayne Ltd, the state-owned successor to the original companies, reported that for the first time they had carried over six million passengers to twenty-three islands in the Firth of Clyde and the Western Isles.

VICTORIA PIER, DOUGLAS, I.O.M.

Edwardian tourists on Victoria Pier, Douglas, Isle of Man, at the peak of mass tourism before World War I

Golfing holidays are another way to lure visitors to islands. A view of the first tee at Ramsey golf course, Isle of Man (*Isle of Man Tourism*)

the best inducements to make a man work hard, and cut the public-house on his return; in fact, not until the dirty slatternly habits of the women are thoroughly revolutionised, can any real progress be anticipated.

No doubt the same sentiments were being expressed in the mission fields of Africa and Asia. At least Smith had some ideas about what was causing the grinding poverty that so offended his sensibilities:

> They are the characteristics of an enslaved people, and the consequences of a state of serfdom . . . Ground down by a landed aristocracy who treated them like dogs, they have gradually increased in poverty and misery.
> Seeing none on earth, they place all their hope on heaven, and possessed of a strange mixture of superstition and religion, through a life of labour, immorality, and devotion, pass wearily to the grave.

Despite his condemnation of endemic drunkenness, Smith seems to have

(Above) There are holidays for special interest groups of all kinds: these birdwatchers are on the Garvellachs, in the Firth of Lorn

Many islands host special events: this is the annual Battle of Flowers parade in St Helier, Jersey, when the island's parishes compete with floral displays

Another popular kind of special interest tourism is the educational holiday. Here an adult education group is learning about Oronsay Priory, in the Inner Hebrides, in the cloisters of the medieval monastery

partaken freely of the produce of Islay's whisky distilleries, of which he is frequently appreciative. However well intentioned, there is in his book no understanding of the cultural extinction that was the policy of Victorian Britain towards its Gaelic citizens. It was assumed that the people would want to espouse Victorian values and if they could not do so at home, perhaps they were better off in the colonies. Sad to relate, there are still vestiges of these attitudes alive and well in the Britain of the 1990s.

Similar passages could be extracted from books on most British islands. There is a vast literature on the subject. Some accounts of the Isle of Man in the nineteenth century follow the same pattern, but it must be conceded that there is a tremendous amount of social history contained in these accounts which would otherwise have been lost completely.

ISLAND TOURISM

The experience of dealing with tourists is something which probably all islanders have in common, wherever they live, and however large or small their island home. In the 1960s and 1970s there was something of a respite, as the mass tourist resorts of the Mediterranean seemed more attractive than the often soggy memories of British islands. But in the 1990s, sand, sun and sex no longer seem so attractive, even to the mass market, and we are constantly being told that the last two of these are positively dangerous, in the age of skin cancer and AIDS.

So island tourism is 'in' again and the island tourist boards are responding. Their business is now increasingly an all-year industry. There is continuing growth in special activity holidays, aiming at golfers, birdwatchers, archaeologists, cyclists, wind-surfers, pony-

trekkers, yachtspersons and any other group that the marketing officers can dream up or invent. By extending the holiday season, tourism has become a more important part of island economies, with a greater claim to resources and improved infrastructure. As this happens, the product improves, as it is no longer feasible to concentrate on parting tourists from their money for a few weeks in the height of summer. Winter visitors need central heating and lots of hot water to wash away the mud accumulated in their outdoor pursuits.

Another sector of the tourist industry which is expanding wherever the facilities are available is the area of luring conferences to islands. Whether it is seven thousand Young Farmers on the Isle of Man or twenty-five Jurassic geologists on the island of Raasay, conferences are big business and an essential component of the tourist scene. The 'big' islands, such as the Isle of Man, the Isle of Wight, Jersey and Guernsey, put a lot of effort and expertise into winning conference delegates. They fill big hotels in the winter months and bring astonishing amounts of money with them to bolster local economies.

The appeal of islands for conferences is obvious. There is a feeling of sharing an adventure, of being cut off from the rest of the world, which concentrates the collective mind and makes for productive conferences. Many bodies return to the same venue again and again, or progress around other suitable islands. A related area of growth is what is termed 'business tourism'. This is closely related in the Isle of Man and the Channel Islands to the growth of their financial sectors and often involves a businessman or woman bringing their family along on what is essentially an elongated business trip.

As more and more people move to islands, for either business or personal reasons, they help to encourage what is known in the trade as 'VFR traffic' – Visiting Friends and Relations.

All around the islands of Britain, tourist authorities are taking their work very seriously, and as traditional industries like fishing and farming come under pressure, tourism is emerging more and more as the only industry capable of stemming the flood of emigration and making island economies viable. In many places there are mixed feelings about this. Some islanders fear and resent the possibility that they may wind up as exhibits in a theme park. Others are happy to charge inflated prices for providing a fairly ordinary level of services and take delight in 'ripping off' the tourists. Things seem to work out for the best where an island has a secure local economy, which can be stimulated and boosted by tourist-related enterprises. The worst possible scenario is where an island has been overwhelmed by incomers who have gained control of the local economy, who monopolise the tourist industry and who eventually force out (through economic means) the native population. Unfortunately, this is already happening on some Scottish islands.

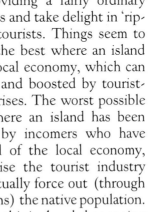

Manx three-legged symbol on the crest of the Isle of Man Steam Packet Company

(Above) Caledonian MacBrayne carry six million ferry passengers annually, over one million of them on this short ferry crossing to Skye from the railhead at Kyleakin

The Snaefell Mountain Railway on the Isle of Man. Built for Victorian tourists, it is still going strong (*Isle of Man Tourism*)

The *Lord of the Isles*
loading at Oban for
Lochboisdale and
Castlebay, one of
Calmac's fleet of fast
modern car ferries

The Isle of Man also
has horse-drawn
trams that pull
tourists along the
Esplanade in Douglas
just as they did before
World War I (*Isle of
Man Tourism*)

5
Dispersal and Emigration

IT is estimated that between 1850 and 1950 the population of the Scottish Highlands and Islands declined by 100,000. But the process of emigration from the Celtic fringe had started in the middle of the eighteenth century with the opening of the New World. Wave upon wave of Scots, Irish, Welsh, Manxmen and Channel Islanders left their homelands and headed for 'The Colonies'.

Not all of the emigration from the islands of the West was to the new land overseas. Internal migration, to the industrial belt of Central Scotland and to the mills of the North of England or to London and the regional centres, probably accounted for at least as many emigrants as left the shores of Britain.

THE HIGHLAND CLEARANCES

In the middle of the nineteenth century, crop failures in Ireland and in most Scottish islands had devastating results. Although the Hebrides never suffered the famines and mass deaths that blighted Ireland, still there was genuine suffering and the chance to leave it all behind was very attractive. In many cases, the desire to emigrate was simply a matter of survival. There were, however, many cruel evictions in what came to be known as 'the Highland clearances'. Many lairds found themselves close to bankruptcy as their tenants were unable to pay even modest rents for farmland and were irresistibly tempted by the economics of sheep farming. For them, too, it was a matter of survival of their way of life. So, land which had been farmed, albeit by a primitive system of subsistence agriculture, for hundreds, if not thousands, of years, was cleared of its inhabitants and turned into sheep farms.

Go to any Scottish island and you will be shown the ruined remains of turf and thatched houses, townships in which hundreds of people once lived. On some islands the decline of population was dramatic. The figures make depressing reading and are repeated throughout the Highlands and Islands.

The population of Islay was nearly 10,000 in 1850 and is 4,000 today. Jura had a population of over 1,000 in 1861, but has just 200 today. Mull had a population of 15,233 at the 1871 census, but now is home to only 1,500, half of them incomers. The population of Skye has declined from 23,000 in 1841 to only 7,000 today. Smaller islands suffered proportionately: Gigha had 534 in 1831, but has only 150 today. Eigg had 233 in 1891, but has only 80 today.

There is a down-side to emigration which has never been adequately documented but which keeps cropping up in unusual places. One might assume that an oppressed minority of people who have been forced out of their ancestral land would treat other minorities with sympathy and consideration in their new home, but there are countless examples from history to suggest that the opposite was the case and the Celtic immigrants were no exception. For example, the Scots took full advantage of the slave trade in the West Indies and the American South, helped to clear the American West of Indians, shot Aborigines for sport in Australia and generally mistreated the natives enthusiastically all over the world. They gained a reputation for being excellent and satisfactorily vicious fighters and Scottish regiments in the British Army gained battle honours all over the world. As opponents, they were feared.

But even a casual reading of Scottish history shows that there are many occasions when Scottish islanders (and their mainland cousins) massacred each other regularly, so it is not surprising that they continued in the same vein when they emigrated to their new worlds. It does help, however, to throw away one's rose-tinted spectacles and view our ancestors more realistically and not through a Scotch mist of nostalgia. Certainly emigrants from the islands of Britain were to the forefront in exploration and innovation in their new homes and were involved in many episodes of individual courage and bravery, but if their achievements are to be celebrated, the darker side of history must be recognised too.

ANCESTOR HUNTERS

Although large-scale emigration took place over a hundred years ago, its impact on modern islanders is considerable. Every summer brings more and

Electricity came too late to improve the lifestyle of the folk in this abandoned cottage near Lochboisdale in South Uist

DISPERSAL AND EMIGRATION

(Right) At Teampull na Trionad, North Uist, in the Western Isles, scholars were reading classical medical treatises in the Middle Ages, translated into Gaelic before they were translated into Latin, at a time when Gaelic culture was vigorous and thriving

Old cultivation ridges on Raasay, looking towards the mountains of the Isle of Skye

(Above) A deserted village on the island of Coll in the Inner Hebrides, at the foot of Beinn Hogh. Johnson and Boswell passed here on their travels in the 1770s

Many islands show traces of abandoned settlements. Here, on the island of Raasay, are the ruins of houses and field systems that were abandoned in the nineteenth century

Gaelic road signs in
Barra, where the
traditional language of
the Western Isles is
still very much alive

(Opposite) A table of
124 Scottish islands,
with the 1891 census
figures, from the
*Ordnance Gazetteer of
Scotland*

more thousands of ancestor hunters, mostly North Americans, searching for the township or cottage from which their forebears left. They may look American and sound American, but they are proud of their background and are determined to trace long-lost relatives. Most come woefully unprepared for the British weather and for a lack of information. Where some countries maintain national research centres to keep records and indexes of emigrants, Britain has only the goodwill of local people and incomplete and impenetrable records. Many parish registers of births, marriages and deaths have simply disappeared and the national census does not start until 1841. The Scottish Record Office (and its equivalents elsewhere) is a mine of information, but it takes a professional genealogist to exploit it to the full.

Many foreign visitors underestimate the time it takes simply to get to many of the islands around Britain and leave themselves with just a few hours between ferries. It is difficult to imagine just what they expect to find. Some islands are far too big to explore on foot

and visitors find themselves trapped in hotels with no transport and no real idea of what to do or where to go. Any island hotelier can furnish dozens of examples of such unhappy visitors, many of whom are used to a sedentary lifestyle and cannot cope with the physical effort involved in travelling and exploring. It is sad to see the disappointment of so many visitors, but there is always the compensation of being able to assist those who are better prepared, who already have contacts and who have taken the trouble to research something of the history and topography of their ancestors' home. It is surprising how often visitors come with accurate details of people and places; in these cases locals can often help and it is very rewarding for them to take an overseas visitor to the very spot where their ancestors lived.

POPULATION STATISTICS

The *Ordnance Gazetteer of Scotland* counted 787 Scottish islands at the 1861 census, defining an island as 'any piece of solid land surrounded by water,

Name	Area		Pop. 1891
	Square miles	Acres	
Long Island, ie Lewis & Harris	859	549,887	30,726
Lewis (Ross)	683	437,221	27,045
Skye (Inverness)	643.28	411,703	15,705
Mull (Argyll)	347.21	222,214	4,691
Mainland (Shetland)	378	242,310	19,741
Islay (Argyll)	246.6	157,851	7,375
Pomona (Orkney)	206.9	132,477	16,498
Harris (Inverness)	176.7	113,142	3,681
Arran (Bute)	168.08	107,572	4,824
Jura (Argyll)	142.9	91,516	619
North Uist (Inverness)	135.7	86,858	3,231
Yell (Shetland)	82.69	52,923	2,511
Hoy (Orkney)	52.8	33,819	1,320
Bute (Bute)	48.68	31,161	11,735
Unst (Shetland)	46.76	29,929	2,269
Rum	41.85	26,785	53
Benbecula (Inverness)	35.7	22,873	1,534
Tiree (Argyll)	33.54	21,471	2,449
Coll (Argyll)	30.6	19,596	522
Sanday (Orkney)	25.77	16,498	1,929
Barra (Inverness)	25.1	16,117	2,131
Westray (Orkney)	24.24	15,516	2,108
Raasay (Inverness)	24.5	15,704	438
South Ronaldsay (Orkney)	20.43	13,080	2,315
Rousay (Orkney)	18.65	11,938	774
Colonsay (Argyll)	16.00	10,878	358
Fetlar (Shetland)	16.77	10,734	363
Stronsay (Orkney)	15.3	9,840	1,275
Eigg (Inverness)	12	7,803	233
Eday (Orkney)	11.5	7,372	647
Shapinsay (Orkney)	11.2	7,172	903
Bressay (Shetland)	10.81	6,919	799
Scalpay (Strath, Inverness)	10	6,489	49
Lismore (Argyll)	9.39	6,014	561
Ulva (Argyll)	7.6	4,924	46
Whalsay (Shetland)	7.62	4,881	927
Baleshare (Inverness)	7.2	4,631	318
Grimsay (Inverness)	7	4,505	281
Muckle Roe (Shetland)	6.81	4,362	213
Seil (Argyll)	5.96	3,820	548
Luing (Argyll)	5.93	3,797	632
Gigha (Argyll)	5.79	3,709	398
Scarba (Argyll)	5.74	3,675	9
Taransay (Inverness)	5.69	3,601	56
Bernera (y) (Harris)	5.27	3,376	501
Foula (Shetland)	5.15	3,300	239
Kerrera (Argyll)	4.9	3,140	92
Great Cumbrae (Bute)	4.87	3,126	1,784
Burra, East and West (Shetland)	4.72	3,024	695
Canna	4.5	2,908	40
South Walls (Orkney)	4.46	2,855	
Burray (Orkney)	4.19	2,683	681
Flotta (Orkney)	4.15	2,661	423
Soay (Inverness)	4.15	2,634	78
Rona (Portree, Inverness)	4	2,564	181
Vatersay (Inverness)	3.9	2,519	32
North Ronaldsay (Orkney)	3.72	2,387	501
Eriskay (Inverness)	3.56	2,299	454
Iona (Argyll)	3.5	2,264	247
Pabbay (Harris, Inverness)	3.37	2,168	3
Oronsay (Colonsay, Inverness)	3.075	1,968	64
Fair Isle (Shetland)	3.02	1,939	223
Scalpa (y) (Harris, Inverness)	3	1,917	517
Egilsay (Orkney)	2.55	1,636	147
Muck	2.4	1,585	48
Mingalay (Inverness)	2.44	1,562	142
Ronay (North Uist, Inverness)	2.3	1,531	6
Monach Island (Inverness)	2.3	1,495	5
Kirkibost (Inverness)	2.2	1,450	6
Gometra (Argyll)	2	1,284	31
St Kilda (Inverness)	1.9	1,200	71
Shuna (Inverness)	1.83	1,173	104
Graemsay (Orkney)	1.8	1,152	223
Wiay (Inverness)	1.6	1,057	10
Sanderay (Inverness)	1.6	1,053	4
Vementry (Shetland)	1.5	960	
Isle of Noss (Shetland)	1.19	762	3
Fuday (Inverness)	1	760	7
Hascosay (Shetland)	1.17	751	
Little Cumbrae (Bute)	1	722	17
Trondra (Shetland)	1.12	722	154
Boreray (North Uist, Inverness)	1	717	152
Lunga (Jura, Argyll)	1	699	15
Holy Island (Arran, Bute)	1.08	691	16
Inchmarnock (Bute)	1.05	675	18
Erraid (Argyll)	1	642	47
Killegray (Inverness)		626	8
Pabbay (Barra, Inverness)		614	13
Calf of Eday (Orkney)		599	
Uyea (Shetland)		598	8
Sanday		577	62
Pabay (Strath, Inverness)		559	7
Oronsay (Morven, Argyll)		539	23
Ensay (Inverness)		537	11
Berneray (Barra, Inverness)		460	36
Wiay (Inverness)		451	
Hellisay (Inverness)		384	
Sanda (Argyll)		381	36
Garbh Eileach (Argyll)		342	
Stromay (Inverness)		348	
Eilean Fladday (Inverness)		336	76
Torsay (Argyll)		275	7
Gighay (Argyll)		264	398
Gunna (Argyll)		260	
Eorsa (Argyll)		259	
Inch Kenneth (Argyll)		248	2
Isay (Inverness)		234	
Hemetray (Inverness)		233	
Fuiay (Inverness)		217	
Soa (Argyll)		210	
Cara (Argyll)		203	3
Muldoanich (Inverness)		203	
Cliasay Mor and Beg		201	
Little Colonsay (Argyll)		200	2
Lunga (Argyll)		195	15
Ascrib Islands (Inverness)		187	
Eilean an Iasgaich (Inverness)		183	
Tahay (Inverness)		171	
Eileach an Naoimh		169	
Longay (Inverness)		164	
Stockinish (Inverness)		155	
Vaccasay (Inverness)		154	
Texa (Islay, Argyll)		151	
Nave (Argyll)		150	

DISPERSAL AND EMIGRATION

(Right) A thatched cottage near Lochboisdale, South Uist. Many traditional cottages, like this one, have been abandoned quite recently

The crofting township of Daliburgh, South Uist. After saving Bonnie Prince Charlie, Flora MacDonald emigrated to America from here

(Above) One of the main causes of depopulation in the twentieth century was the carnage of World War I. Many island war memorials, like this one on Colonsay, have distressingly long lists of names

Traditional cultivation methods that survive in Barra: *fiannagan*, inaccurately termed 'lazy beds', were used for growing potatoes, using seaweed for fertiliser

Ruined cottage at
Drumclach, Colonsay
– a common sight on
any Hebridean island.

which affords sufficient vegetation to support one or more sheep, or which is inhabited by man'. At that time it was reckoned that the Outer Hebrides (from the Butt of Lewis to Barra Head) consisted of 160 islands and islets, of which 100 were inhabited. The number inhabited today is 13. In Shetland the number of populated islands has decreased from 28 to 14 and in the Orkney archipelago it has decreased from 29 to 18. The table on page 69, taken from the *Gazetteer* gives the land area of 125 islands and their population in 1891.

Although the results of the 1991 census are not yet available, the following table shows the current populations and land areas of the inhabited islands of the British Isles.

An analysis of these figures throws up the interesting fact that just under 500,000 people are permanent residents of the islands of Britain, out of a total population for the United Kingdom, the Channel Islands and the Isle of Man of about 56 million. So, just over 1 per cent of Britain's population are islanders. And of the half-million islanders, about 400,000 live on only five islands: the Isle of Man, Anglesey, the Isle of Wight, Jersey and Guernsey. This leaves about 100,000 Scottish islanders who live in the Firth of Clyde, the Inner and Outer Hebrides, and the Northern Isles.

This is why islanders are so special – there are so few of them. Is it too much to ask the wider community to make it possible, through economic and political support, for this rather special group of people to continue to be able to enjoy their island way of life and to share it occasionally with the rest of us?

	Area (sq miles/ sq km)	Population (resident)
Northern Isles		38,992
Shetland	552 (1,429)	20,794
(total for 14 inhabited islands)		
Mainland	378 (979)	6,000
Bressay	11 (28)	300
Whalsay	8 (21)	1,000
Yell	83 (215)	1,185
Fetlar	15 (39)	100
Unst	46 (118)	1,050
Fair Isle	2 (5)	80
Orkney	375 (971)	18,118
(total for 18 inhabited islands)		
Mainland	189 (489)	14,000
Burray	6 (15)	270
S. Ronaldsay	15 (39)	825
Hoy	75 (194)	450
Shapinsay	10 (26)	325
Eday	10 (26)	135
Westray	18 (46)	715
Papa Westray	3 (8)	100
Rousay	18 (46)	210
Stronsay	14 (36)	450
Sanday	15 (39)	485
N. Ronaldsay	5 (13)	110
Outer Hebrides	1,118 (2,895)	31,672
(total for 13 inhabited islands)		
Lewis	680 (1,761)	21,000
Harris	90 (233)	2,450
Scalpay	2 (5)	450
North Uist	118 (305)	1,500
Benbecula	30 (77)	2,250
South Uist	141 (365)	2,400
Eriskay	5 (13)	200
Barra	20 (51)	1,350
Vatersay	3 (7)	72
Inner Hebrides		16,590
Skye	535 (1,385)	8,500
Raasay	30 (77)	150
Canna	4.5 (11)	20
Rum	41 (106)	40
Eigg	8 (20)	80
Muck	2.5 (6)	25
Mull	352 (911)	1,500
Iona	4.5 (11)	100
Lismore	10 (26)	100
Seil	8 (20)	425
Easdale	1 (2.5)	30
Luing	11 (28)	160
Kerrera	7.5 (19)	45
Coll	29 (75)	150
Tiree	29 (75)	780
Islay	401 (1,038)	4,000
Jura	141 (365)	205
Colonsay	16 (41)	120
Gigha	9 (23)	160
Clyde Islands	221 (572)	12,900
Arran	166 (430)	4,500
Bute	47 (121)	6,800
Cumbrae	8 (20)	1,600
Northern Ireland		
Rathlin	5 (13)	100
Isle of Man	221 (572)	72,000
Wales	277 (717)	71,030
Anglesey	276 (714)	71,000
(incl Holy Island)		
Caldey	1 (2.5)	30
England	156 (404)	112,325
Lundy	2 (5)	25
Isles of Scilly	6 (15)	2,100
Isle of Wight	147 (380)	110,000
Lindisfarne	1 (2.5)	200
Channel Islands	77 (199)	142,600
Guernsey	25 (64)	60,000
Alderney	4 (10)	2,000
Sark	2 (5)	550
Herm	1 (2.5)	50
Jersey	45 (116)	80,000
Total populations		
Northern Isles		39,000
Outer Hebrides		32,000
Inner Hebrides		17,000
Clyde Islands		13,000
Isle of Man		72,000
Welsh Islands		71,000
English Islands		112,000
Channel Islands		143,000
		499,000

6
Island Government

THE government of all the islands of Britain varies enormously and is a matter of great complexity. The Isle of Man and the Channel Islands are not part of the United Kingdom of Great Britain and Northern Ireland, and have their own separate arrangements, although they owe their allegiance to the Crown. All the other islands of Britain are part of local government administrative areas, although there is a lot of variation in the powers that are available to various island authorities. Before the reorganisation of local government in the 1970s, the islands of Britain came under the authority of county councils, which produced some ridiculous administrative situations – for example, the Western Isles of Scotland were run partly by Ross and Cromarty County Council from Dingwall and partly by Inverness-shire County Council from Inverness.

The Shetland Islands Council and the Orkney Islands Council are 'all-purpose' local authorities that run all aspects of island life in their respective jurisdictions. The Western Isles are now run by their own Islands Council, which is always referred to by its Gaelic name, Comhairle nan Eilean. Most of its officers are bilingual in English and Gaelic and use Gaelic as their working language.

With the Inner Hebrides the situation is more complicated. Ardnamurchan Point, the most westerly point of mainland Scotland, has once again become the administrative divide it was in the Middle Ages. The islands to the north of Ardnamurchan Point are in Highland Region, while those to the south are in Strathclyde Region, Scotland's largest local government area, which contains over half the country's total population. All the islands south of Ardnamurchan are also part of Argyll and Bute District, which has its headquarters in Lochgilphead. The islands north of Ardnamurchan are generally part of the District on the adjacent mainland, except that Skye and Lochalsh District, which includes the island of Raasay, is made up partly of islands and partly of the adjacent mainland. The detail of these administrative arrangements is even more confusing, and so best avoided, at least for the moment.

As for the islands in the Firth of

Clyde, all are part of Strathclyde Region. Bute is in Argyll and Bute District; Arran and the Cumbraes are part of Cunninghame District, but more importantly come under the jurisdiction of the Highlands and Islands Enterprise, the successor of the Highlands and Islands Development Board.

Anglesey is part of Gwynedd, which is one of the regions of Wales, but it has its own borough council. The Isles of Scilly are part of Cornwall and the Isle of Wight is part of Hampshire. Both have local councils.

There are other jurisdictions which are important to islands. Perhaps the most important is the government of tourism. In some of the Scottish islands this can produce a confusing array of bodies. Thus, tourism in Islay is the concern of the local Islay and Jura Marketing Association, of the Kintyre, Mid-Argyll and Islay Tourist Board, of the Tourism, Leisure and Recreation Committee of Argyll and Bute District Council, of the Local Enterprise Company, of Argyll and the Islands Enterprise, of the Highlands and Islands Enterprise and of the Scottish Tourist Board. This is probably not a complete list!

THE CHANNEL ISLANDS

The constitutional position of the Channel Islands is complex and is the direct result of a number of historical circumstances, beginning with their integration into the Duchy of Normandy in the tenth and eleventh centuries. It was the Duke of Normandy, *their* duke, who conquered England in 1066, and this is why the inhabitants of the Channel Islands continue to give their allegiance to his direct descendant, the British monarch. In the Channel Islands, the loyal toast is to 'The Queen, Our Duke'. Duke William of Normandy, William the Conqueror, was himself the descendant of Viking settlers who overran Normandy. Their influence is

seen in island place-names and possibly in some elements of land divisions and island laws.

In 1204 Normandy was integrated into the emerging Kingdom of France and the English king had eventually to renounce the title of Duke of Normandy in 1259. In 1254 King Henry III of England granted the islands to his eldest son and heir, the future Edward I, 'in such manner that the said lands . . . may never be separated from the Crown and that no one, by reason of this grant made to the said Edward may have any claim to the said lands . . . but that they should remain to the kings of England in their entirety for ever'. This grant meant that in English law the islands were 'annexed to the Crown', so that whoever was the lawful king (or queen) of

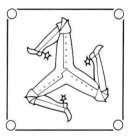

The crest of the parish of St Brelade, Jersey, on the wall of its local government offices. Jersey fishermen ranged far and wide and were famous for their woolly jumpers

SALLE PAROISSIALE DE ST. BRELADE

ISLAND GOVERNMENT

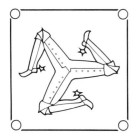

The bailiwick of Guernsey comprises the islands of Guernsey, Alderney and Sark, and the dependencies of Herm and Jethou – all inhabited islands with a total population of about 61,000. The bailiwick of Jersey has a further 80,000. These two bailiwicks are independent of each other and have separate legislatures, judiciaries and executives.

England was, by that fact alone, the lawful ruler of the Channel Islands.

However, the islands were never incorporated into the Kingdom of England then or at any subsequent time. Although he surrendered the ducal title in 1259, King Henry continued to rule the islands as though he were still Duke of Normandy, observing island laws and customs. These were confirmed by subsequent sovereigns in various charters which granted the islands their own judiciaries and other privileges.

The islands maintained close ecclesiastical, trading and personal relations with Normandy well into modern times, but have continuously given their loyalty to the Crown. Guernsey and Jersey are bailiwicks – that is, they are ruled by bailiffs.

The bailiff is the island's chief citizen and representative, appointed by the sovereign by letters patent under the Great Seal of the Realm; he is the administrative head of the island's government – in effect, its chief executive. The islands are not part of the United Kingdom, nor are they sovereign states or colonies. They do not send representatives to the Westminster parliament. However, acts of parliament may contain a provision empowering Her Majesty the Queen by order in council to extend any of the provisions of an act to Guernsey or Jersey.

In practical terms, the main advantage to the Channel Islands of these constitutional arrangements is that Her Majesty's Government does not seek to legislate for the islands 'in any taxation matter, or in any other matter which has long been accepted as the responsibility and concern of the Insular Authorities'. Last confirmed in 1968, this assures the continuation of the islands' privileges. Defence and foreign affairs are administered for the islands by the British government.

The island legislatures are known as the States of Guernsey and the States of Jersey. The States of Guernsey in its present form can be traced back to 1605. It consists of the States of Election, whose only function is to act as an electoral college, and the States of Deliberation, who are in effect the legislature and the executive of Guernsey. It comprises the bailiff, 12 conseillers, 33 people's deputies, 10 douzaine representatives and two crown officials, HM Procureur and HM Comptroller, who are equivalent to the Attorney-General and the Solicitor-General in England. The conseillers are elected by the States of Election and hold office for six years. The people's deputies are elected by universal adult suffrage at a general election which is held every three years. The douzaine representatives are nominated by the ten douzaines or parish councils of the island and serve for one year.

In Jersey there are similar arrangements. The States of Jersey consists of 12 senators, 12 constables and 28 deputies, who are all elected by popular franchise and presided over by the bailiff. In both bailiwicks there are independent courts. In the bailiwick of Guernsey there are special arrangements relating to Alderney and Sark, which also have their own legislatures.

The constitutional position of the Channel Islands has evolved over the centuries and is still evolving and changing. The rather antiquated electoral arrangements, especially on Guernsey, are currently being updated and improved. Recent developments in Europe and the increased harmonisation of the member states of the European Community, mean that the Channel Islands must adapt quickly or run the risk of losing their privileged status, especially in the area of international finances. In 1990 an English Sunday newspaper interviewed one of the Guernsey leaders of the 'Right to Vote' campaign: 'It's just us and Albania left,' he said, 'and it looks as though Albania may crack first.' He may be right!

ISLE OF MAN

Like the Channel Islands, the Isle of Man is a Crown possession and is not part of the United Kingdom. It has its own judiciary and legislature. The roots of its present constitutional arrangements lie in the history of the island, particularly in the Norse period. From AD800 until 1266, the Kingdom of Mann was part of the territory of the king of Norway and was ruled by Norsemen. Many of the island's institutions date from this period.

In 1263 King Haakon of Norway led an expedition to Scotland to assert his claim to the Western Isles, which for a hundred years had been ruled by the MacDonald Lords of the Isles, the descendants of Somerled. He was a guerrilla leader of mixed parentage, the son of a Celtic father and Norse mother, who defeated King Olaf of Mann in a sea battle around 1156, married his daughter and gained control of the Isle of Man. Haakon came to regain control for Norway of Mann and the southern Hebrides, but failed to win a decisive victory over Alexander III of Scotland at the Battle of Largs in 1263. Haakon died on his way back to Norway and in 1266 the Norwegians ceded all their possessions in the Western Isles, including the Isle of Man, to the Scottish king, whose daughter Margaret, the 'Maid of Norway', was married to the King of Norway.

During the Scottish Wars of Independence the English took advantage of the disorganisation of the Scottish state to lay claim to the Isle of Man. After his victory over the English at Bannockburn in 1314, King Robert the Bruce reasserted the Scots claim to Mann and over the next two hundred years it changed hands frequently as the fortunes of war ebbed and flowed over the Scottish border. Finally, in 1405 it was

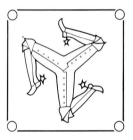

Manx government buildings in Douglas, Isle of Man, home of the oldest parliament in the world (*Isle of Man Tourism*)

ISLAND
GOVERNMENT

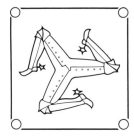

The three-legged
symbol of the Isle of
Man occurs on
government buildings,
here on the harbour
offices at Castletown

A more modern, and
more controversial,
rendering of the
symbol of the
Kingdom of Mann at
Ronaldsway Airport

granted to the Stanley family, later known as the Earls of Derby, who, with their connections, the Dukes of Atholl, ruled the island until 1765. Since then it has come under the direct rule of the British Crown, although it retains its ancient rights and constitution.

For the purposes of government the island is divided into sheadings and parishes. There are six sheadings and all except one contain three parishes each. It is thought that the sheadings correspond to the chief tribal units of the island in pre-Norse days. Now they form electoral districts for the return of sixteen out of the twenty-four members of the island's legislature, the House of Keys. This system was created by Godred Crovan, the King Orry of Manx tradition, to govern (on behalf of the king of Norway) his maritime kingdom of Mann and the Isles. It was reckoned that he controlled thirty-two islands, which had a common parliament. Because it was his capital and also the wealthiest island, Mann sent sixteen representatives to Godred Crovan's parliament. The Hebrides were divided into four groups based on the large islands of Lewis, Skye, Mull and Islay, each sending four representatives to the parliament on the Isle of Man, which was called, after the Norse fashion, the Tynwald.

After the Norse lost the southern Hebrides to Somerled in 1156, the Hebridean element in Tynwald was reduced by eight, giving the House of Keys the twenty-four members it has today. In 1266 they lost eight more members as the northern Hebrides were ceded by Norway to Scotland, but the Manxmen refused to accept that this would be permanent and kept eight places in Tynwald for their northern members, temporarily appointing eight more men from the Isle of Man itself to fill their places.

The system as it exists today is a result of reforms that were carried out in 1866. The government of the Isle of Man now consists of four elements. These are the lieutenant-governor, who represents the Crown; the legislative council, known as the Upper House, which consists of ten members; the House of Keys, with twenty-four elected members; and the Tynwald Court, which consists of the governor and the two branches of the legislature sitting together.

The principal functions of Tynwald are to levy taxes and to decide how to spend the money collected, subject to the governor's right of veto. It appoints committees, known as boards, to administer the various departments of government, including education, roads, harbours, airports, health and social services, fishing, agriculture, advertising, forestry, electricity, water, and town and country planning.

In 1958 further reforms resulted from negotiations with the British government, and the Westminster parliament passed the Isle of Man Act. This dealt with the problems of customs duties and other financial matters, and had the effect of removing British control of the island's finances, giving Tynwald the power to control revenue and expenditure on the island.

Like the Channel Islands, the Isle of Man faces an uncertain future in the new Europe. As well as the usual prob-

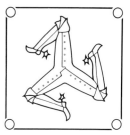

ISLAND GOVERNMENT

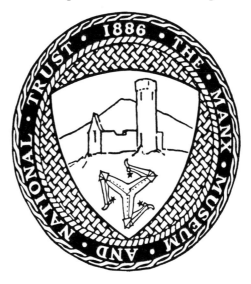

Crest of the Manx Museum and National Trust, founded in 1886

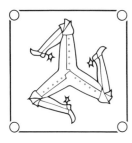

lems of 'harmonisation', it has particular problems in the area of human rights legislation because of its statutes that make homosexual behaviour, even between consenting adults, illegal. The other main area of controversy is the practice of birching offenders, which is infrequently carried out but jealously guarded as one sanction available to island courts. In recent years the House of Keys has tried to defuse these controversies by a combination of keeping a low profile and forcing through reforming legislation, but in so doing has fallen foul of island public opinion, which tends to be uncompromising.

'PRIVATE' ISLANDS

There are a number of islands which are, in one way or another, effectively privately owned, with consequent very close control of their populations and of social and economic developments. At the benevolent end of the spectrum there are uninhabited islands which are kept as nature reserves or bird sanctuaries, with perhaps a seasonal warden and modest facilities for research staff. Examples are the Isle of May in the Firth of Forth, the Calf of Man at the south end of the Isle of Man, or the Pembrokeshire islands such as Ramsey, Skomer and Skokholm. Bodies like the Nature Conservancy Council, the Royal Society for the Protection of Birds, the World Wide Fund for Nature, the Countryside Commission, and local trusts administer many islands and control access, often backed by legislation.

The island of Rum, in the Inner Hebrides, is owned and controlled by the Nature Conservancy Council, and is operated by them as an outdoor laboratory in which they conduct research into, for example, red deer. They have also reintroduced the white-tailed sea eagle into the area, which is slowly spreading outwards throughout the Hebrides. Kinloch Castle, a massive late-Victorian pile, is maintained as an

up-market hotel to generate some income. The population of the island is about forty, all of whom are dependent in one way or another on the Nature Conservancy Council. Most are directly employed by them.

The National Trust for Scotland owns Fair Isle, half-way between Shetland and Orkney, and Canna, in the Inner Hebrides. Fair Isle has been a great success, with its declining population stabilised and now slowly increasing, while in Canna, which was taken into ownership recently, there have been some problems in managing the small community. St Kilda, the remote island west of the Outer Hebrides, has lost its permanent inhabitants but is permanently inhabited by army personnel who run a missile tracking station there. During the summer months the National Trust for Scotland sends working parties to St Kilda to preserve and restore what is left of the original way of life – the last native residents were evacuated in 1930. Lundy, the 'puffin island' in the Bristol Channel, is administered by the Landmark Trust, a private trust that specialises in rescuing historical properties and turning them into up-market self-catering holiday accommodation.

Some islands are more or less completely owned by one individual. Colonsay, in the Inner Hebrides, belongs to Lord Strathcona and Mount Royal, who has converted most of his own home into holiday flats and runs over twenty other properties on the island as self-catering units, despite a serious shortage of housing for local people. It is all done fairly benevolently, but the bottom line is that the estate must pay its own way or be sold. The island of Gigha, off the coast of Kintyre, has been sold several times in the last fifty years, usually to absentee English landlords who have made their money in the financial sector and are looking for a tax-free investment.

The problem of absentee landlords

makes it extremely difficult, not to say stressful, to operate a successful island community. One never knows when the owner will sell up, perhaps to a Dutch or Arab buyer, or, worse still, to a pop star. Despite reassuring noises from proprietors, it is hard for islanders to forget the possibility that, literally at the drop of a hat, they may lose their livelihood, their home and their heritage and be forced out of their island paradise into the real world. It is not a happy prospect. Sometimes islanders are afforded a measure of protection by legislation, as with crofting tenants, or, as in the case of Sark in the Channel Islands, by a balance of rights and obligations which are authentically feudal.

Islanders who are lucky enough to have secure crofting tenancies or who own their own land will find that with freedoms come the complexities of dealing with all the myriad bureaucracies who want to be involved in their lives. On large islands – for example, Mull and Islay – there can be tensions between different groups in the population, which is usually most acrimonious between locals and 'incomers', who are often (although not always) from the south of England.

There can also be friction between different parts of an island as they compete for infrastructure and services. Islay has two competing ferry terminals which, in modern conditions, is one too many, but the islanders could not agree on which one should be closed. Eventually the decision will be forced for commercial reasons, at which point everybody will be able to blame the ferry company. There is also great competition in Islay between the Rinns peninsula and the rest of the island. Most of Islay's Gaelic-speaking population lives there, but the administrative centre of the island is in Bowmore and the two ferry terminals are at opposite ends of the island. When the entire peninsula was made into a Site of Special Scientific Interest, with consequent restrictions on farming practices, the beleaguered locals felt that they were in danger of becoming exhibits in a cultural theme park. There are similar problems on the Isle of Skye and elsewhere.

An essential aspect of the government of islands is the system of networks which operate and the way in which the members of these networks are chosen or selected. It often seems to be the case that the same few individuals turn up over and over again on island committees, sometimes organising a bewildering array of institutions and events. There is a tendency for these people to be incomers, often with a background in management and the professions, whose skills are put to good use. Despite their hard work, there is often resentment on the part of the locals, who are not used to being very well organised. A certain amount of mutual understanding and sensitivity on both sides is desirable, but not always present. But this is an issue which anybody thinking of living on an island should address seriously.

ISLAND GOVERNMENT

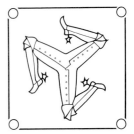

7
Living on an Island

TWO kinds of people live on islands: those who are born on them and cannot wait to get away, and those who go to live on them in order to get away from the urban rat race. Where these two groups come into contact, there is a lot of mutual misunderstanding of motives and much recrimination.

ISLAND CLIMATE

First and foremost, there is the question of climate. It is one thing to view a Hebridean island on a magical Easter break or on a shimmering August day, when the birds are singing, the sun is glistening on the sheltered waters of a sea-loch, backed by majestic mountain scenery. The reality faced by the people who have to live there in October, November, December, January, February and March is very different, because for six months of the year it is among the harshest environments in Western Europe. It is worth remembering that thousands of islanders left their island paradises in the 18th and 19th centuries because survival became marginal, due to crop failures, overpopulation and the excesses of landlords.

Any islander from Shetland to Jersey could recite a string of names of incomers who left their dream island after their second winter, never to return. Incomers are able to cope with the first winter by telling themselves that the conditions must be exceptional, that their renovations and improvements are not yet finished and that next year they will be better prepared. After the second winter the realities of island life, climatic and otherwise, will have penetrated the most persistent romantic illusions and their island home is put on the market, at a price well beyond the means of any islander.

INCOMERS' HOMES

The ethics of selling property to incomers is much debated in the islands. Only in the Channel Islands is the flow of incomers actually controlled by legislation – although many other islanders would wish for such an enlightened attitude by their own rulers. Immigrants are usually able to pay inflated house prices, which even then seem to them a bargain by South of England standards. With generous pensions or redundancy

In the hope that the provision of information can help to draw back the curtains of ignorance, potential incomers are invited to consider their position very carefully before they move to the island of their dreams.

(Above) The city-dweller's image of the Hebrides – but the reality can be cruel. This is one of the last thatched houses in North Uist, at Sollas

(Left) Traditional island architecture was well suited to wind and rain. This thatched cottage is in Tiree. The modern equivalent is double-glazing

Sheep are the
mainstay of many
island economies;
these are at Garvard
on the Hebridean
island of Colonsay

payments and a nice profit from the sale of their suburban home, price is not usually a problem.

If we lived in an Orwellian *1984* state and had a Ministry for Islands, one of the requirements for potential residents would be a crash course in the psychology of human behaviour. In the last chapter the problem of the clash of lifestyles in running island committees and introducing new ideas was hinted at. Nobody likes to have their way of life altered or threatened, even if the new ideas are good ones. It is often said that the Spanish word *mañana* conveys a degree of urgency which does not exist in Scottish Gaelic. To mistake this lack of haste for laziness is a common mistake.

When they move to an island home, most incomers want to modernise their dwelling – for example, by replacing windows, installing double-glazing, upgrading bathroom facilities, improving the kitchen, putting in a damp-proof course, fixing a leaky roof, and so on. It would seem to be elementary that incomers should consider these factors and work out exactly how much it will cost to do all the work required, but repeatedly people make the mistake of spending all their money before they are able to complete the job.

Locals often find the requirements of incomers amusing, until the more thoughtful of them realise that all the improvements will add to the value of the house and put it out of the financial reach of young island couples when the incomers die or move on. Many so-called 'improvements' are seen as unnecessary extravagances. One island laird recounts how he had negotiated housing improvement grants with his local authority and wanted to install indoor toilets for his tenants. He was prepared to cover all the costs involved himself and asked only for a small rise in annual rent to cover the increased insurance costs on the improved cottages. To

This island farmyard,
at Scalasaig, Colonsay,
could be marketed as
an agricultural
museum

one of his aged tenants he explained that in weekly terms this would amount to no more than the price of a packet of cigarettes. The tenant was unimpressed, having managed perfectly well with the existing facilities for over eighty years, and said that he would rather have the cigarettes!

Whatever work *is* necessary, incomers must come to terms with the fact that it is not likely to be done quickly or cheaply. This is not a matter of retaliation by island building contractors. Everything has to be ordered from the mainland and brought on to the island (in most cases) and transport costs are not cheap. If your island is lucky enough to have residents who can undertake building work, you must be prepared to share their time with other people who rely on their skills as much as you. Any emergencies which come up will have to be attended to before your solid-fuel heater is installed. It is usually best to plunge into island social life energetically, make lots of friends, offer whatever help you can to other people and wait for some reciprocation.

TRAVEL FACILITIES

Many smaller islands have a relaxed regime regarding the roadworthiness of motor vehicles, and on such islands it is common for residents to keep one car in good condition on the mainland for use when they travel there and a more basic vehicle on their island. Having two vehicles saves on ferry costs, which can be substantial. The ferry companies all offer attractive concessions for island residents, but transport costs are a big problem. On many Scottish islands, a trip to the mainland – for example, to a market to sell cattle or sheep – involves staying there for at least two days, thus adding substantially to costs, which mainland farmers do not incur. And if a farmer has paid transport costs to get his stock to a mainland auction, he does not really have the option of not selling, and may have to settle for a ridiculously low price.

There are strong arguments for devising some way of relieving island farmers from these disadvantages. The Norwegians have implemented a system

LIVING ON AN ISLAND

(Right) Islanders are learning entrepreneurial skills, as here at Armadale, on the Isle of Skye. The tables are made from recycled fish-boxes

The island post office is often the nerve centre of the community. This one is at Castlebay, Barra

(Above) Cattle are also an important part of island agriculture. These Highland cattle are grazing on Coll, near the ruins of a cottage where Dr Johnson once spent a night

Sheep are the mainstay of the economy of many Hebridean islands. On Coll, one farmer is raising rare breeds

Islands can be busy
places – the bustling
harbour and shopping
area at Stornoway,
Isle of Lewis
(*Highlands & Islands
Enterprise*)

known as the Road Equivalent Tariff,
whereby the cost of transport to
islands is calculated by distance, not
according to the mode of transport.
The tariff amounts to a subsidy for
island-dwellers, but for fragile island
communities to continue in anything
like their present state, this kind of help
from the community at large is essential.

The Road Equivalent Tariff would help
with crippling freight costs.

Ferry timetables are another source of
disaffection with the ferry companies.
Under recent government policies,
however, transport companies are having increasingly to cover their costs, and
public subsidies are harder to get. Caledonian MacBrayne Ltd (known by the

locals as Calmac), who operate ferry services to twenty-three Scottish islands on the west coast and in the Firth of Clyde, try to operate their ferries more or less around the clock, which caused them problems with their crews as well as with the public, who found themselves waiting at ferry terminals at truly ungodly hours. Calmac also wanted to improve their efficiency and cost-effectiveness by operating to the Western Isles on Sundays, but the company fell foul of island sabbatarianism and got themselves in a debate about preserving the islands' way of life that cannot really be reflected on a balance sheet.

Islanders cannot avoid the indisputable

Council houses at
Lochboisdale, with
lobster pots stacked
ready for use. Fishing
for lobsters and clams
is a profitable sideline
for many island
homes.

(Left) A pyramid of nets on the Shetland island of Whalsay. Fishing on a small scale is crucial to many island economies (*Sue Anderson*)

fact that islands are surrounded by water. This can have strange effects on people who are not used to it. It can be exciting to be cut off from the rest of the world on an island holiday for a couple of weeks in summer, but to be surrounded by water for months on end is a new experience for most incomers, and 'island madness' is something to watch for and to take steps to avoid. Even some native islanders have to get away sometimes, although many older people have never been to the mainland. Usually they are female, as male islanders will have served in the Merchant Navy or in the armed services at some time in their lives.

So, this is yet something else for incomers to budget for – essential trips to the mainland, which can be combined with shopping for supplies and visiting relatives. Weddings and funerals are looked forward to for these reasons, but basically any excuse is sufficient.

A salmon-fishing station on the island of Raasay, on the beach in front of Brochel Castle, the stronghold of one branch of the Macleod clan

Island living can be
very isolated. This
Land-Rover is
crossing the tidal
Strand to Oronsay in
the Inner Hebrides

EARNING A LIVING

Unless an incomer has independent means, he or she will have to consider how to generate an income. The era of a proliferation of potters and small (and usually bad) art studios seems, thankfully, to be over. Nowadays, anybody running a small business, especially on an island, has to have a good quality product, good marketing skills and good business practice. One possibility which is opening up new opportunities for island businesses is what is called 'teleworking', where, through the miracles of modern telecommunications, it is possible to sit at a computer terminal on the most remote island imaginable and be in immediate contact with anywhere in the world. Some island communities have established community computer resource centres known as 'telecottages', which are like electronic village halls, but many individuals and small businesses are taking advantage of new technology in many new and innovative ways. A major initi-

ative launched in 1990 and funded jointly by the Highlands and Islands Enterprise and British Telecom brought digital telephone lines to remote areas and, by charging for long-distance transfer at local rates, made the system attractive to islanders.

This development is simply an extension on a smaller scale of the way in which the Isle of Man and the Channel Islands have taken advantage of new telecommunications technology to develop their international banking and financial service industries. The prospects for the future are exciting and the response by islanders to these new opportunities is extremely encouraging. Clearly, this is an aspect of island life which will become more and more important and the day will come when a computer terminal is as essential as a telephone in an island home.

For potential island residents who might be tired of hearing of some of the negative aspects of island life, the electronic revolution may give some much-needed encouragement. But they would

be well advised to think things through carefully, to make sure that they are adequately funded, to be prepared to muck in with other islanders, to buy adequate wet-weather clothing – and to keep smiling! Islands do have many positive features which modern society desperately needs – peace, tranquillity, quality of life, clean air, pure water, community feeling and a safe environment in which to bring up children. Perhaps the rest of us can find ways to enjoy islands without destroying the features that attract us to them.

Cutting and stacking peats for fuel is an important communal activity on many islands; these have been left to dry on the Isle of Lewis *(Highlands & Islands Enterprise)*

PART II

Island Groups

8
The Northern Isles

OFF the northern coast of mainland Scotland there are two archipelagos. The Orkney islands are separated from Caithness by the turbulent Pentland Firth, which is 6 miles (9.6km) wide, and consist of 52 islands, of which 18 are currently inhabited. The second island group is Shetland, which lies 48 miles (77km) north-north-east of Orkney, consisting of 100 islands, 14 of them inhabited. In between the two groups is Fair Isle, which administratively is part of Shetland.

ORKNEY

The largest of the Orkney islands is known as Mainland and has a resident population of 14,000 who live in a land area of 189sq miles (489sq km). The landscape is flat but not featureless, with rolling hills of fertile farmland, interspersed with freshwater lochs. There are two large towns, Stromness and Kirkwall. Of the 52 islands in the Orkney archipelago, 18 are inhabited, with a total population of 18,000.

Mainland was originally called Hrossey, meaning 'horse island' in Norse, which is a far more imaginative

name. The Viking raiders and settlers who came to the islands in the tenth century had vivid imaginations and a way with words, which they set down for posterity in their sagas. The Orkneys were at the heart of the Vikings' sea empire and the sagas are full of exciting stories about their exploits and their way of life. The major event of the Viking era in Orkney was the murder of Earl Magnus Erlendson by his cousin Earl Haakon Paulson, in 1117. The two earls had ruled jointly, but quarrelled, and Magnus was killed by treachery on the island of Egilsay, where a church commemorates the event. Magnus was buried inside the little church in Birsay. Subsequently, miracles and cures convinced the local bishop that Magnus must have been a saint and in 1137 a cathedral was founded in his memory in Kirkwall. It is the most impressive church on any of the islands of Britain.

Next door to St Magnus Cathedral is the twelfth-century Bishop's Palace and the sixteenth-century Earl's Palace, which was built by Earl Patrick, nephew of Mary, Queen of Scots, one of the Stewart earls who terrorised Orkney. Opposite the cathedral is the fine

(Previous Page) Looking towards the mountains of Rum from the neighbouring island of Eigg, under a powdering of snow (*Highlands & Islands Enterprise*)

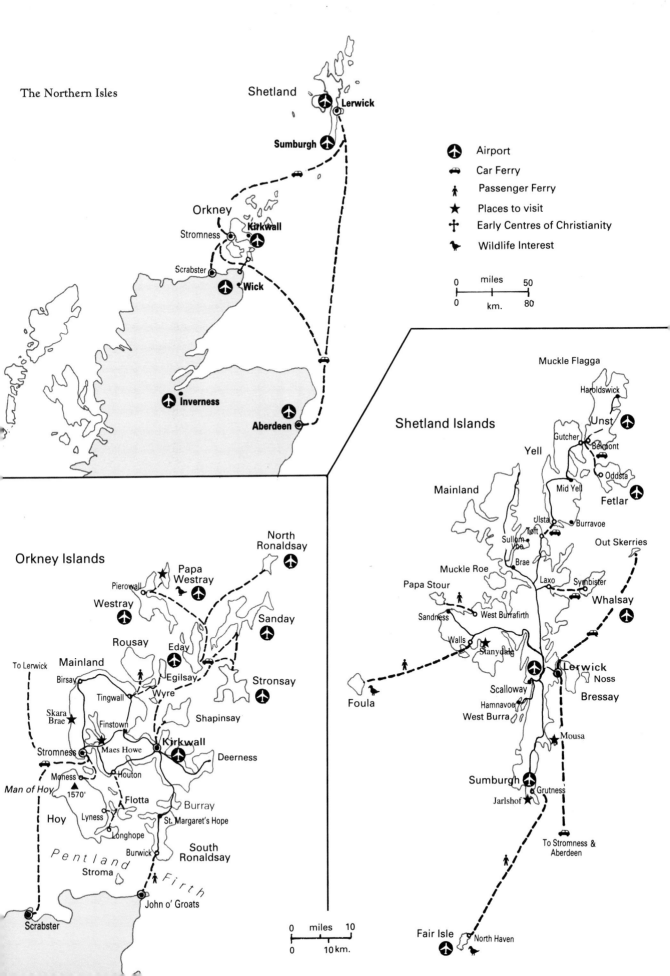

The Northern Isles

Shetland
Lerwick
Sumburgh

Orkney
Stromness
Kirkwall
Scrabster
Wick

Inverness

Aberdeen

✈ Airport
🚗 Car Ferry
🚶 Passenger Ferry
★ Places to visit
✝ Early Centres of Christianity
🐦 Wildlife Interest

0 — miles — 50
0 — km. — 80

Shetland Islands

Muckle Flagga
Haroldswick
Unst
Gutcher
Belmont
Oddsta
Yell
Mainland
Mid Yell
Fetlar
Ulsta
Burravoe
Out Skerries
Sullom Voe
Toft
Muckle Roe
Laxo
Symbister
Papa Stour
Brae
Whalsay
Sandness
West Burrafirth
Walls
Stanydale
Lerwick
Noss
Foula
Scalloway
Bressay
Hamnavoe
West Burra
Mousa
Sumburgh
Jarlshof
Grutness
To Stromness &
Aberdeen

Orkney Islands

North Ronaldsay
Papa Westray
Pierowall
Westray
Sanday
Rousay
Eday
Egilsay
Stronsay
Wyre
To Lerwick
Mainland
Birsay
Tingwall
Shapinsay
Skara Brae
Finstown
Kirkwall
Stromness
Maes Howe
Deerness
Moness
Houton
Man of Hoy
1570'
Flotta
Burray
Hoy
Lyness
St. Margaret's Hope
Longhope
Burwick
South Ronaldsay
Pentland
Stroma
Firth
John o' Groats
Scrabster

0 — miles — 10
0 — 10 km.

Fair Isle
North Haven

The waterfront at Stromness, Orkney, where the ferry arrives from the Scottish mainland. In the background are the hills of Hoy, the most rugged of the Orkney Isles (*Sue Anderson*)

Tankerness House Museum, with archaeological exhibits and restored rooms.

Orkney is full of interesting archaeology. Within a few miles of each other on the main island are three monuments which would be on any prehistorian's list of the top ten archaeological attractions in the British Isles. These are the Neolithic village of Skara Brae, the Neolithic chambered tomb of Maes Howe and the Bronze Age Ring of Brodgar, a stone circle inside a deep ditch.

Skara Brae was discovered after a massive storm shifted sand dunes in the winter of 1850, uncovering the best-preserved prehistoric village in northern Europe. The circular houses have been cleared of sand and the connecting passages excavated. A small museum on the site displays some of the material found; more of the finds are on display in Kirkwall and also in the National Museum of Scotland in Edinburgh. The reasons for the incredible state of preservation are twofold. First, the village was obliterated by sand five thousand years ago and remained buried until

The harbour at Kirkwall, the administrative capital of the Orkneys, which is famed for its medieval cathedral, St Magnus (*Sue Anderson*)

A lobster fisherman preparing his gear on the island of Westray, in the Orkneys (*Sue Anderson*)

ORKNEY

Getting there

P & O Scottish Ferries Scrabster (Caithness)–Stromness; passage time: 2 hours.

Thomas & Bews John o'Groats (Caithness)–Burwick (passengers only); passage time: 40 minutes.

Ferry information For reservations contact P & O Scottish Ferries, Pier Head, Stromness, Orkney KW16 3AA. Tel: (0856) 850655; or P & O Scottish Ferries, PO Box 5, Jamieson's Quay, Aberdeen AB9 8DL. Tel: (0224) 572615; fax: (0224) 574411; Thomas & Bews, John o'Groats, Caithness. Tel: (0955) 81353

Airport Kirkwall.

Tourist Information Centres Orkney Tourist Board, 6 Broad Street, Kirkwall, Orkney KW15 1NX. Tel: (0856) 2856; fax: (0856) 5056. Also at Ferry Terminal Building, Stromness KW16 3AA. Tel: (0856) 850716; fax: (0856) 850777.

1850. The inhabitants literally had to flee for their lives, leaving their possessions behind them. Secondly, because of the shortage of wood in the northern isles, Skara Brae was built entirely in the local Orkney flagstone, right down to the internal furnishings. There are stone beds and dressers which exactly mirror their wooden equivalents, not only indicating exactly what the houses at Skara Brae looked like, but also giving an insight into Neolithic villages elsewhere, whose wooden furnishings and structures have long rotted away.

Skara Brae sits on the coast, on the Bay of Skaill. Not far away is the mound of Maes Howe, which is penetrated by an entrance passage down which the sun shines at midwinter, into a large burial chamber. There are many other chambered tombs in Orkney and hundreds throughout the British Isles, but the only other one which matches it for architectural splendour is at La Hougue Bie, in Jersey. Maes Howe was broken into in Viking times and looted, probably by brave young men who were anxious to prove their manhood. They left behind runic inscriptions that comment on the attributes of the local females, suggesting that they proved their manhood in other ways as well. Near Maes Howe is the early nineteenth-century Tormiston Mill, which now incorporates a restaurant and craft shop in a sympathetic restoration.

In the same area are the Stones of Stenness, three monoliths which are probably the remains of a stone circle, and the more impressive Ring of Brodgar, named after a Viking hero but dating to the Bronze Age, around 1500BC. Only thirty-six of the original sixty stones are still standing, arranged in a circle inside a deep ditch. There are other stones and cairns in the surrounding landscape, which was clearly an important centre of ritual and religion 3,500 years ago.

Birsay, further up the west coast of Mainland from Skara Brae, is a tidal island with a Viking church and settlement, as well as a sixteenth-century Stewart palace, overlooking the Brough of Birsay. Earl Thorfinn and his cousin MacBeth, who later became king of Scotland, dined in the great hall here. The genealogy is complicated and the documentary sources are not always reliable, so that some people argue that these two great war leaders were, in fact, one and the same person. But this theory is not much liked by scholarly historians, which of course does not in itself make it wrong. We do know that at the very least the two men were close friends.

A ring of islands encloses the sheltered waters of Scapa Flow, where the German fleet scuttled itself after World War I and where the battleship *Royal Oak* was sunk by a German submarine in October 1939 with the loss of eight hundred lives. Subsequently it was decided to close off the eastern entrance to Scapa Flow by sinking ships and by building concrete barriers linking Mainland to the islands of Burray and South Ronaldsay. These Churchill Barriers now carry the main road from Kirkwall to St Margaret's Hope on South Ronaldsay, which was named after the Maid of Norway who died there in 1290 while she was on her way to ascend the throne of Scotland. Her death precipitated the succession crisis which led to the Scottish Wars of Independence, a situation which was not resolved until 1314, when the English were defeated at Bannockburn.

There are many spectacular burial chambers in the various Orkney islands, but none is more stunning than the chambered tomb at Isbister on South Ronaldsay. Excavated by a local farmer, it is known as 'The Tomb of the Eagles', from the remains of sea eagles that were found therein. It is thought the birds may have been a tribal totem. The dead were left on platforms before burial, to be dried by the wind and eaten by birds of prey, a process known as excarnation.

Finds from the cliff-top tomb are on view at the farm.

The Churchill Barriers were built by Italian prisoners-of-war, who transformed a Nissen hut into a chapel, which still stands on the small island of Lamb Holm and is a poignant reminder of the war years. It says a lot for the human spirit that the captured Italians were able to rise above the misery of Orkney winters and their own predicament to erect this religious shrine.

Kirkwall is the administrative centre of the Orkneys and has a harbour, from where small ferries connect with the smaller islands in the group. The main island harbour and ferry port is at Stromness, on the south-western side of Mainland. Stromness is a beautiful little town, with much of its medieval townscape surviving. In the eighteenth century it became one of the busiest harbours in northern Europe, the last port of call for whalers and fishing-boats heading for Arctic waters. The Pier Art Centre and the Stromness Museum are both well worth visiting. Stromness is home to George Mackay Brown, one of Scotland's most respected writers, whose short stories, novels and above all poetry have done so much to interpret Orkney to the outside world.

To the south of Stromness is the large island of Hoy, which is unlike the other Orkney islands. Hoy is rugged and even mountainous, rising to a height of 1,565ft (477m). On the slopes of Ward Hill is the Dwarfie Stane, a strange rock-cut tomb thought to date to the Neolithic period. On the west coast of Hoy is a 450ft (137m) high sea stack, the Old Man of Hoy, which was first climbed in 1966. It can be seen from the Scrabster–Stromness ferry.

To the east of Hoy is the island of Flotta, which, together with Sullom Voe in Shetland, is one of the main terminals for North Sea oil and gas. Orkney's other main natural resource is uranium, which is present in the rocks in mineable quantities. So far, it has not been exploited commercially, but a great deal of assessment and exploration has been carried out in recent years.

Of the islands to the north of Kirkwall, it seems unfair to single out any particular one – they are all lively and interesting communities, full of history. Orkney's holy island is Eynhallow, between Mainland and Rousay. It is now deserted, but there are boat-trips there in summer to the twelfth-century monastery, and also to Egilsay, where St Magnus was murdered. Papa Westray – the name recalls the Celtic hermits who lived there in early Christian times – is in the record books for having the shortest scheduled airline flight – two minutes by Loganair flight from the neighbouring island of Westray.

North Ronaldsay, the most northerly of the Orkney group, is encircled by a stone dyke, which keeps its sheep off the agricultural land – they graze on seaweed on the seashore. Like Shapinsay, Stronsay, Sanday and Eday, North Ronaldsay looks like a tiny scrap of land on a small-scale map of the British Isles, but it has enough fertility to support a thriving community. Westray has a population of 800, and a prosperous fishing fleet – in many ways similar to the island of Scalpay in the Western Isles.

Loganair operates inter-island connecting flights, as well as flights from Edinburgh and Wick. British Airways fly from Glasgow, Edinburgh, Inverness and Aberdeen. Both airlines have connections to London and other UK airports. The Orkney islands are outstanding for their natural history and archaeology. The bird life is diverse and attracts many specialist 'twitchers' in the migration season. During the summer months it is never completely dark, even at midnight, and of course the further north you go the lighter it gets.

FAIR ISLE

Halfway between Orkney and Shetland, Fair Isle has a population of about 80 in

The lighthouse and cliff scenery on Fair Isle, half-way between Orkney and Shetland, the most remote of all the islands of Britain (*Sue Anderson*)

its 2sq miles (5sq km). It is the most remote inhabited island in British waters. Once on the verge of being evacuated, it was rescued by the National Trust for Scotland and now has a thriving population, an airstrip, a wind generator and a new jetty. There is a mail boat from Shetland, weather permitting, and Loganair flights from both Orkney and Shetland. A bird observatory attracts serious ornithologists from all over the world. Its hostel and research facilities are operated by the Fair Isle Bird Observatory Trust.

In 1588 one of the scattered ships of the Spanish Armada was wrecked on Fair Isle. Seventeen island families rescued 286 souls and looked after them until help came, although 50 Spaniards had died of disease and starvation by then. Some people believe that the introduction of the colourful knitting patterns for which the island is famous began after this episode. Demand exceeds supply for hand-knitted Fair Isle sweaters, so prices are high. Authentic Fair Isle knitting is simpler than it looks. It uses only knit stitches – no purl – and just two colours at any one time in any one row. The garments are knitted on a circular pin so that the right side always faces the knitter, who can see how the pattern is developing.

SHETLAND ISLES

The sea passage to Shetland can be exciting, to say the least, and the added expense of the air fare is therefore very tempting. The Tourist Organisation publishes a travel guide which explains all the options. They also provide a wide range of material on the history of the various islands. Shetland is Britain's

THE NORTHERN ISLES

Sheep rock, Fair Isle. The cliffs of this remote island are home to thousands of nesting sea-birds (*Sue Anderson*)

The P & O ferry at the harbour in Lerwick, the capital of the Shetland Isles, an area made prosperous by North Sea Oil (*Sue Anderson*)

SHETLAND ISLES

Getting there

Ferry information P & O Scottish Ferries run an all-year-round service daily to Lerwick from Aberdeen; passage time: 14 hours, usually departing at 6pm. For reservations, contact P & O Scottish Ferries, PO Box 5, Jamieson's Quay, Aberdeen AB9 8DL. Tel: (0224) 572615; fax: (0224) 574411. During the summer season some sailings go via Orkney. From June to August the Smyril Line includes Lerwick in some of its routes from Norway and Denmark to Iceland and the Faeroe Islands. For information, contact P & O Scottish Ferries.

Airports Sumburgh (British Airways) and Tingwall (Loganair).

Tourist information Centre Shetland Tourist Organisation, Information Centre, Lerwick, Shetland ZE1 0LU. Tel: (0595) 3434

most northerly archipelago, consisting of fourteen inhabited islands with a total population of about 21,000 and a total land area of 552sq miles (1,430sq km).

As with Orkney, the largest island is called Mainland, and has the only two towns, Lerwick and Scalloway. Lerwick lies half-way up the east side of Mainland and is the administrative capital, with a sheltered harbour currently used by ferries and luxury cruise ships, as well as fishing boats and visiting yachts. Much of the old town survives. The Shetland Museum is excellent and gives a good introduction to the long history of the islands. Just outside the town are the ruins of an Iron Age broch tower at Clickimin. Lerwick hosts the reconstituted 'Up Helly Aa' annual fire festival each January, when a replica Viking longship is launched to its fiery doom amid much partying and all-night celebrations.

Scalloway is on the west side of the narrow peninsula of South Mainland, directly opposite Lerwick. Formerly the capital of Shetland, its busy harbour, which is full of fishing-boats, is dominated by a ruined castle built by the same Stewart earls who also terrorised Orkney in the Middle Ages. At nearby Tingwall Loch was the site of the Norse island parliament, the Thing. Just north of the loch is an interesting agricultural museum.

Geologically, Shetland is a landscape of flooded river valleys, in many ways not unlike the Isles of Scilly at the opposite end of the British Isles. The land is everywhere penetrated by long sea-lochs called 'voes' and the coastline is tortuous in the extreme. At several points the Mainland island is almost severed by indentations, but manages to hang together over a total north–south length of 50 miles (80km). Near the north end of Mainland is Sullom Voe, which contains the largest oil terminal in Europe. It may not exactly blend with the environment, despite excellent landscaping, but it has brought pros-

perity to Shetland beyond the wildest dreams of the hard-working crofter fishermen of a century ago. Most of the UK's oil comes ashore here in two pipelines and is processed. Oil and natural gas are separated, then loaded into tankers to be transported to refineries and petrochemical plants elsewhere.

Shetlanders take their independence seriously and although they are legally completely integrated into the United Kingdom, there is strong local feeling about local control of their island affairs, which is expressed through the Shetland Movement. Shetlanders have legally questioned the UK's right to their island, which derives (like Orkney) only from 1469, when the islands were pledged in lieu of a dowry by King Christian of Denmark when his daughter Margaret married King James III of Scotland. Shetlanders are still far more Scandinavian than Scottish and the local dialect (Norn) is impenetrable to mainland Scots – except to some natives of Caithness who share the Norse background.

Like Orkney, the Shetland landscape is riddled with well-preserved archaeological monuments of all periods. Most spectacular of all is the almost intact broch tower on the island of Mousa, near the south tip of Mainland. It stands 40ft (12m) high and is built of a double-wall construction which allows great height while at the same time keeping down the weight of the walls. It is the best preserved broch of over five hundred which are found throughout the northern isles and Hebrides, and on mainland Scotland. There are over ninety broch towers in Shetland alone. In profile brochs are slightly bell-shaped, again providing extra strength. They are thought to date from the first century BC, although who exactly built them and why, remains a mystery. As a defensive structure brochs are well suited to relatively flat ground without any obvious natural defences. They may have been erected to counter the threat

of the Roman army and navy – the Romans concluded treaties with the tribes of the northern isles in the first century AD. The uniform style of brochs throughout a geographically wide area suggests both specialist architects and a stable political structure in the Scottish Iron Age. Some brochs have been excavated (as at Clickimin), but as usual these exercises seem to raise more questions than answers, showing that the towers were changed and adapted over several centuries by a succession of residents. They remain a mystery.

Off the west side of South Mainland, half-way between Sumburgh and Lerwick, is St Ninian's Isle, another island with an early Christian site. Today, it is joined to the mainland by a sand-bar, but was probably cut off at high tide in earlier times. In the 1950s a schoolboy discovered a hoard of metalwork, with richly ornamented silver bowls and brooches, which was probably hidden in the eighth century by monks fleeing from Viking raiders. In their usual efficient way, the Vikings ensured that no one survived to reclaim the buried treasure. The originals of the find can be seen in the National Museum of Scotland in Edinburgh, with replicas in Lerwick.

Of the other islands in the Shetland group, the most northerly is Unst; off the northern tip of Unst is Muckle Flugga with its lighthouse, the most northerly point of the British Isles. The Hermaness bird sanctuary attracts ornithologists from all over the world. Important research is being carried out here and at bird sanctuaries throughout the northern isles, to try to understand if North Sea fishing is having an effect on the numbers of breeding birds, or if recent declining numbers are due to other, natural causes. If the fishermen are blamed, there will be far-reaching consequences for island economies.

The islands of Yell, Fetlar and Whalsay are all well populated and thriving. Fetlar has only eighty-five inhabitants, but that is a reasonable number for its 15sq miles (39sq km). Less well favoured than the other Shetland Islands, its residents have to be innovative to survive, and are espousing cottage craft industries and 'teleworking' in a bid to diversify. In 1990 the local Community Council

The most northerly post office in the British Isles, at Haroldswick on the Shetland island of Unst (*Sue Anderson*)

Walls, Shetland, a small community of crofter-fishermen on the western peninsula of the Mainland of Shetland (*Sue Anderson*)

Muckle Flugga lighthouse, the most northerly point of the British Isles, seen from the Hermaness nature reserve (*Sue Anderson*)

placed advertisements in *Scottish Field* and *Country Life* magazines: 'Start a new life on a Scottish island. Exciting opportunities for the adventurous. Youngish people/families with some capital and an entrepreneurial spirit needed.'

Whalsay is another enterprising island, with a modern and prosperous fishing fleet, although with the industry in decline throughout the North Sea there are serious problems to be faced in the coming years. Like the other Scottish islands, it has spectacular coastal scenery.

At a latitude of just over 60°N, Lerwick is 200 miles (198km) north of Aberdeen, 600 miles (965km) north of London and only 250 miles (402km) west of Bergen, in Norway. The Faeroe Islands are 250 miles (402km) to the north-west. It may seem to be an isolated place when viewed from the south of England, but it was at the hub of the Norse world and its harbours are still full of boats from all the countries of the North Atlantic.

Eshaness Stacks, off the north-west coast of Shetland's main island (*Sue Anderson*)

9

The Western Isles: The Outer Hebrides

THE five largest islands of the Western Isles are served by ferry boats operated by Caledonian MacBrayne Ltd (known as 'Calmac' throughout the islands). Most of the ships currently in operation are fast, purpose-built, modern car ferries using link-span pier facilities which allow quick and safe loading and unloading of cars and freight – a far cry from the rather primitive arrangements which existed in many places in the not too distant past.

Especially in the summer months, Caledonian MacBrayne offer a wide range of special offers, package holidays and island-hopping tickets, which are perfect for the independent traveller. Although Calmac will always do its best to accommodate individual needs, it is almost always essential to book well in advance for vehicles. For up-to-date information on sailing times and to book vehicle and passenger tickets, always contact the Calmac Head Office at Gourock: Caledonian MacBrayne Ltd, Car Ferry Reservations, The Ferry Terminal, Gourock, PA19 1QP. Tel: (0475) 34531; fax: (0475) 37607; telex: 779318.

Ferries may be unavoidably delayed by bad weather at any time of the year, but of course especially during the winter months. Calmac do try to remedy matters as soon as possible, especially for the more remote islands, but safety always comes first. Part of the appeal of a Hebridean holiday is the *frisson* of never being absolutely sure when you will arrive and when you will leave. But one thing is for sure: after a week or two or three on a Hebridean island, few will be disappointed at the prospect of an enforced extension to their holiday.

Cars have to be checked in at ferry terminals usually thirty minutes to one hour in advance of sailing. This is to allow vehicles to be loaded efficiently and safely. Most ferry terminals have waiting-rooms, toilets, coffee/soft drinks machines and confections. However, this is not always the case, so come prepared. Nearby hotels are used to dealing with ferry passengers and are usually able to provide teas, coffees and

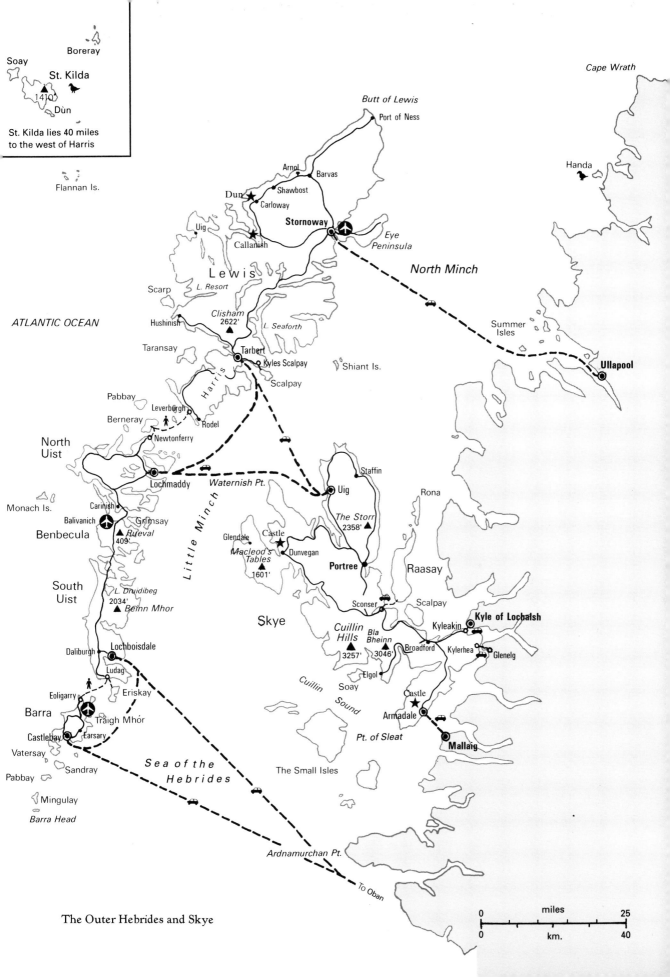

Soay

Boreray

St. Kilda

1410

Dùn

St. Kilda lies 40 miles
to the west of Harris

Flannan Is.

Cape Wrath

Handa

Butt of Lewis

Port of Ness

Arnol

Barvas

Shawbost

Dun

Carloway

Stornoway

Eye
Peninsula

North Minch

Uig

Callanish

L e w i s

Scarp

L. Resort

Summer
Isles

ATLANTIC OCEAN

Clisham
2622'

L. Seaforth

Hushinish

Ullapool

Taransay

Tarbert

Kyles Scalpay

Shiant Is.

Scalpay

Pabbay

Harris

Berneray

Leverburgh

Rodel

Newtonferry

North
Uist

Lochmaddy

Waternish Pt.

Uig

Staffin

Rona

Monach Is.

Carinish

Grimsay

Balivanich

Rueval
409'

Benbecula

Glendale

Castle

The Storr
2358'

Macleod's
Tables
1601'

Dunvegan

Portree

Raasay

South
Uist

L. Druidibeg
2034'
Beinn Mhor

Little Minch

Skye

Sconser

Scalpay

Cuillin
Hills
3257'

Bla
Bheinn
3046'

Kyle of Lochalsh

Kyleakin

Broadford

Kylerhea

Glenelg

Daliburgh

Lochboisdale

Ludag

Eoligarry

Eriskay

Cuillin

Soay

Barra

Traigh Mhór

Sound

Elgol

Castle

Castlebay

Earsary

Armadale

Pt. of Sleat

Vatersay

Mallaig

Pabbay

Sandray

Sea of the
Hebrides

The Small Isles

Mingulay

Barra Head

Ardnamurchan Pt.

To Oban

The Outer Hebrides and Skye

miles
0   25

0   40
km.

Street scene in the town of Stornoway in the Isle of Lewis, the capital of the Gaelic-speaking Western Isles and a stronghold of Gaelic culture. There is not a kilt in sight (*Highlands & Islands Enterprise*)

simple meals in their lounge bars, as well as more potent refreshment.

Whenever possible, telephone and confirm reservations. Calmac ticket offices and most of their modern ships are linked together by a computer network, which (usually) makes the process more efficient.

There are thousands of books dealing with all aspects of Scotland's islands, so for more information than there is room for in this book, which is intended mainly to whet your appetite on the subject, please take advantage of the facilities provided by your local public library or visit your local bookshop. Tourist Information Centres (TICs) usually sell books and leaflets relating to 'their' islands.

On the island of Lewis, the *Stornoway Gazette* is still very much the traditional, somewhat old-fashioned local newspaper. But within its sometimes boring layout and typography the island pulse beats strongly. It is particularly good on local history and folklore and has good coverage for Gaelic readers.

Needless to say, national newspapers are also available on the islands, although not always on the day of publication. If it is important to you to keep up with the news, it is better to telephone ahead and place an order. However, the majority of island visitors seem to welcome the opportunity to 'escape' from the news for a week or two.

LEWIS

The 'island' of Lewis (Gaelic *leodhas*, 'marshy') makes up the northern two-thirds of the most northerly island in the Outer Hebrides; Harris lies to the south, divided from its larger and more populous northern neighbour by Loch Seaforth and Loch Resort. Lewis has a land area of 680sq miles (1,761sq km)

and a population of 21,400.

Stornoway is the largest town in the Hebrides and the administrative capital of the Western Isles, which today are ruled by Comhairle nan Eilean, the islands' council. With a population of nearly 6,000, it has a fine, natural deep-water harbour. A ferry service connects with Ullapool, on the Scottish mainland, and Stornoway Airport is linked by scheduled services with Benbecula, Barra and Glasgow. Stornoway has some interesting buildings, notably Lews Castle, which was built with money made from opium and tea by Sir James Matheson, founder with another Scot of the firm of Jardine Matheson & Co.

Geologically, Lewis is the most interesting of the Outer Hebrides. The underlying rock is Lewisian gneiss, the oldest rock in Europe, at 2,900 million years, over half the age of the earth itself. Around Barvas, on the west side of Lewis, is a large exposure of granite,

THE WESTERN ISLES: THE OUTER HEBRIDES

The Caledonian MacBrayne ferry from Ullapool berthed at Stornoway (*Highlands & Islands Enterprise*)

Stornoway, the main
town and
administrative centre
of the Western Isles
(*Highlands & Islands
Enterprise*)

while around Stornoway is Torridonian sandstone. There is evidence in glacial striations on rocky outcrops of at least two ice ages, while the most recent geological deposition is the blanket peat which covers much of today's landscape but which started to form only five thousand years ago.

Lewis is well known for its spectacular archaeological monuments, notably the Bronze Age standing stones at Callanish. The concentration of Bronze Age archaeological remains around the shores of Loch Roag, on the west coast of Lewis, suggests a regional centre of considerable significance in the second millennium BC. More than twenty sites have been recorded in this area, mainly stone circles and standing stones, but beyond doubt the finest monument and the centre of this ritual landscape is the site at Callanish itself. The forty-seven

surviving stones, which date from around 1800BC, are arranged in a cruciform pattern, measuring 405ft (123m) from north to south and 140ft (42m) from east to west. The tallest stone is over 15ft (4.5m) in height. The true height of the stones was not appreciated until 1857, when 5ft (1.5m) of peat which had accumulated since the end of the Bronze Age was removed.

Most of the stones are slabs of Lewisian gneiss. The natural grain of this rock gives the stones an ancient and eery appearance, especially at dusk. The lower parts of the stones, which were buried in the peat, are paler. Controversial theories about the archaeo-astronomical use of standing stones appear to have slowly gained acceptance in recent years. There are many other stone circles and single standing stones from the same period. At Ballantrushal, on

the west coast of Lewis just north of Barvas, the tallest standing stone in the Hebrides (19ft/5.7m high) overlooks the sea.

The dry-stone broch tower of Dun Carloway, on the west coast of the Isle of Lewis, is one of the best preserved examples of this type of late first millennium BC Iron Age homestead. In places the walls survive almost to their original height of 29ft (9m), but the main feature of interest is that the collapse of the northern side of the broch has revealed, in section, the way in which the tower was built. Details of the entrance with its guard cell, the hollow-wall construction with internal staircases, and scarcement ledge supporting a floor, are all clearly visible.

West of Callanish is the township of Uig, where a magnificent Norse chess set of walrus ivory, dating from the twelfth century, was found in the sand dunes in 1831. Much reproduced, the original pieces were divided between the British Museum in London and the Royal Scottish Museum in Queen Street, Edinburgh. The King, Queen, Bishop, Knight and Castle depict a medieval monarch and his entourage, defended by Viking warrior pawns. These are particularly fearsome, depicted biting hard on the edge of their shields, eyes popping, in true Viking 'berserk' fashion.

The extent of Viking domination in Lewis is revealed by a study of place-names, many of which, including Uig (Norse *vik*, 'a bay') are of Norse origin. Many fine artefacts of the period have been found on Viking age archaeological sites, including distinctive 'tortoise'-shaped brooches, bone pins and portable scales for itinerant traders in precious metals. But the Uig chess set is the most superb of all the finds from Viking Scotland. It represents the final flourishing of Norse settlement in the Western Isles, for shortly afterwards Somerled, the son of Gillebride, defeated a Norse naval force and re-established Celtic control of Norse territories. The Western Isles were first raided by Vikings in the ninth century and then settled extensively by Norse colonists. Legally, the Western Isles were under Norwegian sovereignty until 1266.

Not far from Stornoway, the medieval chapel on the Eye peninsula, dedicated to St Columba, is an important ecclesiastical site. At the Butt of Lewis, the northern tip of the island, is an important lighthouse. Outside the nearby township of Eoropie is the restored twelfth-century church of St Moluag (Teampull Mholuidh).

To the west of Barvas is the township of Arnol, where there is a small folk museum in a black house (*tigh dubh*), which was last occupied in 1964. The walls are 6ft (1.8m) thick and the roof was thatch over turf. There was no chimney, but smoke from a peat fire in the middle of the floor escaped through the roof. This architecture, apparently primitive, was, in fact, better adapted to the Hebridean wind and rain than the modern bungalows which are now to be seen throughout the islands.

On the road to Point, to the east of Stornoway, stands a monument to the saddest disaster ever to befall the Hebrides, where the ebb and flow of history has witnessed many tragic scenes. In 1919 the Admiralty yacht *Iolaire*, carrying 260 naval ratings who were returning to their villages from service in the Great War, foundered near Arnish Point early on New Year's Day, with the loss of 208 lives. Every village in the island, indeed, almost every home, was affected. Combined with the death toll of the war and the emigrations which followed it, the *Iolaire* disaster affected succeeding generations profoundly. Its influence can still be traced.

The economy of Lewis is still based on the traditional industries of crofting and fishing, and tweed, despite various attempts to broaden the industrial base. The Highland and Islands Development

LEWIS
Getting there
Calmac ferry Ullapool-Stornoway; passage time: 3½ hours. **Ferry information** For vehicle reservations contact Caledonian MacBrayne, The Ferry Terminal, Ullapool, Ross-shire. Tel: (0854) 2358. Or Uig-Tarbert (Harris); passage time: 1¾ hours, then by road to Stornoway. **Local ferry office** The Ferry Terminal, Stornoway, Isle of Lewis. Tel: (0851) 2361; fax (0851) 5523.

Railhead Inverness; connecting bus to Ullapool.

Airport Stornoway Airport has daily flights to Glasgow, operated by British Airways; flight time: 70 minutes. Loganair has connecting flights to Benbecula and Barra.

Tourist Information Centre No 4 South Beach Street, Stornoway, Isle of Lewis. Tel: (0851) 3088.

Board has done much to encourage the island's economy, despite some spectacular failures. The growth of co-operatives and craft associations are evidence of the realisation that in a fragile community co-operation is essential. Unemployment figures are well above the national average, and the emigration of young people to the mainland and beyond is a perennial problem. Unfortunately, Stornoway is showing signs of following mainland trends as regards social problems.

Although the Harris Tweed industry has had its ups and downs in recent years, there is now an increasing demand from the fashion industry for quality tweed. To qualify as Harris Tweed, cloth must bear the orb trademark of the Harris Tweed Association, which was founded in 1909, and be made in the Outer Hebrides from virgin Scottish wool, woven on hand-looms in the weavers' own homes.

Tweed is hard-wearing, warm, water-resistant – and fashionable. The cloth is produced in rolls of 38 weaver's yards, each of 72in (182cm), 28½in (47cm) wide. About 650 home weavers produce 4.5 million yards of cloth annually. Traditional Gaelic 'waulking' songs arose out of the communal treatment of the finished cloth.

Attempts to rationalise the industry by concentrating production in a factory in Stornoway met with almost total opposition from the weavers, but since 1934 the wool has been dyed, carded and spun in Stornoway. The hand-looms are often housed in sheds or out-houses on crofts, leaving the operators free to look after their sheep, cut peat and tend the croft.

Although Lewis is now the centre of the tweed industry, where weaving is often carried on by men, it had its origins in Harris, where the earl of Dunmore at Amhuinnsuidhe Castle asked one of the local traditional weavers to copy some Murray tartan for his army's kilts. The pioneers were Marion and Christina Macleod of Strond, who were originally from the island of Pabbay and were known as the 'Paisley' sisters because they were sent there for training by the Dowager Countess of Dunmore, Catherine Herbert, a daughter of the Earl of Pembroke.

The history of the Harris Tweed industry is displayed at An Clachan, Leverburgh. It is also described in detail in Francis Thompson's *Harris Tweed: The Story of a Hebridean Industry*.

Lewis is the most powerful bastion of Gaelic life and culture surviving, in which the promotion of the Gaelic language through Gaelic broadcasting and publishing is all important. Radio nan Eilean, the Gaelic local radio station run by the BBC, Gaelic television programmes, constantly expanding, and the Stornoway publisher Acair are all-important influences in island culture. One of the finest evocations of island life is *Devil in the Wind*, by Charles Macleod. The foremost Celtic scholar of the present generation is a Lewisman, Professor Derick Thomson, while the Gaelic (and English) poet and novelist Iain Crichton Smith has a deservedly international reputation. Comhairle nan Eilean's bilingual policy is very supportive of Gaelic culture.

The sabbatarianism of the Free Church has proved controversial in recent years, especially as regards Sunday ferry sailings and public use of council-owned facilities. In Lewis, the Free Church is still immensely powerful, the issue being inextricably linked with the very survival of Gaelic culture in all its richness.

HARRIS

The 'island' of Harris (Gaelic *Na Hearadh*), is not an island at all: together with Lewis it forms the largest and most northerly of the Western Isles, Harris taking up the southern third. The long sea lochs of Loch Seaforth and Loch Resort divide the two districts.

With a land area of 90sq miles (233sq km) and a population of 2,400, Harris has a landscape which in places is almost mountainous – very different from the flat, peaty lands of Lewis. Clisham (2,622ft/799m) is the highest hill in the Outer Hebrides. Around it is some of the finest unspoilt wilderness to be found anywhere in Scotland. Archaeological monuments and Norse place-names dot the landscape.

The largest town and ferry terminal is at Tarbert, which is connected by Caledonian MacBrayne's ferries to Lochmaddy in North Uist and Uig on the Isle of Skye. A passenger ferry plies from Leverburgh in Harris to Newtonferry in North Uist. Another ferry serves the offshore island of Scalpay.

One of Scotland's architectural gems is St Clement's Church, at Rodel, on the south-east corner of Harris. Although it has been restored on several occasions, most recently in 1873, most of the walls and the greater part of the tower are medieval, dating from the early sixteenth century. The windows are square-headed, except for the east window, which has a pointed arch with three trefoil-headed panels, above which is a wheel window with six spokes.

St Clement's is the finest pre-Reformation church in the Western Isles and is memorable also for two magnificent medieval tombs that are built into its south wall. Rodel was the burial place for many of the MacLeods of Dunvegan and Harris, and the tomb of Alexander MacLeod of Dunvegan (also known as Alasdair Crotach) is an outstanding example of medieval stone carving. It was built in 1528, although curiously, Alexander MacLeod did not die for another twenty years. His tomb consists of a stone effigy of his body in chain mail and plate armour, lying with his head on

HARRIS

Getting there

Calmac ferry Uig (Skye)-Tarbert; passage time: 1¾ hours, Lochmaddy (North Uist)-Tarbert; passage time: 1¾ hours.
Ferry information For vehicle reservations contact Caledonian MacBrayne, The Ferry Terminal, Uig, Isle of Skye. Tel: (047 042) 219; fax: (047 042) 387.
Local ferry office The Ferry Terminal, Tarbert, Isle of Harris. Tel: (0859) 2444; fax: (0859) 2017.

Railhead Kyle of Lochalsh; ferry to Kyleakin, then by road to Uig (Skye).

Airport Stornoway Airport has daily flights to Glasgow, operated by British Airways. Loganair has connecting flights to Benbecula and Barra.

Tourist Information Centre The Pier, Tarbert, Isle of Harris. Tel: (0859) 2011.

a stone pillar. Behind the stone figure is a recessed arch decorated with panels illustrating a variety of scenes, including ecclesiastical and biblical figures, a castle, a galley under sail and a hunting scene, with men holding hunting dogs observing a group of deer. Because this tomb was built into the fabric of the church in the Middle Ages and has never been subject to the ravages of Hebridean weather, the carvings have a freshness and detail that is rarely seen.

There are many other interesting architectural details in St Clement's Church, including a carving of St Clement himself, with a bull's head beneath his feet, and a *sheila-na-gig* – a nude female figure, with a child, in a crouched attitude, blatantly displaying her vagina. It is thought that the purpose of such figures was to attract the attention of the satanic spirits, representing the evils and temptations of life, who might follow worshippers into the building.

The recent history of Harris is closely bound up with that of Lewis; both now form part of the all-purpose local authority that is administered from Stornoway by Comhairle nan Eilean, the islands' council. Much of present-day attitudes towards local government and administration are conditioned by the era of Lord Leverhulme, the soap magnate, who bought Lewis and Harris is 1918–19 and proceeded to introduce ideas of social engineering which unfortunately met with a mixed reception and came to an abrupt end with his death in 1925. His 'Lewis & Harris Welfare & Development Company Limited' was an early version of the local enterprise trusts which are now in fashion again.

William Hesketh Lever, 1st Viscount Leverhulme, was born in 1851, the son of a Bolton soapmaker. He founded Port Sunlight in 1888 and Lever Brothers in 1890. His international business empire, Unilever, brought him fame and fortune. In 1918 he bought Lewis and Harris,

and in the next five years spent £875,000 with the intention of redeeming the islands from poverty and creating wealth for the islanders through enterprise and the exploitation of the natural resources of the sea. Lord Leverhulme bought fishing boats and built a cannery, ice-factory, roads and bridges, and a light railway. He planned to use spotter planes to locate herring shoals and created MacFisheries, his own chain of retail fish shops. A full account of his activities can be found in Nigel Nicolson's *Lord of the Isles*.

In 1923 Leverhulme was forced to abandon his plans for Lewis and he gifted 64,000 acres (26,000ha) of Stornoway parish to the people, to be administered by the elected Stornoway Trust. His withdrawal from Lewis caused an economic slump, leading to the emigration of over a thousand able-bodied men to North America.

After the collapse of his schemes for Lewis, Lord Leverhulme turned his attention to Harris, where the peaceful little village of Obbe was renamed Leverburgh and transformed into a bustling harbour town with all kinds of public works projects. But in May 1925 Lord Leverhulme died and all developments stopped. Instead of becoming a town with a projected population of 10,000, Leverburgh reverted to being a sleepy village.

The economy of Harris is based on crofting and fishing, supplemented by income from tourism and from the district's most famous export, Harris Tweed. Originally a domestic activity, which was carried on mainly by women, the weaving of tweed became a full-time specialist male occupation, partly because the flying shuttle in 'modern' looms made the work heavier. In 1909 the Board of Trade approved a trade mark defining Harris Tweed as 'tweed, hand-spun, hand-woven and dyed and finished by hand in the Outer Hebrides', with 'made in Harris' or 'made in Lewis' added as appropriate. A Harris Tweed

Association was formed and the distinctive orb surmounted by a cross has been in use since 1911. Today, the industry is subject to the vagaries of the fashion industry, but in general clothes made from Harris Tweed are highly regarded and priced appropriately. In recent years the amount of tweed produced has contracted, as market forces dictate that what was once a common and serviceable cloth is now a luxury item, but the islanders have proved adaptable in meeting this crisis. Some even produce tweed in the old way, hand-dyeing and carding, spinning on the wheel, hand-weaving and finishing, thus producing a high-quality cloth that sells for up to three times the price of ordinary tweed.

Just off the shore of North Harris, on the west coast, opposite the township of Hushinish, is the small rocky island of Scarp, which rises to a height of 1,011ft (308m) on its north side. First settled in 1810, it was abandoned in 1971. In 1884 the population was estimated at around 200. As late as the 1940s the population was over 100; now the crofters' cottages are used as holiday homes and there are periodic threats to develop the island as a luxury holiday resort. Scarp was the scene of a strange experiment in 1934, when the German rocket scientist Gerhardt Zucher tried to persuade the British government that rockets could be used to transport mail and emergency medicines to remote islands. Amid much publicity, 30,000 letters were launched into the Hebridean air. But the rocket exploded and this attempt to use modern technology to solve the perennial problem of communication with remote communities was not repeated.

Until recently, the most remote community in Harris was Rhenigidale, which was accessible only by sea or by a rough hill-track. But after lengthy representations a road was built, probably just in time to save this community from abandonment. There is a Gatcliffe Trust Hostel in the village.

SCALPAY

The island of Scalpay (Norse *skalp-r ay*, 'the island shaped like a boat') lies in the Outer Hebrides, just off the south-east corner of Harris, at the entrance to East Loch Tarbert. Access is by a small vehicular ferry from Kyles Scalpay on Harris, 5 miles (8km) east of Tarbert. Although only 2sq miles (5sq km) in size, the population of Scalpay is about 450, a small but tightly knit community with a deserved reputation for innovation and enterprise. Its fishing fleet has been modernised, with the result that during the fishing industry's recent difficulties Scalpachs have maintained their island as a lively and viable community. In 1861 the population was 388, including some families who had been evicted from the island of Pabbay in the Sound of Harris; by 1921 it had peaked at 624.

On the south-east corner of Scalpay is Eilean Glas lighthouse, now automatic. Its predecessor was one of the four original lighthouses built by the Commissioners of Northern Lights in 1789. The keepers' cottages are now holiday houses.

In December 1962 six Scalpay men went out in a small open boat in a gale to rescue the crew of the trawler *Boston Heron*; their consummate seamanship and bravery was recognised by the RNLI.

NORTH UIST

The island of North Uist lies in the Outer Hebrides, between Harris and Benbecula, with a land area of 118sq miles (305sq km) and a population of about 1,500. The chief village is Lochmaddy, which is linked by ferry to Tarbert in Harris and Uig in Skye. Calmac operates a 'triangular' service; enquire to them for full details. A causeway links North Uist to Benbecula, where there is an airport. The highest hill is Eaval (1,138ft/347m) in the

SCALPAY

Getting there

Calmac ferry Kyles Scalpay–Scalpay; passage time: 10 minutes.
Ferry information Frequent sailings, vehicle booking not required. No Sunday service.
Local ferry office Contact Caledonian MacBrayne Ltd, The Ferry Terminal, Tarbert, Harris. Tel: (0859) 2444; fax: (0859) 2017.

Tourist Information Centre Pier Road, Tarbert, Harris. Tel: (0859) 2011.

A fantastic Hebridean sky over Loch Olabhat in North Uist. The small island in the loch is a crannog (artificial island) connected to the shore by a causeway

Another island crannog, at Dun an Stoicir, North Uist

south-east corner of the island.

There is an RSPB reserve near Balranald, on the western side of North Uist. It takes in 1,625 acres (657ha) of varying habitats: rocky coast, sandy beaches and dunes, machair, marshland and freshwater lochs. In fact, the headland of Ard an Runair within the reserve is the most westerly point of the Outer Hebrides and an ideal place for birdwatching, especially during the spring and autumn migrations. Manx shearwater pass at the rate of over 1,000 per hour. Gannets, fulmars, skuas and storm petrels are also commonly seen. In all, 183 species of birds have been recorded on the reserve, of which about 50 nest each year. Balranald is especially good for waders, such as redshank, dunlin, oystercatcher and ringed plover. There are 300 pairs of lapwing, and a dozen pairs of corncrakes, with their distinctive rasping call.

North Uist is a Protestant island, in contrast to its southern neighbours, and as such has more in common with Harris, although the intervening Sound of Harris is too deep to be bridged easily with a causeway. A passenger ferry links Newtonferry in North Uist with Leverburgh in Harris.

The north and west coasts have attractive sandy bays backed by wide expanses of machair, which are ablaze with colour in spring and summer. The landscape is dotted with interesting archaeological sites of different periods, notably the Neolithic chambered cairn of Barpa Langass, between Clachan and Lochmaddy, the only chambered cairn in the Western Isles with an intact burial chamber and an impressive monument, 25ft (7.6m) in diameter and 13ft (4m) high.

Another cairn, at Clettraval, has been severely robbed but is of interest because it belongs to the Clyde type and is thus unique in the Western Isles. It is possible to get close to this cairn by using the road to the small defence installation on the summit of the hill

South Clettraval, from where there is a panoramic view.

On the western slopes of Blashaval (358ft/109m), in the north-west of the island, are three Bronze Age standing stones called Na Fir Bhreige, the false men, improbably said to be the graves of three spies who were buried alive. The Iron Age Dun an t-Siamain, on a small island in a loch on the west side of Eaval, can be reached by a curved causeway. Another site on an island in a loch is the broch of Dun an Sticir, not far from Newtonferry.

In recent years archaeologists have explored Eilean Domhnuill, a small crannog, or man-made island, in Loch Olabhat, near Griminish. Usually regarded as Iron Age and dated to the early centuries BC, this example has foundations which are nearly five thousand years old, putting it back into the Neolithic period and making it possibly the oldest artificial island in Europe. Connected to the shore of the loch by a stone causeway, the site yielded up hundreds of sherds of pottery and dozens of flint flakes, giving the experts a real insight into life in ancient times.

From the road just west of Loch Olabhat can be seen a small tower standing in the loch at Scolpaig – not a well-preserved prehistoric site, but a 'folly' which was constructed for famine relief. Apparently there *was* an Iron Age 'dun' on the site, which was quarried to build the tower. This is also a good point for viewing and hopefully photographing the Monach Islands, 8 miles (13km) off the coast.

During the centuries of Norse occupation, North Uist was farmed by colonists from Norway, who have left their mark on the landscape in the many Norse place-names. The name 'Uist' is from the Norse *i-vist*, an abode or 'indwelling'. There is an important but ruinous medieval church site at Teampull na Trionaid in the south-west of the island, near the township of Carinish, which was reputedly founded

NORTH UIST
Getting there

Calmac ferry Uig (Skye)-Lochmaddy; passage time: 3¾ hours. Tarbert (Harris)-Lochmaddy; passage time: 1¾ hours. Alternatively, Oban-Lochboisdale (South Uist) then by road across causeways to North Uist. A small passenger ferry connects Newton Ferry (Port na Long) to Berneray and Harris (Leverburgh).
Ferry information For vehicle reservations contact Caledonian MacBrayne Ltd, The Ferry Terminal, Uig, Isle of Skye. Tel: (047 042) 219; fax: (047 042) 387.
Local ferry office The Pier, Lochmaddy, North Uist. Tel: (087 63) 337; fax: (087 63) 412.

Railhead Kyle of Lochalsh, from there Calmac ferry to Skye and bus to Uig.

Airport Benbecula has daily flights to Glasgow Airport, operated by British Airways; flight time: 1 hour. Loganair operates flights to Barra and Stornoway.

Tourist Information Office The Pier, Lochmaddy, North Uist. Tel: (087 63) 321.

by Somerled's daughter Beathag early in the thirteenth century. There was a monastery and college here, where the sons of chiefs were sent to be educated.

By 1850 the population had increased to 5,000, but evictions carried out with much acrimony and bloodshed took place under the direction of the landowner, Lord MacDonald of Sleat. There was a violent confrontation between crofters and police at Malaclete. Nearby is the excavated archaeological site of the Udal, a settlement site which was occupied from the Bronze Age until the nineteenth century. The economy of the island today is based on crofting and fishing (mainly for lobsters and crabs), tourism, scallop farming, knitwear and tweed, and the alginate factory at Sponish on Loch Maddy.

With a circular road and hilly interior, North Uist is perfect for hillwalking. There is a regular bus service around the island and occasional post buses as well. Offshore from Sollas is the tidal island of Vallay, an interesting destination for an easy walk – but watch the tides! The larger of the two houses on Vallay was built by Erskine Beveridge, who conducted early archaeological surveys of the Outer Hebrides, Coll and Tiree.

BENBECULA

The island of Benbecula (Gaelic *Beinn a'bhfaodhla*, 'mountain of the fords') lies between North and South Uist. Today, a road causeway replacing the previous fords connects all these islands together. The north causeway, which links Benbecula to North Uist, was opened by the Queen Mother in 1960. Despite the island's name, its only hill is called Rueval (409ft/125m). Benbecula is about 8 miles (13km) wide by 5 miles (8km) from north to south. The native population of 1,300 is divided more or less equally between the Protestantism of North Uist and the Roman Catholicism of South Uist. Gaelic survives as the language of everyday life, although a

high proportion of the place-names are of Norse origin. An additional 500 Royal Artillery army personnel and dependents are stationed at their base at Balivanich, providing support for the missile range on South Uist. The operation has expanded greatly from its small beginnings in 1959. An RAF radar station was established in 1972: new radars were constructed on Clettraval, South Uist, in 1981, while the control building and associated facilities are at East Camp, Balivanich. A small World War II airfield, staffed by RAF technicians, links the island with Barra, Stornoway and Glasgow. And, of course, the ferries from Lochmaddy in North Uist and Lochboisdale in South Uist provide links to Harris, Skye and Oban.

The underlying geology is Lewisian gneiss, the coastline is indented and the land surface of the island a maze of tiny lochans. From the summit of Rueval there is a fine view of the whole island. Peat is exposed on the shore at Borve, proof that the Outer Isles are slowly sinking into the Atlantic along their western edge, although at an extremely slow rate.

Benbecula's natural beauty is somewhat marred by the military facilities, but economically the island has benefited. The army's NAAFI supermarket is the only one in Britain that is open to the general public.

There are several sites of archaeological interest in Benbecula's watery landscape. An exceptionally well-preserved chambered long cairn and a ruined passage grave lie close together in the centre of the island, ½ mile (800m) east of the main road. Near the northern causeway at Gramisdale are two stone circles. Most of their stones have fallen. There is a good example of an Iron Age dun on an island in Loch Dun Mhurchaidh, near Knock Rolum township, which is joined to the shore by a causeway. Superimposed on the ruins of the dun are the ruins of a seventeenth-century township.

In 1746 Bonnie Prince Charlie sailed over the sea to Skye from Benbecula with Flora MacDonald, disguised as Betty Burke, after he had hidden in a cave for two days. He came within an ace of being captured there by the forces of General John Campbell of Mamore. The island was held by Clan Ranald, whose ruined fourteenth-century castle, which was occupied until 1625, is at Borve. Near their eighteenth-century house at Nunton is a fourteenth-century chapel. The MacDonalds of Clan Ranald owned Benbecula until 1839, when it was sold to Colonel Gordon of Cluny, along with Barra, South Uist and Eriskay. Clan Ranald took its name from Ranald, the second son of the first marriage of John, 1st Lord of the Isles, to Amie MacRuari.

SOUTH UIST

The island of South Uist is the second largest island in the Outer Hebrides and is linked to Benbecula to the north by a causeway. With a land area of 141 sq miles (365sq km), it has a population of 2,400, which is concentrated into a narrow strip on the western side between 20 miles (32km) of virtually unbroken beach and peaty moorland that rises to a mountainous spine running down the eastern side of the island. Beinn Mhor (2,034ft/620m) and Hecla (1,988ft/600m) are the two highest hills, with fine views from their summits. The underlying bedrock is Lewisian gneiss.

The Loch Druidibeg National Nature Reserve to the north of Drimsdale provides an ideal habitat for many species of waterfowl, including native greylag geese, which breed here. The corncrake, which is increasingly rare on the mainland, is common here. There is a large colony of mute swans on Loch Bee, at the north end of South Uist.

The east coast is deeply indented by four sea lochs. At the head of the most southerly of these is the main village and ferry terminal, Lochboisdale, with a population of over 300. It has a hotel, police station, post office, doctor, dentist, garages, school, shops and the island's Tourist Information Centre. There are ferry connections from Lochboisdale to Oban and Castlebay (Barra). From the south tip of South Uist there are passenger ferries to Eriskay and Barra.

At Daliburgh, 2 miles (3km) west of Lochboisdale, there is a hotel, post office, shops, school, petrol station, maternity hospital and old people's home. To the south, the road goes 6 miles (9.6km) to Pollachar, where there is a picturesque early nineteenth-century inn and stupendous views across to Eriskay and Barra. Near the inn is a standing stone.

North of Daliburgh the main road runs up the west side of the island, with many side roads leading down to crofts and beaches. Of special interest is the road through Bornish to the shore at Rubha Ardvule, which has beautiful beaches, both freshwater and seashore habitats, and an Iron Age fort.

There are many sites of archaeological interest, including the excavated prehistoric aisled house at Kilpheder and the Reinaval passage grave on the northern shoulder of the hill just south of the township of Mingary. Dun Mor is an Iron Age fortified island in a loch just south of the township of West Gerinish, while Dun Uiselan is a similar site in another loch, west of the township of Ollag. Two churches at Howmore, dedicated to St Mary and St Columba, may date from early Christian times, perhaps as early as the seventh century. The graveyard at Hallan contains one of the few sixteenth-century carved graveslabs to be found in the Western Isles.

Just north of Milton, a cairn marks the birthplace of Flora MacDonald, who helped Bonnie Prince Charlie to evade capture and assisted his escape. Disguised as her maid 'Betty Burke', they sailed to Skye from Benbecula in a small

THE WESTERN ISLES: THE OUTER HEBRIDES

SOUTH UIST
Getting there

Calmac ferry Oban-Lochboisdale; passage time: 5¼ hours. Most sailings are via Castlebay (Barra); passage time: 7½ hours. A small passenger ferry connects Ludag to Eriskay and Eoligarry (Barra). Contact Tourist Information Office, Lochboisdale, for details.

Ferry information For vehicle reservations, contact Caledonian MacBrayne Ltd, The South Pier, Oban, Argyll. Tel: (0631) 62285; fax: (0631) 66588.

Local ferry office The Pier, Lochboisdale. Tel: (087 84) 288.

Railhead Oban.

Airport Benbecula has daily flights to Glasgow Airport, operated by British Airways; flight time: 1 hour. Loganair has connecting flights to Barra and Stornoway.

Tourist Information Centre The Pier, Lochboisdale. Tel: (087 84) 286.

(Above) Abandoned croft house, South Uist

A distant view of the hills of Barra from the pier at Ludag, South Uist

boat on 28 June 1746. South Uist suffered badly from clearances in the nineteenth century as a result of the policies of Colonel Gordon of Cluny, who bought the island, together with the neighbouring islands of Benbecula and Eriskay, from the MacDonalds of Clan Ranald in 1838. Between 1841 and 1861 the population fell from 7,300 to 5,300 as townships were cleared for sheep. Many islanders emigrated to North America.

South Uist's economy is dominated by the army missile range on the northwest corner of the island, from where rockets are fired out over the Atlantic, their progress monitored by a tracking station on St Kilda. Other sources of

(Above) Loch Druidibeg nature reserve, North Uist, looking towards the hills of Hecla and Beinn Mhor

Lord of the Isles approaching Lochboisdale pier, South Uist, after a five-hour journey from Oban

income are crofting, fishing (mainly for lobsters and crabs), shellfish farming and seaweed processing. The missile range control installation, known locally as 'space city', dominates the skyline of Rueval and dwarfs the 30ft (9m) granite statue of Our Lady of the Isles by Hew Lorimer (1959). It is possible to drive right to the top of this hill, where, turning one's back on the communications 'golfballs', there are spectacular panoramic views. In clear weather St Kilda is visible to the west.

This mainly Roman Catholic island with its many roadside shrines has a more relaxed attitude to Sabbatarianism than the Protestant islands to the north.

ERISKAY

The island of Eriskay (Norse: *Eiriks-ey*, 'Eric's island') lies in the Outer Hebrides between South Uist and Barra. A local ferry boat, the *Eilean na h-Oige* suggests an alternative Gaelic meaning, 'the Isle of Youth'. Only 2½ by 1½ miles (4 by 2.4km) in size, Eriskay is the most densely populated Hebridean island with a population of 200. The economy of the mainly Roman Catholic community is based on an enterprising fishing industry, supplemented by crofting and hand-knitted woollen jumpers. There are ferry connections to South Uist and Barra.

Ben Scrien (610ft/186m) is the highest hill, overlooking the township of Balla, with a shop, school, post office and church. St Michael's Church was built in 1903 by Father Allan MacDonald; the altar is supported on the bow of a lifeboat.

Bonnie Prince Charlie first landed on Scottish soil at Eriskay in 1745. The beach where he stepped ashore is called *Coilleag a'Phrionnsa*, where a small pink convolvulus reputedly, but inaccurately, said to be found nowhere else in the world flowers in July. The 'Eriskay Love Lilt' is a famous Gaelic folk song. In 1941 the merchant ship *Politician*, carrying 20,000 cases of whisky, foundered off Eriskay; 5,000 cases were salvaged locally and unofficially. The event formed the basis of Sir Compton MacKenzie's novel *Whisky Galore!* and an Ealing comedy film, based on the book, was made in Barra in 1948. In 1991 the Islanders experienced an influx of journalists, camera crews and sightseers, as salvage operations on the wreck continue and its fiftieth anniversary was celebrated. As well as 24,000 cases of whisky, the ship was also carrying some £3 million in Jamaican currency. The local pub, which opened in 1988, an ugly modern building but a very welcome addition to the island's facilities, is called, unsurprisingly, Am Politician, and has a small collection of photographs and memorabilia.

The island's small Catholic church is worth a visit. Opened in 1903, it owes its existence to Father Allan MacDonald, a well-known folklorist and collector of Gaelic stories and songs. The design is based on churches he saw in Spain during his training at Valladolid. The church bell comes from the German battleship *Derflinger*, which was scuttled at Scapa Flow in Orkney at the end of World War I. The altar is the bow of a lifeboat from the aircraft carrier *Hermes*, which was washed ashore on Eriskay after it became lost on an exercise off St Kilda.

Eriskay ponies are the last survivors of the native Scottish pony, and are the subject of a conservation breeding scheme. They stand 12–13 hands tall, with small ears, and are still used to carry peat and seaweed.

BARRA

Barra is an island at the southern end of the Outer Hebrides, separated from South Uist by the Sound of Barra and the island of Eriskay. Only 8 miles (13km) from north to south and 4–5 miles (6.4–8km) wide, it supports a population of about 1,200 on its 20sq miles (52sq km). About 12 miles (19km) of road encircle the island, with a northern spur to the airport at Traigh Mhor and the jetty at Eoligarry.

The island takes its name from St Barr (Finbarr); the church of Cille Bharra near Northbay airport dates from the twelfth century. It was the parish church for the island in the Middle Ages. Inside are carved grave-slabs and a small display explaining the history of the church, including the famous Runic Stone, which has Norse runes on one side and a Christian cross on the other. The runes have been translated as: 'This cross has been raised in memory of Thorgeth, daughter of Steinar'. Sir Compton MacKenzie is buried in the graveyard.

There are several ancient sites on Barra: cairns, standing stones and forts. The broch at Dun Cuier, Allasdale, has been excavated. Barra has always been a fertile island and was an attractive proposition in prehistoric times. Even today it has an air of tidiness and prosperity that is missing from its northern neighbours.

On the west side of the island are miles of sandy beaches, backed by machair land which bursts into colour with a carpet of wild flowers in May and June. At one end of the white sands of Hallaman beach is the modernistic and controversial Isle of Barra Hotel. The east coast is rockier, with more dramatic coastal scenery. Inland the land is rocky and covered with heather and peat.

The main village, Castlebay, is linked to Oban and Lochboisdale in South Uist by car ferry. It takes its name from the picturesque and much-photographed Kisimul Castle, the ancestral stronghold of the MacNeills of Barra from 1427, when they received a charter from Alexander, Lord of the Isles, which was confirmed by James IV in 1495. When it was sold to Colonel Gordon of Cluny in 1838 to pay for debts, the island was offered to the government as a penal colony. Clearances later in the nineteenth century led to massive emigration.

Kisimul Castle, which dates from the eleventh century, consists of a square keep within a curtain wall, which is shaped to fit the contours of the islet on which it stands. It is similar in design to other early castles in the west of Scotland, such as Dunstaffnage, Castle Tioram, Mingarry and Breachacha (Coll). It was bought in 1937, together with 12,000 acres (4,850ha) of land, by the 45th MacNeil of Barra, an American architect, who restored it to its present state before his death in 1970. According to clan tradition, a retainer used to announce daily from the castle walls: 'MacNeil has dined, the kings, princes and others of the earth may now dine.' You can take a boat trip to the castle, departing from the pier at Castlebay.

Castlebay provides a full range of services: shops, doctor, church, bank, post office, secondary school, library and accommodation. High on the hill above the town is a massive statue of the Virgin Mary with the infant Jesus, which was erected in 1954 to mark the Roman Catholic Church's Marian year. The marble statue, which was made in Italy, was carried up the mountain by relays of twelve men. From the summit of Heaval (1,260ft/384m) there are magnificent views to the north and south.

Gaelic culture is strong and healthy in Barra, and is sustained by the Church and by a rich store of folklore and song. Barra has a reputation as a place which knows how to enjoy itself, and, with its Catholic tradition, is unhindered by Sabbatarianism. The church in Castlebay, Our Lady, Star of the Sea, was built in 1889.

Castlebay was once the site of a thriving herring industry, but now supports only a small-scale commercial fishery that catchess mainly white fish, prawns and lobsters. Most islanders are crofter-fishermen, who keep sheep and cattle

BARRA
Getting there

Calmac ferry Oban-Castlebay; passage time: 5 hours. Lochboisdale (South Uist)-Castlebay; passage time: 1¾ hours. A small passenger ferry connects Eoligarry (Barra) to Ludag (South Uist).

Ferry information For vehicle reservations, contact Caledonian MacBrayne Ltd, The South Pier, Oban, Argyll. Tel: (0631) 62285; fax: (0631) 66588. The Sunday service formerly operating Mallaig-Castlebay no longer runs.

Railhead Oban.

Airport Northbay, Barra. Daily service to Glasgow Airport, operated by Loganair; flight time: 65 minutes. Also flights to Benbecula and Stornoway.

Tourist Information Centre Main Street, Castlebay, Isle of Barra. Tel: (087 14) 336.

THE WESTERN ISLES: THE OUTER HEBRIDES

(Right) The main settlement on the island of Eriskay; just around the corner is the beach where Bonnie Prince Charlie landed from France in 1745

Scattered croft houses on Eriskay, overlooking the seashore with a beach of clean, white sand

(Above) The main
street of Castlebay,
Barra. Kisimul Castle
guards the harbour

The Loganair plane
from Glasgow arriving
at Barra Airport

and grow a few vegetables, especially potatoes. Tourism is increasingly important. There are several craft shops on the island and a perfume factory at Tangusdale.

There is a daily air service to Glasgow; the airstrip is on the beach at Traigh Mhor, at the northern end of the island, the only one in the United Kingdom where schedules are shown as 'subject to tides'. The air service to Barra was started by Northern and Scottish Airways Ltd in 1936 and since 1975 has been operated by Loganair. Landings are not possible within three hours either side of high tide.

Barra was the location for the famous Ealing comedy film *Whisky Galore!* which was based on Compton Mac-Kenzie's novel and made in 1948. It gives a very amusing and only slightly exaggerated account of events on the neighbouring island of Eriskay, where the 12,000-ton SS *Politician*, carrying 250,000 bottles of whisky, was wrecked in 1941. Many of Barra's older residents were extras in the film, which is the subject of documentaries celebrating the fiftieth anniversary of the wreck.

VATERSAY

The island of Vatersay, to the south of Barra, can now be reached by a 250yd (228m) long causeway, which was opened in 1990, at a cost of £4 million, including a new road over the hill from Castlebay. Over 200,000 tons of rock were blasted for this project, which the islanders view as a life-saver for their small community. Vatersay is 3sq miles (7.7sq km) in area with a Gaelic-speaking population of around 70.

In 1908 the Vatersay Raiders were imprisoned for occupying some of the island's fertile land. They came from Barra and Uist in search of land. In 1911 there were 288 people on this tiny island, including many immigrants from Barra and Mingulay. The present crofts, shop, post office, church, school and village hall are scattered around the island's 5 miles (8km) of road. The highest point is Heishival Mor (625ft/190m); to the south are the Bishop's Isles and Mingulay, all now uninhabited. It is sometimes possible to organise boat-trips to these islands; for information, enquire locally or at the Tourist Information Centre in Barra.

10
The Western Isles: the Inner Hebrides

SKYE

THE island of Skye (Gaelic: *An t-Eilean Sgitheanach*) is a large island covering 535sq miles (1,385sq km), with a complicated topography featuring fingers of land that are separated by sea lochs penetrating far inland, forming 350 miles (563km) of coastline. Loch Snizort, Loch Dunvegan, Loch Harport, Loch Eishort, Loch Ainort, Loch Sligachan – the names reveal the mixture of Norse and Gaelic culture which has influenced the island over many centuries.

It is possible to run up a hefty mileage during a week's holiday on Skye. It is the largest of the Inner Hebrides, measuring 50 miles (80km) long and from 7 to 25 miles (11–40km) broad.

Geologically, Skye is renowned for its lava landscapes, especially in the Trotternish area, where the Old Man of Storr and the unusual formations of the Quiraing attract many visitors. Also greatly admired, whenever they are visible through the ubiquitous mist, are the Cuillins – jagged mountains of hard gabbro that have been beloved by generations of climbers. The Red Cuillins, which are made of only slightly less hard granite, have eroded into more rounded shapes and have slopes of scree. The fertility of some parts of the island derives from underlying sandstones and limestones which surface around the volcanic rocks.

A rich variety of archaeological and historical monuments testifies to Skye's long and turbulent history. Of particular interest are the brochs of Dun Ardtreck, near Carbost, and Dun Beag, just west of Bracadale, both of which have been very neatly built with square-sided facing-stones. These were originally stone towers up to 29ft (9m) high. Clach Ard, Tote, is a Pictish symbol stone, unusual in the Hebrides.

Skye is part of the heartland of Gaelic culture, with a large proportion of the population of 8,500 speaking the Gaelic language in everyday life. As in other parts of the Hebrides, this culture is under threat, particularly from

The old bridge at
Sligachan, looking
towards the Cuillins, a
favourite haunt of
climbers in summer
and winter

SKYE

Getting there

Calmac ferry Kyle of
Lochalsh-Kyleakin;
frequent sailings,
passage time: 5
minutes, no reservation
necessary; 24-hour
service from Easter
1991, Uig-Tarbert/
Lochmaddy; passage
time: 1¾–2¼ hours.
Mallaig-Armadale;
passage time: 30
minutes. Summer
Sundays: Mallaig-
Armadale-Tobermory-
Coll-Tiree round trip.
A private seasonal
vehicle ferry service
operates from Glenelg
to Kylerhea.
Ferry information For
vehicle reservations
contact Caledonian
MacBrayne Ltd, The
Ferry Terminal, Uig, Isle
of Skye. Tel: (047 042)
219; fax: (047 042) 387.
Local ferry offices
Armidale, tel: (047 14)
248; Kyleakin, tel:
(0599) 4482.

Railheads Kyle of
Lochalsh and Mallaig.

**Tourist Information
Centre** Meall House,
Portree, Isle of Skye.
Tel: (0478) 2137. Also
Broadford and Kyle of
Lochalsh.

incomers, but there is a resurrection of
interest in Gaelic culture, assisted by a
Gaelic college (Sabhal Mor Ostaig),
Gaelic poetry (eg Sorley MacLean),
Gaelic rock music (eg Run Rig), a local
newspaper (*The West Highland Free
Press*) and with economic support from
the Highlands and Islands Development
Board and spiritual underpinning from
the extreme Sabbatarian Free Church.
Local museums at Luib, Colbost,
Glendale and Kilmuir help to interpret
crofting society to visitors.

Kilmuir burial ground has the grave of
Flora MacDonald and a monument to
the most famous lady in Skye's long history. The monument has Dr Johnson's
epitaph engraved on it: 'Her name will
be mentioned in history and if courage
and fidelity be virtues, mentioned with
honour'. It was she who helped Bonnie

Prince Charlie to escape capture after
the defeat of his army at Culloden in
1746, by transporting him in a boat from
North Uist, 'over the sea to Skye'. After
Flora's part in the prince's escape
became known, she was arrested and
spent almost a year in the Tower of London. After a busy life, including some
dozen years in North Carolina, she
returned to her husband's house at
Kingsburgh and died in Skye in 1790. It
is said that her funeral was the largest
ever witnessed in the Highlands.

Also in the Kilmuir graveyard are
some members of the MacArthur family
who were hereditary pipers to the Mac-
Donalds at Duntulm Castle. Kilmuir
also has a major visitor attraction in the
restored thatched cottages that make up
the Skye Museum of Island Life, which
was opened in 1965. Here the way of life

of a traditional crofting community of the past can be experienced.

Another famous piping family was the MacCrimmons of Borreraig, who were hereditary pipers to the MacLeods of Dunvegan for over two hundred years. They operated a college of piping, with a course of instruction that lasted for three years. A cairn commemorates their activities and every year in August a special piping competition is held in their honour in the drawing-room of Dunvegan Castle. Classical piping music, traditionally played only by the greatest pipers, is known as pibroch or *piobaireachd*, or *Ceol mor*, 'the great music', pronounced 'kyoll more'. A new Piping Centre at the old school in Borreraig tells the story of the bagpipes, which survived their banning after Culloden to be the internationally recognised symbol of the Highland Scot.

In the nineteenth century the native culture came under serious threat, with an estimated emigration of thirty thousand islanders between 1840 and 1888. In 1882 the Battle of the Braes saw a confrontation over grazing rights between local farmers in the Braes dis-

The hills of the Trotternish peninsula, Isle of Skye

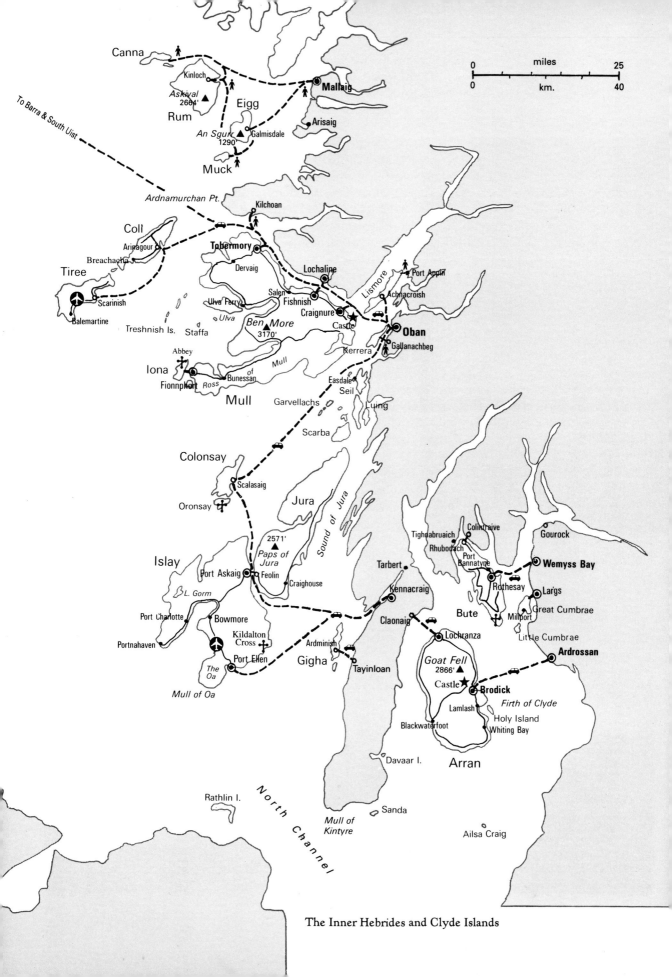

The Inner Hebrides and Clyde Islands

trict near Portree and fifty Glasgow policemen who were imported to keep control. After a pitched battle, gunboats were sent and a force of marines landed at Uig. After a public outcry, a royal commission was established by Gladstone, resulting in the Crofters Act of 1886, which provided security of tenure at a fair and controlled rent. This system, which replaced the original communal townships, remains in force today.

The principal residence of the MacDonalds of Sleat from 1815 was

Armadale Castle, the surviving portion of which has been renovated and opened to the public as the Clan Donald Centre. Previous MacDonald castles included Dun Scaich, on the west side of the Sleat peninsula, Knock Castle or Castle Camus, also in Sleat, and Duntulm, a spectacular site at the north end of Trotternish, which was abandoned in about 1730. Dunvegan Castle, the ancient seat of the MacLeods of Dunvegan and Harris, occupies a rocky site on the east shore of Loch Dunvegan. The keep dates to the fourteenth century. In part of the later eighteenth-century buildings is an exhibition covering the history of the Clan MacLeod, including the famous 'Fairy Flag', a silk banner of eastern origin which is thought to convey protection on the clan.

Skye has five ferry terminals that connect it to the mainland and the surrounding islands. The main crossing is from the railhead at Kyle of Lochalsh to Kyleakin, a short, five-minute crossing eventually to be replaced by a toll bridge. Calmac operate a 24-hour service on this route. This is where the Norwegian King Haakon anchored his longships in 1263, on his way to the

(Left) A Victorian engraving of Dunvegan Castle on the Isle of Skye, ancestral home of the MacLeod clan

The harbour at Uig, Isle of Skye, from where ferries depart for Tarbert, Harris and Lochmaddy, North Uist (*Highlands & Islands Enterprise*)

fiasco of the Battle of Largs; the place-name commemorates his visit. A few miles to the south is a seasonal ferry connection from Glenelg to Kylerhea – another short crossing through treacherous, tidal races. At the southern end of the Sleat (pronounced 'slate') peninsula a ferry connects Armadale to Mallaig, another railhead, with connections through Fort William to Glasgow and London. This ferry only takes vehicles in the summer, but operates as a passenger service for the rest of the year. At the opposite end of Skye, from the harbour of Uig in the Trotternish peninsula, there are ferry connections to the Outer Hebrides (Tarbert, Harris and Lochmaddy, North Uist). Another short crossing connects Sconser on Skye to the island of Raasay.

All these ferries and the island's extensive road system are stretched beyond capacity in the summer tourist season, when over one million visitors sail 'over the sea to Skye'. Although crofting and fishing still form the basis of the island's economy, tourism and light industry, including electronics, are now vitally important. There is a

The old harbour at Armadale, in the sheltered Sleat peninsula

Looking across the
Sound of Raasay to
Braes and the
mountains of the Isle
of Skye

Room with a view:
Skye from the terrace
at Raasay House

(Right) Glendale,
Skye: this is real
'White Settler'
country, where few
native islanders
remain (*Highlands &
Islands Enterprise*)

'Over the sea to
Skye'? There are
plans to replace the
Kyle-Kyleakin ferry
with a toll bridge
(*Highlands & Islands
Enterprise*)

famous whisky distillery at Carbost –
the Talisker Malt Whisky Distillery –
which was established in 1833. Most of
its production is blended for export.
There are guided tours during the tourist season.

Portree, with a population of over
1,000, is the main town, with hotels,
shops, banks and all the usual services,
including a Tourist Information Centre.
Its name derives from a visit by King
James V in 1540, on an expedition to

quell insurrections among the rebellious
population of the Western Isles. In this
aim he was not notably successful.

Skye Week, an annual festival of culture and leisure events, is one of the
major events of the year. From
Broadford, a lively village of 900 people,
with craft shops and an annual folk festival, a scenic road leads eventually to
Elgol, from where there is a fine view of
the Cuillin ridge. A track leads from
Elgol to the Sligachan Hotel past Loch

Coruisk. There are many other thriving crofting townships throughout the island.

There are many scenic and interesting areas in Skye of outstanding natural beauty, but none is more spectacular than the Neist peninsula west of Dunvegan. On the western tip of Skye is the Neist Point lighthouse, which overlooks towering cliffs full of sea-birds. Nearby are the 967ft (294m) cliffs of Waterstein Head. Far out to the west are North and South Uist, and Benbecula. In the Sleat peninsula, the small village of Isleornsay is very picturesque and attractive, situated in a more fertile, sheltered, landscape. The nearby small tidal island of Ornsay has a ruined chapel and an unmanned lighthouse.

RAASAY

The island of Raasay lies east of Skye and is separated from the Trotternish Peninsula by the Sound of Raasay. The mainland district of Applecross is 8 miles (13km) to the east. Raasay is 13 miles (21km) long and up to 3 miles (5km) wide, with a population of 180 in 30sq miles (77sq km). It is a hilly island, rising in the centre to the flat-topped Dun Caan (1,456ft/443m), where Boswell 'danced a Highland dance' in 1773.

There is a short ferry connection to Sconser on the Isle of Skye. The principal settlement is Inverarish, between the ferry slip and Raasay House, where the Macleod laird, his wife and large family (three sons and ten daughters) entertained Boswell and Dr Johnson in lavish style. They expressed in rather flowery prose what generations of visitors to the Hebrides have felt: 'Such a seat of hospitality amids the winds and waters fill the imagination with a delightful contrariety of images!' Raasay House stands on the site of a tower house that was built in 1549. On the east side of the island is Brochel Castle which was built by the MacLeods of Lewis in the fifteenth century.

Mineworkers' cottages on Raasay: the ironstone mines nearby were worked by German POWs during World War I (*Highlands & Islands Enterprise*)

RAASAY

Getting there

Calmac ferry Sconser (Skye)–Raasay; passage time: 15 minutes.
Ferry information For vehicle reservations, contact the Ferrymaster, Raasay. Tel: (0478) 62226. No Sunday service.

Railhead Kyle of Lochalsh; ferry to Kyleakin (Skye), then by road to Sconser.

Tourist Information Centre Portree, Isle of Skye. Tel: (0478) 2137.

The original Raasay House was burned by government troops after the Battle of Culloden. Because the outlawed Bonnie Prince Charlie was given refuge on Raasay, 300 houses were burned, 280 cows and 700 sheep were slaughtered, several horses were shot and most of the island's boats were holed and sunk.

After John MacLeod of Raasay sold the island in 1843, it passed through the hands of numerous owners, none of whom was able to reverse a trend of emigration, depopulation and poverty which continued until recent times. Raasay House was run as a hotel from 1937 to 1960, when it was allowed to collapse into a dilapidated ruin. It is now used as the base for an outdoor adventure school. There is a hotel and youth hostel. Raasay is strictly Sabbatarian due to the influence of the Free Church. The poet Sorley Maclean is a native of Raasay. His brother Calum, who died in 1960 at the age of 45, was the author of *The Highlands*, one of the most evocative and perceptive accounts of the Highlands ever written.

The 2 miles (3km) of road that join Brochel to Arnish are the work of one man, Calum MacLeod, who died in 1988 soon after he had built 'Calum's Road' single-handed over a period variously estimated at ten to fifteen years. With just a pick and shovel and a wheelbarrow, and a manual on roadmaking which cost him 25p, he decided to build the road himself after the local council turned down his requests for a proper access to his home. Raasay Community Council decided to honour his achievement with a cairn, which was unveiled in 1990, with a suitable plaque in Gaelic and English.

THE SMALL ISLES: EIGG, MUCK, RUM, CANNA

The Small Isles parish consists of the islands of Eigg, Muck, Rum and Canna, which are located south-west of Skye and west of Mallaig, from where there is a passenger ferry. The islands, which are all inhabited, are all part of Highland Region. If small is beautiful, then this is the place to be. Although the populations of these communities are small, the islands are viable working units – just.

The tumbled remains of an Iron Age fortress at the southern end of the island of Raasay

(Above) Ponies in front of Kinloch Castle, on the island of Rum: formerly an Edwardian holiday home, now owned by the Nature Conservancy (*Highlands & Islands Enterprise*)

Gallanach Farm on the small island of Muck in the Inner Hebrides, part of the parish of the Small Isles. The island of Eigg is in the background (*Sue Anderson*)

THE SMALL ISLES: EIGG, MUCK, RUM, CANNA

Getting there

Calmac ferry Mallaig-Eigg-Muck-Rum-Canna; passage time: Eigg, 1½ hours, Muck, 2¼ hours, Rum, 3-3½ hours, Canna, 4-4½ hours. On summer Saturdays early morning ferry (5am) sails Mallaig-Canna-Rum-Muck-Eigg.
Ferry information No vehicles carried. Summer sailings: Monday, Wednesday, Friday, Saturday; winter sailings: Monday and Wednesday only. For timings, contact Caledonian MacBrayne Ltd, The Ferry Terminal, Mallaig, PH41 4QB. On summer Saturdays there are two sailings from Mallaig, making it possible to spend 9½ hours on Canna, or 7½ hours on Rum, or 5 hours on Muck, or 3½ hours on Eigg. At Eigg, Muck and Rum passengers are transferred to small boats as there are no suitable piers.

Railhead Mallaig. Through connections to Fort William, Glasgow and London.

Tourist Information Centre Mallaig. Tel: (0687) 2170. Fort William & Lochaber Tourist Board, Travel Centre, Fort William. Tel: (0397) 3781.

EIGG

The island of Eigg (Gaelic *eige*, a hollow), 6½ by 4 miles (10.4 by 6.4km) in size, has been in the headlines recently on account of the domestic difficulties of its laird. When it is placed on the open market, it is expected to fetch over £1 million. The population is about 35. In the 1950s there were 35-40 children in the school; in 1990 there were 8-10. In the 1840s the population was over 500.

In 1577 practically the entire population of Eigg was suffocated in a cave by the MacLeods from Skye. The atrocity took place in winter; the hide-out was given away by footprints in the snow. The MacLeods piled brushwood at the entrance to the cave and set fire to it. The smoke killed all within – about 395 men, women and children, all tenants of the MacDonald laird. MacDonalds cave is ½ mile (800m) south-west of the pier. In early Christian times a monastery was established on the island by St Donnan, who was killed there by islanders.

Looming over the harbour and the main settlement of Galmisdale (which has a shop and post office) is the 'sgurr' or Eigg, An Sgurr, a distinctively shaped ridge of columnar pitchstone which is identifiable from far and wide, reaching a height of 1,290ft (393m). There is a superb view from the summit. It is home to a colony of Manx shearwater, which burrow into the ground for nesting. At the foot of An Sgurr are the abandoned townships of Upper and Lower Grulin. Over one hundred men, women and children from Grulin were evicted to make room for sheep in the 1850s and moved to Nova Scotia, in Canada. At the north end of the island is the small crofting township of Cleasdale, on the Bay of Laig. In 1841, when the population of the island was 546, there were over 150 people there, now there are less than 20. At Camas Sgiotaig there are strange sandstone rock formations and singing sands.

MUCK

Muck is the tiniest of the Small Isles, less than 2 miles by 1 mile (3 by 1.6km) with a land area of 1,586 acres (642ha). The high point is Beinn Airein at 451ft (137m). Muck is 2½ miles (4km) south-west of its neighbour, Eigg. Its name comes from the Gaelic *Eilean a muic*, 'the island of the pig'. During the Napoleonic wars 280 people lived on Muck, working in the kelp industry, but by 1826 the industry collapsed and with it the economies of Muck and many other islands. In 1861 the population was 58; today it is 26. There is a traditional laird's house at Gallanach and a guest-house at Port Mor.

RUM

Calmac still spell this island's name 'Rhum' – the 'h' reputedly was introduced in Victorian times to take account of sensibilities over strong liquor. Properly pronounced 'Room', the name may derive from the Norse *Röm oe*, 'wide island'. Measuring 6 by 6½ miles (9.6 by 10.4km), it is the largest of the Small Isles.

Today, Rum looks like a trackless wilderness, but it once supported over 300 people. Most of them went to Canada and were replaced by 8,000 sheep. In 1888 the island was bought by John Bullough of Oswaldtwistle, who made a fortune in the textile industry designing machinery. His son, Sir George Bullough, took over Rum in 1891 and built Kinloch Castle, a massive late-Victorian mansion on which no expense was spared. The red sandstone was brought from the island of Arran, in the Clyde. The fittings are opulent. In 1957 his widow Lady Monica sold the island to the Nature Conservancy Council, which now runs it as an enormous outdoor laboratory and research station, supporting a population of about 40.

On the west side of Rum is what has all the appearance of a Greek temple but is, in fact, the Bullough family mausoleum. To say it looks out of place is an understatement. The Nature Conservancy Council has maintained Kinloch Castle as an Edwardian mansion and runs it in the summer as an up-market hotel. Cheap hostel accommodation is also available. Although Rum is an artificial community wholly dependent on the scientific staff and their families, it is an interesting and congenial place to spend a week, if you are interested in natural history and outdoor pursuits.

Ongoing studies of the red deer population of Rum are providing crucial information for the future of a venison industry in the Highlands. The thousands of breeding sea-birds are constantly studied and over 130,000 pairs of Manx shearwater nest on the mountain tops. The mountains have Norse names: Orval, Askival (2,664ft/812km), Hallival, Ruinsival, Barkeval, Trallval. The last of these takes its name from the troll of Norse mythology, which visiting Norsemen heard at night in these hills. What they really heard was the eery call of the Manx shearwater. In recent years the white-tailed sea eagle has been re-introduced to the Hebrides from Norway and is slowly spreading outwards from Rum.

In recent years archaeologists have found evidence at a site near Kinloch of human occupation on Rum before 6000BC in the form of thousands of flint and bloodstone flakes. Sixty million years ago, Rum was a volcano.

CANNA

With a population of about twenty on an island 5 miles (8km) long by 1 mile (1.6km) wide, Canna is the most westerly of the Small Isles. The deep-water harbour and pier are sheltered by the tidal island of Sanday. There are spectacular views to Rum and Skye. The high point of the island is Carn a Ghaill at 690ft (210m). Above the pier is Compass Hill (458ft/139m); the highly

metallic rock affects navigation in its vicinity.

Like Rum, Canna is an artificial community, owned by the National Trust for Scotland. The folklorist and Gaelic scholar John Lorne Campbell bought the island in 1938, but has recently handed it over to the National Trust for Scotland, from whom limited accommodation is available. Dr Campbell has assembled one of the finest collections of books on the Hebrides, Highland history and Gaelic culture generally. Under his regime the island was run as a single working farm and it is hoped that this will continue, despite some controversy about how the new owners are discharging their responsibilities.

On a fine summer Saturday, it is possible to join the day-trippers from Mallaig and spend over nine hours ashore on Canna, which is just long enough to have a good wander, a picnic and enjoy the panoramic views before you catch the ferry back to Mallaig. It is a long day, though, with a 5 o'clock start from Mallaig and the ferry arriving back at 7.30pm.

COLL

The island of Coll lies in the Inner Hebrides, north-west of the island of Mull. The population is about 150. A car ferry from Oban calls at the main township, Arinagour, before it continues to the neighbouring island of Tiree. In size the island measures 13 miles by 4 miles (21 by 6.4km), the terrain is generally low-lying but knobbly due to the underlying Lewisian gneiss, especially in the northern half of the island. A thin vein of lead at Crossapol was once mined. Garnets are found on the shore south-west of Breachacha. The highest hill is Ben Hogh (341ft/104m), on top of which a large glacial erratic is precariously perched.

The only settlement on Coll is Arinagour, with three piers, shops, hotel, guesthouse, school, post office,

COLL

Getting there

Calmac ferry Oban-
Tobermory-Coll;
passage time: 3 hours.
Tiree-Coll; passage
time: 1¼ hours.
Tobermory-Coll;
passage time: 1¼ hours.
Sailing days vary
seasonally, but are three
times a week in winter
and four times a week
in summer. Summer
Sundays: Mallaig-
Armadale-Tobermory-
Coll-Tiree round trip.
Ferry information For
vehicle reservations,
contact Caledonian
MacBrayne Ltd, The
South Pier, Oban, Argyll.
Tel: (0631) 62285; fax:
(0631) 66588. Most
ferries leave Oban at
6am. Overnight berths
bookable on ferry. New
roll-on, roll off facilities
are now operational.
Local ferry office The
Pier, Arinagour, Isle of
Coll, Argyll. Tel: (087
93) 347.

Railhead Oban.

Airport None. There is a
private airstrip at
Breachacha and an
airport on Tiree.

**Tourist Information
Centre** Oban, Mull &
District Tourist Board,
Bothwell House, Argyll
Square, Oban, Argyll.
Tel: (0631) 63122.

perfume factory and doctor. It is possible to charter boats locally for fishing trips and sightseeing. The island is ideal for walking and cycling and has lots of interesting nooks and crannies to explore. There are fine views eastwards to Mull, the Treshnish Islands and Staffa, and north to the Small Isles and Skye.

One of the most picturesque scenes in the Hebrides is at Sorisdale, at the north end of Coll, probably named after a Norseman who settled there soon after 1000. A single thatched cottage remains of what was once a thriving and populous settlement. Surrounding the sandy bay are boat 'noosts' for sheltering small boats during winter storms. Some of these may be of Norse date. In the sand dunes north of Sorisdale a 'beaker' burial, dating from the Bronze Age, was found after the series of storms in September 1976.

The north-east coast of the island, between Sorisdale and Arinagour, is an uninhabited wilderness which is excellent for easy hill-walking or just wandering. The prehistoric fort at Dun Dulorichan, on an isolated steep-sided rocky outcrop overlooking the south-east end of Loch Airidh Raonuill is poorly preserved, but worth a visit for its setting.

The natural history of the island reflects a fairly wide range of habitats and is typical of the Inner Hebrides. There is a small native population of greylag geese.

Coll has a rich archaeological heritage. Notable are the chambered cairn at Arinagour and the two standing stones at Totronald, mentioned by Johnson and Boswell who were storm-bound here in 1773. The stones are known as Na Sgeulachan, 'the Tellers of Tales', and date probably from the Bronze Age – around 1500BC. Both are granite slabs, aligned WNW-ESE, possibly indicating important positions in the movements of the sun and moon.

There are several Iron Age forts on Coll; those at Dun an Achaidh and Feall Bay are best preserved. A feature of Dun an Achaidh is the marked contrast between the natural quartzite of the ridge on which it stands and the stones and boulders of Lewisian gneiss which was used in its construction. Casual finds from the site have included plain and decorated pottery, a slate whorl and a stone pounder. An alternative name for this fort is *Dun Bhorlum mhic Anlaimh righ Lochlinn* – the fort of the ridge of the son of Olaf, King of Norway. Badly ruined, but in a spectacular location, is the fort of Dun Morbhaidh, on a small craggy hill near the shore to the north-west of Cornaigbeg farm. Pottery with incised animal designs has been found here.

To the north of the road near the cattle-grid at Kilbride farm are the remains of a hut-circle and enclosure. The hut-circle is fairly well-preserved, with the stone wall surviving to a height of two courses on the north side. The internal diameter of the hut was 14ft (4.3m) while the wall, which probably supported a conical thatched roof, is 7ft (2.2m) thick. The entrance faces east and is about 3ft (1m) wide, with well-defined stone jambs.

Unusual in the islands, there is a souterrain at the Arnabost crossroads: enquire locally to obtain access. It was discovered in 1855 and excavated in 1896 by the island's postmaster, Robert Sturgeon. There are several crannogs (fortified islands) in Coll's hill lochs.

The medieval parish church is at Killunaig, on the north-west coast; it was first recorded in 1433 when the parsonage and the vicarage belonged to the nunnery of Iona. There are fine views from the top of the sand dunes behind the church. In the dunes 295yd (270m) west of the burial ground at Killunaig are two cists, dating from the Bronze Age, which, when they were excavated in 1976 were found to contain the remains of three individuals.

The beaches on the west side of the

Breachacha Castle, Coll, now the headquarters of Project Trust, an adventure school that sends youngsters overseas for a year. It was built by the Macleans of Coll in the Middle Ages

island, especially at Killunaig, Hogh Bay and Feall Bay, are among the finest in the Hebrides. At Grishipoll, between Arnabost and Acha, there is a fine, though roofless example of a mid-eighteenth-century laird's house. It was built by Hugh MacLean and occupied when he succeeded his brother as 14th laird of Coll in 1754. When James Boswell and Samuel Johnson stayed there in October 1773, it was tenanted by Sween McSween.

At the south end of the island is Breachacha Castle, in design comparable to Kisimul Castle in Barra. In 1965 it was bought and restored by Major N. V. MacLean-Bristol, a descendant of the Macleans of Coll who owned it from 1631 to 1856 and is now used as the headquarters for an adventure-training school, the Project Trust, which sends two hundred young people annually overseas in the year between school and university. Tours of the castle run in conjunction with some ferries. On certain days it is possible to spend 3½ hours on Coll on a day trip from Tobermory or Oban. In the surrounding fields many rare breeds of sheep and cattle are kept. Nearby is a dilapidated eighteenth-century mansion.

The population of Coll was much greater in the past than it is now. In 1793 the First Statistical Account – a kind of inventory of all the parishes in Scotland – quotes a population of 1,041. In 1792, 36 people had emigrated to America. Near Acha House is an abandoned mill, with most of the original machinery intact. When it was built in

TIREE

Getting there

Calmac ferry Oban-Tiree (via Tobermory and Coll); passage time: 4¼ hours. On summer Fridays, direct Oban-Tiree service; passage time: 3½ hours. Sailings three times a week in winter, four times a week in summer. Sailing days vary. Summer Sundays: Mallaig-Armadale-Tobermory-Coll-Tiree round trip.
Ferry information For vehicle reservations, contact Caledonian MacBrayne Ltd, The South Pier, Oban, Argyll. Tel: (0631) 62285; fax: (0631) 66588. Most ferries leave Oban at 6am. Overnight berths bookable on ferry. New roll-on, roll-off facilities are now operational.
Local ferry office The Pier, Scarinish, Isle of Tiree, Argyll. Tel: (087 92) 337.

Railhead Oban.

Airport Tiree Airport has daily flights to Glasgow Airport, operated by Loganair; flight time: 50 minutes.

Tourist Information Centre Oban, Mull & District Tourist Board, Bothwell House, Argyll Square, Oban, Argyll. Tel: (0631) 63122.

---

the nineteenth-century, the population of the island justified such a major investment, reaching a peak of 1,409 in 1841. Over the next twenty years, 700 emigrated, mainly to Canada and Australia.

Agriculture is the main industry, with a little tourism. There are about 1,000 beef cattle, 7,000 sheep and a few dairy cattle. One or two local fishermen make a precarious living from lobsters, clams and prawns. Tourism is still small-scale, mostly due to lack of accommodation for holidaymakers, coupled with an unattractive ferry timetable – it requires a high level of commitment to turn up at Oban pier at 6am, especially if you are travelling from the South of England. But those who do come, return again and again and are not particularly keen to see the island changed. However, the declining and ageing local population desperately needs to attract young couples with families, and the problem of providing them with employment is serious.

TIREE

The island of Tiree lies in the Inner Hebrides, to the west of Mull. Reached by ferry from Oban, it is a popular destination for wind-surfers. With a population of 800 on a land area of 29sq miles (75sq km), it is busier and much more fertile than its northern neighbour, Coll. The island is about 12 miles (19km) long and 3 miles (5km) wide. Tiree is a wind-swept, flat island, its level landscape broken only by sand dunes, occasional rocky knolls and the hills of Ben Hynish (462ft/140m) and Beinn Hough (390ft/118m) at its western extremities. On the western skyline a massive dimpled military communications 'golfball' is prominent. In Gaelic, Tiree was sometimes given the nickname *Tir fo Thuinn*, 'Land below the waves'. When seen from a distance, the low ground disappears below the horizon, leaving the south-western hills stranded.

The long, flat sandy beaches all around the island mean that visiting wind-surfers can always find somewhere to practise their sport. The locals were initially worried about the influx of brightly coloured visitors with their strange obsession, but the years have mellowed suspicion on both sides and Tiree is now a regular venue for surfing championships.

The underlying bedrock is Lewisian gneiss, but wind-blown sand has allowed fertile, well-drained machair to cover most of the island. Tiree was known in Gaelic as the land of corn (*Tir-Iodh*) and supported a population of 4,450 in 1831. Following famines and evictions the population declined to 2,700 by 1881. At the height of the tourist season today it approaches the levels of the last century.

There are several interesting archaelogical sites, including the excavated broch of Dun Mor Vaul: the finds are in the Hunterian Museum at Glasgow University. The broch sits on an outcrop of Lewisian gneiss on the north coast of Tiree, about 437yd (400m) north of the township of Vaul. The rig and furrow marks of crofting agriculture are visible on the grassy areas around the rocky knoll on which the broch stands. Excavations showed the site to be complex, with an initial Iron Age occupation dating from around 500BC. The broch itself, of which substantial walling remains, was probably built in the 1st century AD; it continued in use until 300. The wall was 10–13ft (3–4m) thick and had a continuous gallery inside it, running almost the whole way around the building. The original height of the broch was 25–30ft (7.6–9m), with perhaps three or four galleries on top of the surviving one at ground level. A stairway, of which only the first eleven steps survive, would have run up to the wall head by means of mural galleries. A ledge running around the inside wall and a ring of post-holes would have supported a wooden floor.

In times of danger fifty or sixty people may have lived in the broch. It is one of the most impressive archaeological monuments anywhere in the Hebrides.

On the shore between Vaul and Balephetrish is a granite glacial erratic, the 'ringing stone', *Clach a'Choire*, which is covered with over fifty Bronze Age cup marks. It makes a metallic sound when struck. There is a legend that if it ever shatters or falls off the pedestal of small stones on which it rests, Tiree will sink beneath the waves.

Further west along this northern shore, above Balephetrish farmhouse, is another poorly preserved prehistoric fort, with a well inside the ruined walls.

The most spectacular island scenery is at the headland of Kenavara, in Gaelic *Ceann a' Mhara*. On the headland itself is a prehistoric fort, Dun nan Gall. All around are massive sea cliffs, which are battered endlessly by Atlantic rollers. In the breeding season, thousands of sea-birds wheel overhead and seals play on the rocky shore. The natural history of Tiree is typically Hebridean, with abundant bird life and a profusion of wild flowers in the spring, especially on the grassy coastal pastures known as the machair. One strange feature of the island is that there are no rabbits.

Tiree has a long and interesting history. The early Christian Columban church was present on the island and has left traces at Kirkapol, in the form of simple Latin crosses carved on rocks to mark the extent of the consecrated ground. There are also two late-medieval chapels at Kirkapol and some carved grave-slabs. After the centuries of Norse rule, from 850 until 1150, Tiree was part of the territory of Somerled, the founder of the MacDonald Lords of the Isles. When the Lordship of the Isles was abolished in 1493 and reverted to the Crown, Tiree was granted, in 1517, to the MacLeans of Duart (on Mull). The MacDonalds resisted and feuding continued for many years. The Campbells took over the island in 1674, after

rising debts diminished the power of the MacLeans. Island House was built by the Earl of Argyll for his factor in 1748 at Loch an Eilein, Heylipol, on the site of an earlier stronghold.

In 1886 Scarinish was the scene of a confrontation between local crofters and the government. About 250 marines and 50 policemen were drafted on to the island to restore law and order. As a result, 8 crofters were arrested and sentenced to four to six months' imprisonment in Edinburgh. The relative prosperity of the island today is due in large measure to concessions that were won from the government, especially after World War I.

The ferry terminal and main township is at Scarinish. The pier area at the west end of Gott Bay is rather unkempt, but the village ½ mile (800m) away has interesting shops, offices, post office, bank and other services, and an old harbour. The islanders are proud of their secondary school, which is the smallest in the country. There are several crofting townships around the island, many with thatched cottages. Balevullin has several brightly painted renovated traditional houses. The thick walls and rounded corners are perfectly adapted for the windy Hebridean environment.

At Hynish, at the southern tip of the island, there is an interesting harbour and signalling tower containing relics and information about the lighthouse on Skerryvore, 10 miles to the south-west. It was built in 1838-43 by Alan Stevenson, an uncle of the writer Robert Louis Stevenson. A large telescope is provided to facilitate viewing.

Tiree has a weather station, which regularly records more hours of sunshine than at almost any other part of Britain. Its report comes right at the beginning of the 'coastal stations' listed on the BBC shipping forecast. Rainfall is well below the average for the west coast of Scotland, but there is no getting away from the fact that it is a windy place to live. The wind varies from

strong to unrelenting, which is bad news for midges, the scourge of the Western Isles in the tourist season. Although Tiree's flatness is good news for cyclists, the wind more than compensates for the absence of hills.

Tiree airport is in the middle of the island, in an area known as 'The Reef'. The strange name is a corruption of the Gaelic *ruighe*, 'summer pasture'. More than four thousand servicemen were stationed here during World War II. The airfield was built in 1941 on the site of a grass landing strip. Planes flew long patrols out over the Atlantic from Tiree. The island is littered with debris from the war years. Old huts, building foundations, gun emplacements and other bits and pieces are scattered around the island although much has found a use around the island's many crofts.

MULL

The island of Mull lies off the coast of Argyll, forming the western entrance to the Firth of Lorn and Loch Linnhe. To its north, across the narrow, fjordlike Sound of Mull, lies Morven and the Ardnamurchan peninsula. To the south are Colonsay, Islay and Jura, while to the west are Coll, Tiree, Iona and the waters of the North Atlantic. With a land area of 353sq miles (914sq km) its

The mountains of Mull, seen from the island of Colonsay

Lobster-pots, hotel and church at Bunessan, Mull – three elements found on every Hebridean island (*Highlands & Islands Enterprise*)

An aerial view of Tobermory, Mull (*Highlands & Islands Enterprise*)

MULL

Getting there

Calmac ferry Oban–
Craignure; passage time:
40 minutes. Oban–
Tobermory; passage
time: 1¾ hours.
Lochaline–Fishnish;
passage time: 15
minutes. Kilchoan
(Ardnamurchan)–
Tobermory (summer
only); passage time: 35
minutes. Summer
Sundays: Mallaig–
Armadale–Tobermory–
Coll–Tiree round trip.
Ferry information For
vehicle reservations
contact Caledonian
MacBrayne Ltd, The
South Pier, Oban, Argyll.
Tel: (0631) 62285; fax:
(0631) 66588. The ferry
from Oban–Coll/Tiree
calls at Tobermory on
most sailings.
Local ferry office
Craignure. Tel: (068 02)
343; Tobermory (0688)
2017.

Railhead Oban.

Airport Private airstrip
at Glenforsa.

Tourist Information
Centre Tobermory. Tel:
(0688) 2182. Oban, Mull
& District Tourist Board,
Bothwell House, Argyll
Square, Oban, Argyll.
Tel: (0631) 63122.

population of just under 2,400 is scattered thinly but unevenly across the landscape, with the largest settlements at Tobermory (700), Craignure, Salen, Bunessan, Dervaig and Fionnphort.

A feature of the topography is the way in which sea lochs bite into the middle of the island. Loch na Keal, Loch Scridain, Loch Buie and Loch Spelve all provide sheltered anchorages. There are 300 miles (482km) of coastline.

Mull is well served by ferry services. The main connection is from the railhead at Oban to Craignure, at the eastern entrance of the Sound of Mull: this is a 40-minute crossing. A shorter voyage across the Sound of Mull from Lochaline to Fishnish gives access from Morven, Lochaber and Fort William. In addition, ferries heading for Coll and Tiree call at Tobermory. A summer service links Kilchoan (Ardnamurchan) with Tobermory.

Mull is a picturesque and hilly island, dominated by the central mountain of Ben More (3,170ft/966m), from which there is a spectacular view. Its scree slopes are the remains of an ancient volcano which exploded sixty million years ago. All around the central plateau are basaltic lavas which form gigantic terraced steps. The interesting geology attracts many students and field-workers during the summer months. Near the headland of the Ardmeanach peninsula is MacCulloch's Tree, a remarkable geological fossil tree that was discovered in 1819. Today, only the base of the trunk survives, consisting of a partially silicified cylinder of fossil wood glistening with quartz crystals, surrounded by a sheath of soft, black charred wood. It is rooted in a carbonaceous mud with a film of coal, overlying a bed of red volcanic ash.

Mull has many sites of archaeological and historical interest, ranging from chambered cairns and standing stones to vitrified forts, duns and brochs, and several important castles. The stone circle at the head of Loch Buie and the linear settings of standing stones in the forestry plantations around Dervaig, are evidence of ceremonial observances in Mull in the Bronze Age, dating to the second millennium BC. The Iron Age Dun Aisgain, near Burg, is exceptionally well preserved, dating as it does from around 200BC.

Duart Castle, near Craignure, was probably built as a McDougall castle in the thirteenth century. The main feature is the tower house that was built in the late fourteenth century, when it became the chief residence of the MacLeans of Duart. The MacLeans lost their estates in the 1670s, but in 1911 Duart Castle was purchased and restored by Colonel Sir Fitzroy MacLean, 26th chief of the clan MacLean. It is now a place of pilgrimage for Maclean Diaspora.

Aros Castle, on the Sound of Mull, near Salen, dates from the fourteenth century and was one of the strongholds of the Lords of the Isles. Moy Castle, at the head of Loch Buie, was built in the fifteenth century by the MacLeans of Lochbuie. The strangely-named Frank Lockwood's Island, east of the entrance to Loch Buie, recalls the solicitor-general in Lord Rosebery's administration (1894–5). He was the brother-in-law of the 21st MacLaine (sic) of Lochbuie.

Torosay Castle, to the south of Craignure, was built in 1856 in the Scottish baronial style. There are fine gardens, through which runs a narrow-gauge railway which has become a major tourist attraction. Another modern castle is Glengorm, on the Mishnish promontory west of Tobermory; it was built in 1860.

The long, low peninsula of the Ross of Mull is traversed by an ancient pilgrim track, which aims for the island of Iona lying at its western extremity. The modern road system of Mull amounts to over 120 miles (193km), much of it greatly improved in recent years. Close to the south-west tip of the Ross of Mull is the island of Erraid, which was immortalised by Robert Louis Steven-

son in *Kidnapped*. It was here that David Balfour was shipwrecked from the brig *Covenant* and began his adventures. The cottages were built as a shore station by the Commissioners of Northern Lights for keepers who were serving the lighthouses at Skerryvore and Dubh Artach. The engineer on these projects, and others, was Alan Stevenson, uncle of the writer. The island is now occupied by members of the Findhorn Foundation.

As well as being one of the smallest Scottish burghs, Tobermory is also one of the most colourful: brightly painted houses line the sheltered harbour. The town was built in 1787–8 by the British Fisheries Society. An annual music festival and yacht races are among the events held there. There are many hotels and guest-houses, and a youth hostel, that provide accommodation. There is a good range of shops and facilities, including a Tourist Information Centre.

The population of Mull grew dramatically in the eighteenth century and peaked at 10,600 in 1821, but has been declining ever since. In recent years numbers have stabilised around 2,300–2,400, although the replacement of native islanders by both English and Scottish incomers is more apparent, and thus has aroused more controversy on Mull than on the many other Hebridean islands with which it shares this trend. The locals refer to the incomers as 'White Settlers' and sometimes refer to the island as 'The Officers' Mess'. During the summer the resident population rises to over 8,000.

The lack of adequate medical facilities for the population is an ongoing subject of controversy, as on many other islands. Often elderly patients have to be sent to the mainland, to hospitals in Oban or Glasgow, from which they may never return, causing great distress to relatives. At Dunaros Hospital, Salen, there are only five beds, and the local GPs provide emergency cover. Ambulances are often seen on the Craignure–Oban

ferry, taking patients to the mainland for treatment or to the maternity hospital there. In 1990 Calmac delayed one of their sailings for thirty minutes for an expectant mother, precipitating lengthy correspondence in the *Oban Times* when a bus courier wrote in complaining bitterly because his paying customers were late for dinner at their Oban Hotel. Not all visitors are so insensitive.

Dervaig is home to the thirty-five-seat Mull Little Theatre, which was founded in 1966 by Barrie and Marianne Hesketh and run by them until 1984. Their successors are carrying on the tradition of providing high quality dramatic entertainment in what was a disused cow byre. It is Britain's smallest professional theatre. As their publicity material says, if you draw a line from Inverness to Glasgow, the only theatre between you and Broadway is the Little Theatre, Mull.

In modern times, the Forestry Commission, small-scale crofting and fishing, sheep farming, fish farming and tourism (over 600,000 annual visitors) are the major industries on Mull.

The island of Ulva (Norse: 'wolf island') lies in Loch Tuath, off the west coast of Mull, which is now connected by a bridge to the neighbouring island of Gometra. The population of over 500 was completely cleared between 1846 and 1851. Owned by MacQuarries for over eight hundred years, it was the birthplace of the father of Major-General Lachlan MacQuarie (*sic*), Governor-General of New South Wales, an important figure in Australian colonial history. The grandfather of the famous missionary and explorer David Livingstone was a crofter in Ulva.

From Ulva ferry it is possible to arrange boat trips to the offshore island of Staffa. This tiny island consists of 71 acres (29ha) of columnar basalt. The hexagonal columns result from the slow cooling of Tertiary basalt lavas, sixty million years ago. Geologically, they are similar to the Giant's Causeway in

The colourful
waterfront at
Tobermory, the main
town on the Isle of
Mull, one of
Scotland's largest
islands. There is
Spanish treasure in
the harbour, from one
of the ships of the
Spanish Armada that
came to grief in 1588

Antrim and to formations on the
Ardmeanach peninsula on Mull, 6 miles
(10km) to the south-east. Landing is
possible only in calm sea conditions.
Boat trips to Staffa visit the musical
cave, An Uamh Binn, in which the
sound of the sea among the columns
made such an impression on Felix
Mendelssohn in 1829. The island is
immortalised in his *Hebrides Overture*.

IONA

Iona is a small island, barely 3½ by 1½
miles (5.6 by 2.4km) overall, with historical importance out of all proportion
to its size. It lies just off the end of the
Ross of Mull – the long peninsula at the
south-west corner of Mull along which
a pilgrim's way leads to the holy island of
Iona.

The place-name, according to the latest scholarship emanating from the Royal Commission on the Ancient and Historical Monuments of Scotland, is from a misreading of the Latin *Ioua insula*, meaning something like 'yewy island', from the ancient Irish *iwos*, 'yew tree'. They point out that the reason the mistake gained acceptance was that the word *Iona* (*Jonah*) is the Hebrew equivalent of the Latin *Columba*, 'a dove', which was the church name of Colum, the Irish monk who came here with his companions in 563. St Columba is known in Gaelic as *Colum Cille*, which explains the Gaelic name for the island, *I Chaluim Chille*.

Although there are one or two prehistoric sites on the island, notably the Iron Age fort on the summit of Dun Cul Bhuirg, Iona owes all of its known history to one man, the early Christian saint and missionary, St Columba, who founded a monastery there in 563. It was typical of the small offshore islands that apparently were irresistible to early Celtic Christians. The first religious community on Iona would have consisted of a few monks living in separate huts, grouped around a small church – quite unlike the great monasteries of the Middle Ages. Apart from the elaborately carved stone crosses and the earthen bank which surrounded their foundation, few traces now remain. The impressive medieval church and monastic complex, which is viewed annually by over 600,000 tourists, was founded around 1200 as a Benedictine abbey by Reginald, son of Somerled who freed the southern isles from Norse rule.

After the forfeiture of the MacDonald Lords of the Isles in 1493 the abbey lost its independent status and after the Protestant Reformation in the 1560s it fell into disrepair. The ruins were gifted by the 8th Duke of Argyll to the Iona Cathedral Trust in 1899, on condition that they reroof the medieval church and restore it for worship. This was accomplished by 1910. In 1938 Dr George MacLeod (the late Very Reverend, Lord MacLeod of Fuinary) founded the Iona Community as an evangelical Church of Scotland brotherhood, with the abbey buildings as its headquarters. This body organised working parties and by 1965 had succeeded in restoring the other monastic buildings in the abbey complex. In 1979 the island of Iona (except for the abbey buildings) was sold by the trustees of the 10th Duke of Argyll to the Fraser Foundation, who then presented it to the Scottish nation in memory of the late Lord Fraser of Allander. Subsequently, the Secretary of State for Scotland transferred ownership to the National Trust for Scotland.

Several guides to Iona Abbey are sold locally, of which by far the best is that prepared for the RCAHMS. The abbey bookshop is well stocked with books on Scottish history, and sells a range of souvenirs. The abbey Museum, in what was probably the monastic infirmary, houses the restored St John's Cross and assorted architectural fragments. A large number of early Christian cross-marked stones are also displayed there.

The oldest part of the abbey is the small, steep-roofed building which is tucked away in a corner just north of the main west door of the abbey church. Although much restored (only the footings of the original structure survive), this is likely to be an oratory of ninth to tenth century date and almost certainly marks the site of St Columba's tomb.

The small building south-west of the abbey is St Oran's Chapel, which was probably built as a family mortuary chapel by Somerled, the ruler of the Isles (d.1164) or his son Reginald. Surrounding it is the *Reilig Odhrain*, 'the burial-ground of Oran', which reputedly contains the burials of forty-eight Scottish kings, including Macbeth's victim, Duncan. Four Irish and eight Norwegian kings are also supposedly buried here. The stone slabs in the ground are not the graves of these kings, but mark

THE WESTERN ISLES: THE INNER HEBRIDES

IONA

Getting there

Calmac ferry
Fionnphort (Mull)–Iona; passage time: 5 minutes.

Ferry information
Vehicles are not usually carried. Frequent sailings. In summer, excursions from Oban are available, allowing two hours ashore at Iona.

Railhead Oban. Calmac ferry Oban–Craignure, local bus.

Tourist Information Centre Oban, Mull & District Tourist Board, Bothwell House, Argyll Square, Oban, Argyll. Tel: (0631) 63122.

The medieval abbey on Iona, before restoration

the last resting place of various important people from around the West Highlands and Islands who were buried at Iona in the late Middle Ages and later.

Without a doubt the most important Christian monuments on Iona are the early Christian high crosses. They date from the beginning of the eighth century. The most spectacular and the most often reproduced are St Martin's Cross, which has a small 'wheel', and St John's Cross. A replica of St John's Cross stands in front of the abbey; the restored original is in the Abbey Museum. The east face of St Martin's Cross shows the Virgin and Child, Daniel in the lions' den and Abraham's sacrifice of Isaac.

An Augustinian nunnery, which was founded about 1200, stands just outside the village. Between it and Iona Abbey is MacLean's Cross, a late-medieval intricately carved cross, with a crucifix on the west face.

Geologically, Iona is quite different from Mull. Whereas Mull is basically a volcanic landscape, Iona has more in common with the Outer Hebrides, at least as far as its rocks are concerned. Some of it is made up of Torridonian sandstone, but the basement rock is Lewisian gneiss. In many ways it is geologically very similar to the Rinns of Islay. Iona marble was formerly quarried on the south-east corner of the island at

Rubha na carraig geire, 'the point of the sharp rock'. Early records show quarrying on Iona in 1693, but the rusting machinery, gunpowder store and rough quay date from 1907 to 1914. Polished pebbles of the yellowish-green serpentine stone can be picked up on most of Iona's beaches.

Today's resident population numbers about 100, excluding the temporary visitors staying in the accommodation blocks at the abbey. Obviously, the island is swamped in the summer months by day-trippers, but it is astonishing how few of them venture more than a few yards from the paved roads, leaving the rest of the island relatively unspoiled. But visitors should remember that the local people are going about their daily lives and should show appropriate consideration. In 1990 a new visitor centre opened, in the old manse, with exhibits and displays illustrating the daily life of the working people of the island from 1770 to the present day. Old photographs show the traditional activities of crofting, fishing, schooling and the coming of the steamboats from Oban that began the tourist boom.

Many visitors come to Iona as a genuine pilgrimage and it is only the totally insensitive who fail to be moved by the spiritual qualities of the place, despite the tourist hordes. One of the first tourists to Iona was Dr Samuel Johnson, who spoke eloquently about the island on behalf of the millions who have followed in his footsteps:

> We were now treading that illustrious island, which was once the luminary of the Caledonian regions, whence savage clans and roving barbarians derived the benefits of knowledge, and the blessings of religion. To abstract the mind from all local emotion would be impossible if it were endeavoured, and would be foolish if it were possible. Whatever withdraws us from the power from our senses, whatever makes the past,

the distant, or the future, predominate over the present, advances us in the dignity of thinking being . . . That man is little to be envied whose patriotism would not gain force upon the field of *Marathon* or whose piety would not grow warmer among the ruins of *Iona*!

Although undoubtedly genuinely moved by the place and its history, both Dr Johnson and his companion, James Boswell, were disappointed with what they saw at Iona. Having heard that kings of Scotland were buried there, they apparently expected something more grand, along the lines of Westminster Abbey!

LISMORE

The fertile island of Lismore (Gaelic *leis mor*, 'the big garden'), lies in Loch Linnhe, 1–2 miles (1.6–3km) off the coasts of Benderloch and Appin on the Scottish mainland. The population is about 140. The ferry terminal is at Achnacroish, half-way up the eastern side of the island. Most of the houses and farms are concentrated in the low-lying and more fertile northern half of Lismore. Until the end of the sixteenth century the island was covered by oak woods, which were cut down for charcoal to fuel Lorn's iron furnaces, for shipbuilding and to clear the hills for cattle and sheep.

The fertility and productiveness of Lismore is due to the ridges of Dalradian limestone which make up most of the island. Limestone was quarried formerly at An Sailean on the west coast and exported to the mainland from Port Ramsay. There are fine raised beaches around the shoreline, reflecting changes in sea level at the end of the last Ice Age. The highest point of the island is Barr Mor (416ft/126m).

A single road runs down the centre of the island, ending in a track that leads to the south point, opposite Eilean

Musdile, where there is a lighthouse that was built in 1833 and is now automatic. Lismore is just under 10 miles (16km) long and 1½ miles (2km) wide, with a land area of 10,000 acres (4,000ha). The island has a long and interesting history. In prehistoric times a broch tower was built at Tirefour, about 1½ miles (2km) south of Point or 2½ miles (4km) north of Achnacroish pier. Although ruinous, many typical broch features survive, including the concentric dry-stone walls an mural galleries, and it is, in fact, regarded as one of the best-preserved prehistoric monuments in Argyll. On the south-east side it survives to a height of nearly 16ft (5m). The walls have been quarried for building stone.

For several centuries in the Middle Ages, Lismore was the ecclesiastical capital of Argyll. A cathedral for the new diocese of Argyll was founded around 1189 and dedicated to St Moluag. It continued in use until the sixteenth century. Several interesting medieval architectural features survive, including the north choir doorway, and a piscina, sedilia and doorway in the south choir wall. The choir of the medieval cathedral is now used as the parish church, as the result of renovations that were carried out about 1900. The cathedral probably occupies the site of a church founded by the Irish saint Moluag (Lugaidh), who founded a religious community on Lismore in the second half of the sixth century, at about the same time St Columba was establishing his monastery in Iona, in 563. Local tradition holds that the wooden staff, the *Bachuil Mor*, which can be seen in Bachuil House, belonged to St Moluag. A bell and bell shrine which are believed to have belonged to the saint are in the Royal Museum of Scotland, in Edinburgh.

A rather gory tradition relating to St Columba and St Moluag has it that the two saints were racing to see who could set foot first on Lismore, to establish a

LISMORE
Getting there

Calmac ferry Oban-Lismore (Achnacroish); passage time: 50 minutes.
Ferry information For vehicle reservations, contact Caledonian MacBrayne Ltd, The South Pier, Oban, Argyll. Tel: (0631) 62285; fax: (0631) 66588. There is also a passenger ferry from Port Appin on the mainland to Point at the north end of Lismore; passage time: 10 minutes.

Railhead Oban.

_____

Tourist Information Centre Oban, Mull & District Tourist Board, Bothwell House, Argyll Square, Oban, Argyll. Tel: (0631) 63122.

monastery there. As St Columba's coracle forged ahead, Moluag cut off a finger and threw it on to the island, thus claiming first possession. Similar stories abound in Celtic folklore and should not be taken too literally.

In the south-west of the island, near the shore, is the thirteenth-century Achadun Castle, which was built for the bishops of Argyll. It fell into ruins after Bishop David Hamilton had a new castle built at Saddell, in Kintyre, in 1508. It is reached by taking the road to Achanduin farm and following a track from there. From the castle it is a short walk to Bernera Island, which can be reached at low tide. Visitors should take care not to get themselves stranded. There is a tradition that St Columba preached under a great yew tree on Bernera Island and in the stained-glass window in the east gable of the parish church of Lismore he is shown blessing this tree.

On the west coast of Lismore, opposite the cathedral of St Moluag, is Castle Coeffin, a thirteenth-century hall-house and bailey. It was probably erected by one of the MacDougalls of Lorn, for the island of Lismore occupied an important strategic position within their territories. According to local legend, the unusual name comes from the legendary Norse Prince Caifean. In 1470 it was acquired by the Campbells of Glenorchy and remained in their hands until the early eighteenth century.

Lismore makes an interesting destination for a day-trip. It is ideal for walkers and cyclists, although it has to be said that the rainfall is double that of the east of Scotland. There are spectacular views up and down Loch Linnhe, taking in the Paps of Jura to the south, the mountains of Mull and Morven, Ben Nevis to the north and Cruachan to the east. Accommodation on the island is limited and booking is required. The guest-house beside St Moluag's cathedral provides teas, coffees, lunches and dinners. There is a small general store and post office

situated at Clachan, a mile (1.6km) south of the church. Visitors coming to stay on the island are advised to order bread, milk and newspapers well in advance.

ISLAY

The island of Islay (pronounced 'eye-la') lies 15 miles (24km) off the west coast of Argyll, while Northern Ireland is only 23 miles (37km) to the south, across the North Channel. It is the most southerly of the Inner Hebrides and with a land area of 246sq miles (637sq km), one of the largest Scottish islands, covering 25 miles (40km) from north to south and 19 miles (30km) from west to east.

Islay's geology is complex and includes the most southerly outcropping of Lewisian gneiss, in the southern half of the Rinns peninsula. The gneiss of Islay is younger than that of the Outer Hebrides, but at 1,600 million years old it is twice as old as Torridonian sandstone, which was formed from eroded gneiss 800 million years ago. Gneiss is pink or grey in colour, sparkles and is of a striped appearance. The glitter is caused by mica or quartz crystals, while the striped bands are caused by minerals which floated into layers as the rock cooled slowly after being subjected to tremendous heat and pressure deep down in the earth.

The gneiss of the Rinns of Islay and of the islands of Coll, Tiree, Iona and a tiny part of the north end of Colonsay, was made from metamorphosed sedimentary rocks, which were originally sand or mud on an ocean floor; it is known as paragneiss, while the orthogneiss of the Outer Isles was metamorphosed from igneous rocks.

The crystalline appearance of gneiss is not dissimilar to granite. The constituents may be the same: quartz, felspar, mica and hornblende. Its fresh appearance, which apparently is inconsistent

(Above) Carraig Fada lighthouse, Port Ellen, Islay, built in mock-Egyptian style in memory of the wife of an island laird

Loading the Islay ferry at Port Askaig

ISLAY

Getting there

Calmac ferry
Kennacraig (Kintyre)–
Port Ellen and Port
Askaig; passage time:
2–2¼ hours.

Ferry information
Vehicle reservations
necessary, all year
round. In stormy
weather ferry for Port
Ellen often diverts at
fairly short notice to
Port Askaig, which is
more sheltered. Two
sailings a day (one only
on winter Sundays). For
timings, contact
Caledonian MacBrayne,
The Ferry Terminal,
Kennacraig, Argyll. Tel:
(088 073) 253; fax: (088
073) 202.

Local ferry office The
Pier, Port Ellen. Tel:
(0496) 2209 (also
provides information
about Port Askaig
sailings).

Railhead Glasgow. Bus
from Glasgow–
Campbeltown calls at
Kennacraig Ferry
Terminal. Some buses
connect with Islay ferry.

Airport Glenegedale.
Daily services to and
from Glasgow Airport
operated by Loganair;
flight time: 35 minutes.
Tel: (041) 889 1311; fax
(041) 887 6020.

with its great age, is explained by the fact that for almost the whole of geological time the gneiss has been buried under later rocks. The geological history of Islay is the story of how successive layers of rocks were created and eroded. In Islay it is only in the southern half of the Rinns that the 'basement rock' – the gneiss – has been exposed again.

The long sinuous thrust or slide which separates the gneiss of the south end of the Rinns from the Torridonian series of the north end can be seen on the shores of Lochindaal just north of Bruichladdich and weaves its way across the peninsula to emerge at Kilchiaran Bay.

Most of the higher ground on Islay is quartzite, this being the hardest rock in the island and therefore most resistant to erosion. In the quartzites of south-east Islay are intrusions which are now represented by epidiorite, their metamorphic equivalent.

Islay was covered by several thousand feet of ice during the last Ice Age and there are some excellent examples of glacial landforms, notably around Loch Gorm, on the east side of the road from Bridgend to Port Ellen, and especially between Port Ellen and Leorin Farm, on the slopes of the hill there. Related to the retreat of the ice sheets and subsequent changes in sea level are the marine-cut platforms and raised beaches, which form level areas of well-drained land. This kind of landscape is best seen on Islay around the head of Lochindaal. Other areas where raised beaches can be seen clearly include the shores of Loch Gruinart, Lossit Bay on the west coast of the Rinns and the shores of Laggan Bay. The last post-glacial raised beach stands about 25ft (8m) above today's strands, but there are other raised beaches at the 50ft (15m) and 100ft (30m) levels.

The Port Askaig boulder bed supplies evidence of an ice age in late Pre-Cambrian times, while the broad bands of Islay limestone make the pas-

tures of the central corridor of Islay green and fertile. In the south-east, bands of epidiorite provided the raw material for the finely carved late-medieval grave-slabs which grace the island's churches.

There are some very fine areas of sand dunes on Islay, especially at Lossit Bay, where blown sand reaches a height of 220ft (67m) and has polished the exposed gneiss. There are other dune systems on the shores of Laggan Bay and at Machir Bay, where the sand comes inland as far as Kilchoman church and has polished Torridonian slates and grits. Probably the finest sand-dune formations are on the north-west coast of the Rinns, at Saligo and Sanaigmore, while the dunes at Ardnave Point are also impressive. Several of these locations have yielded archaeological sites.

The natural environment is very varied, with a wide range of habitats ranging from mountainous moorland to the sheltered woodland around the head of Lochindaal. Ornithologists find Islay especially appealing; the rare native chough breeds there, while from early October to the end of April it plays host to large populations of migrating geese. The wintering population of barnacle geese, which come to Islay from breeding grounds in the east of Greenland, is now approaching 25,000, while up to 4,000 Greenland white-fronted geese are also present. About 110 species of birds breed on Islay, and even on a short visit it should be possible to see over 100 species.

Islay's strategic location and agricultural fertility combined to give it a rich cultural heritage. Archaeological riches range from standing stones and stone circles as at Ballinaby and Cultoon, to chambered cairns, forts, duns and, unusually, a broch at Dun Bhoraraig, near Port Askaig.

The stone circle at Cultoon, in the western peninsula of the Rinns of Islay, was excavated in the 1970s. After several inches of peat were removed, the original Bronze Age ground surface, dating from around 1500BC, was revealed, into which sockets were dug to accommodate standing stones. These are now marked with concrete markers. A feature of this site was that it was never completed, and all except two stones were left lying on the ground. The single tall standing stone at Ballinaby, at the north end of the Rinns, is easily visited and is in a spectacular setting.

The quaintly named fort of Dun Nosebridge is exceptionally well preserved; its Norse name (*knaus-borg*, 'the fort on the crag') is one of many place-names which derive from the Viking conquest and settlement of Islay from 800 to 1156. The medieval chapel and early Christian cross at Kilnave, on the shores of Loch Gruinard, lie near the site of a clan battle which was fought in 1598, in the course of which some Macleans were trapped in the chapel and burned to death.

The Iona-style wheel-cross at Kildalton is one of Scotland's most important early Christian monuments. Carved from a single slab of locally obtained epidiorite, the high relief carvings are still well preserved 1,100 years after the cross was erected, presumably on the site of an early Christian monastery, of which no traces now remain. The carvings depict scenes from the Bible, such as Cain and Abel, and Abraham about to sacrifice Isaac, which illustrate the concept of sacrifice. The medieval parish church of Kildalton is nearby.

The intricately abstract carving of the fourteenth-century cross at Kilchoman is also noteworthy. Several different motifs are all interconnected in carved interlacing reminiscent of knitting or macramé. There are also grave-slabs from the late-medieval period, some depicting armed warriors and clerics. These are to be found in lesser numbers in most of Islay's graveyards.

Historically, Islay's main importance was as the administrative capital of the Lords of the Isles, the ancestors of Clan Donald. From Somerled's victories in the twelfth century until the forfeiture of the lordship in 1493, the military and naval base at Dunivaig on the south coast and the civil headquarters on two small islands on the inland Loch Finlaggan were the centres of power for an administration which, at its maximum extent in the early fifteenth century, ruled all of the islands off the west coast of Scotland and almost the whole of the western seaboard from Cape Wrath to the Mull of Kintyre. Technically under the sovereignty of Norway until the Treaty of Perth in 1266, the subduing of Clan Donald and the eventual integration of its vast territories into the Kingdom of Scotland was a process not finally completed until after the final defeat at Culloden in 1746.

The Finlaggan Trust maintains a small visitor centre at Finlaggan, which is open from May to September. Access to the islands on Loch Finlaggan is restricted at the moment. For information, you should enquire locally. Archaeological excavations by the National Museum of Scotland are currently under way at this nationally important site. Preliminary results indicate a wealth of artefacts and the remains of over thirty buildings, some of them from the period of the Lords of the Isles. There is a fine collection of sculptured medieval grave-slabs on Eilean Mor, near the ruins of a medieval chapel. The most spectacular stone is an effigy of a man in armour, dating from around 1550. The Latin inscription, part of which is now broken, translates as 'Here lies Donald, son of Patrick, son of Celestinus'.

A smaller island, Eileen na Comhairle – 'the Council Isle' – is where the Lords of the Isles met with their advisers and where the fourteen members of the Council of the Isles deliberated at a stone table and issued edicts, instructions and rulings that affected

Tourist Information Centre The Square, Bowmore (May–September). Tel: (049 681) 254; Kintyre, Mid-Argyll and Islay Tourist Board, The Pier, Campbeltown, Argyll (open all year). Tel: (0586) 52056.

Loch Finlaggan and the Paps of Jura. The two small islands in the isolated hill loch contained the palaces and council chamber of the Lords of the Isles, who ruled the Hebrides from 1156 to 1493

their territories, and administered justice.

The Lords of the Isles were descended from Somerled, son of a Celtic father and Norse mother, who drove the Norse out of the southern Hebrides after a guerrilla war that culminated in a great sea battle off the coast of Islay in 1156. Somerled was killed at Renfrew in 1164. He is often credited with inventing the West Highland galley which used a hinged rudder, making it more manoeuvrable than the Viking longship with its steering oar. The galley came to be one of the emblems of Clan Donald, and often appears on grave-slabs.

Somerled's main naval base and fortress was probably at Dunivaig, although the spectacular visible remains date from the sixteenth and early seventeenth centuries. He and his MacDon-ald descendants ruled from Islay for nearly 350 years, although after Norway ceded its island possessions to Scotland under the Treaty of Perth in 1266, the MacDonalds technically owed allegiance to the king of Scotland. But continual rebellions, conspiracies with Edward IV of England and persistent threats to the security of the Scottish nation, eventually caused James IV to lose patience with his wayward subjects and in 1493 the lands of the lordship were forfeited and reverted to the Scottish crown. After nearly a century in the hands of MacIain of Ardnamurchan and his descendants, Islay eventually came into the possession of the Campbells of Calder (or Cawdor) in 1614 and was bought by Daniel Campbell of Shawfield, an important Glasgow ship-owner and merchant, in 1726.

Currently, the population of Islay has

steadied at 4,000, having declined from a maximum of 15,000 in 1831. The largest town is Port Ellen with a population of 1,020 and a ferry terminal; the administrative capital of the island is Bowmore (population: 970). These centres of population and the villages of Port Charlotte, Portnahaven and Port Wemyss, were established by Campbell of Shawfield lairds in the eighteenth and nineteenth centuries. Other settlements include the distillery villages of Caol Ila and Bunahabhainn in the north, Bruichladdich in the Rinns, and Laphroaig, Lagavulin and Ardbeg in the south-east; their names are a catalogue of some of the finest malt whiskies in Scotland, which constitute Islay's best known and most lucrative export. Keills and Ballygrant are small villages that were based originally on weaving and quarrying. Port Askaig, with a tiny resident population, is one of the busiest places on the island, with ferries connecting with both the mainland at Kennacraig and with Feolin in Jura. The airport at Glenegedale has a twice daily link with Glasgow Airport; an emergency air ambulance operates as required.

Bowmore is an important centre, with banks, Tourist Information Centre, hospital, post office, police station, local government offices, Islay High School and many shops and services. There are several small hotels and guest-houses. It is very much the hub of the island, largely because of its geographical location. The new swimming-pool, in an old warehouse next door to Bowmore Distillery, is the result of years of fundraising and community effort. Bowmore was founded in 1768, at which time its famous Round Church was built, replacing the old parish church at Kilarrow, at the head of Lochindaal.

Port Charlotte (1828), in the Rinns, is very popular with visitors. The Museum of Islay Life, which is housed in an old church, is well worth a visit and has a fine reference collection of books

A medieval child's grave-slab at Finlaggan, where some of the Lords of the Isles were buried

A decorative cross-head from Finlaggan, containing some of the elements found in the crest of Clan Donald

Intricately carved
medieval stone cross
at Kilchoman, Islay

islands as Iain Og Ile. Sadly, his father went bankrupt and this friend of the Gael did not inherit. In 1853 Islay was sold for £451,000 to James Morrison, a London merchant banker, whose descendants still control Islay Estates.

Although it is a definite advantage to have a private car, there are plenty of opportunities for walkers and cyclists. The road to Bunnahabhainn is particularly scenic. The scenery to the east is dominated by the Paps of Jura, while by walking a few yards off the road the full length of the Sound of Islay can be seen. To the north, Colonsay is visible behind the Rhuvaal lighthouse and the mountains of Mull can be seen over the raised beaches of Jura.

From Bunahabhainn it is possible to walk across open moorland to the north coast of Islay, where the main attractions are caves, raised beaches, sea-bird colonies and fantastic coastal scenery. The whole of the north-east corner of Islay is a wilderness, with only occasional tracks. The south-east of the island is also wild and uninhabited, except for the narrow coastal strip from Port Ellen to Ardtalla. The view from the summit of Beinn Bheigeir (1,609ft/ 491m) is spectacular. The most interesting ascent is from the south-east, up the River Claggain. During the shooting season visitors are advised to check with the offices of the various sporting estates regarding access to the hills.

Islay's main industry is agriculture, with beef cattle and sheep predominating. Dairy herds sustain the creamery at Port Charlotte which makes and exports a fine cheese. Agriculture employs around 250 people on around 110 holdings. There are about 12,000 beef cattle on the island, including 7,000 breeding cows and heifers; 5,500 cattle are sold off the island each year as yearlings to Lowland farmers, to be fattened up before they are slaughtered. There are around 35,000 breeding ewes, mostly Blackface, which produce over 25,000 lambs a year. Fishing, once the

and photographs. Across the road from the museum, it is possible to visit the creamery and see cheese being made. The Islay Field Centre provides hostel accommodation and study facilities for students who are interested in natural history, archaeology and geology, or for the independent traveller. There is a most welcome tea-room in Port Charlotte, which is noteworthy also for a large number of self-catering cottages and Gaelic street signs.

Port Wemyss (1833) and Portnahaven (1788) at the south end of the Rinns, are both picturesque villages, founded by Campbell lairds. Port Ellen, the main ferry terminal for freight, was founded in 1821. Several of Islay's villages were named after ladies who were associated with Walter Frederick Campbell, laird of Islay from 1816 to 1848. Charlotte was his mother, while Eleanor his first wife is remembered both in Port Ellen and in Port Wemyss – she was the daughter of the 8th Earl of Wemyss. Walter Frederick Campbell's son and heir was the famous Celtic scholar and folklorist John Francis Campbell, who was known in the mainstay of the island's economy along with farming, is carried on in a small way, mainly for the export market. Forestry is a branch of agriculture relatively new to Islay, and the spread of private forestry – for example, to 3,000 acres (1,214ha) that were taken over near Loch Finlaggan in 1983 – gives cause for concern. Tourism is a growth industry: 45,000 summer visitors come by the Caledonian MacBrayne ferries and an additional 11,000 arrive by air.

JURA

The island of Jura (Norse *dyr-ey*, 'deer-island') lies to the east and north of its more fertile neighbour, Islay. It is reached by the Western Ferries car and passenger ferry from Port Askaig in Islay to Feolin at the south end of Jura (tel: 049 684 681 for timings). Most visitors to Islay will spend at least half a day there, so a short description of one of Europe's wildest landscapes is not out of place.

Jura is 27 miles (43km) from north to south and 5–6 miles (8–10km) wide, tapering towards its northern end, which approaches to within 4 miles (2.5km) of the Scottish mainland. One of the last great wildernesses in the British Isles, it is almost cut in two by Loch Tarbert. Its southern half is dominated by three rounded, conical peaks, which have been known as the Paps of Jura since at least the end of the sixteenth century. Formed of quartzite, they owe their distinctive form to frost shattering at the end of the last Ice Age, which has left spectacular scree slopes on their higher levels. These mountains dominate not only their immediate environment, but also form part of the seascape for many miles around. From Kintyre, Colonsay, Coll, Tiree and Mull, and from the high tops on the western seaboard of Scotland from Skye to Arran and even from the Isle of Man and Ben Lomond, they form part of the distant horizon.

The other important topographical feature that is associated with Jura is the renowned whirlpool of Corrievreckan – Corrie-Bhreacan, the cauldron of Breckan. This area of raging marine turbulence lies at the northern tip of the island, between Jura and the uninhabited island of Scarba. It is named after a Viking who sought to prove his manhood and win an island princess by anchoring in the area for three days and three nights. Unfortunately, the last of his ropes, which was supposedly woven from the hair of virgins, parted under the strain, thus casting doubt on the veracity of at least one of the contributors, and Breckan was drowned.

Scattered archaeological remains show that Jura was inhabited in prehistoric times, starting with Mesolithic sites around 7000BC. There is a single Neolithic burial cairn south of Strone farm, while seven sites with standing stones attest to a Bronze Age population in the south-east of the island. There are several Iron Age forts and duns, of which the most spectacular is An Dunan on Lowlandman's Bay, to the south-east of Ardmenish.

The population of Jura has dwindled over the last 150 years from around 1,000 to less than 200 today. On the other hand, the island's 5,000 red deer are the main attraction for the sporting estates, which attract wealthy visitors. With only one hotel and limited bed and breakfast accommodation, tourism, apart from day visitors from Islay, is a very small-scale industry. Most of the inhabitants work in agriculture, forestry, or as estate workers. A distillery in Craighouse provides employment and produces a fine, peaty, malt whisky.

George Orwell wrote his novel *1984* at Barnhill, at the northern end of Jura, during the summer months from 1946 to 1949. Every summer brings its quota of literary pilgrims, who would all agree with Orwell's description of his cottage: 'it's in an extremely un-getatable place'. He almost drowned in Corrievreckan,

One of the Paps of Jura modestly covered in mist, seen from across the Sound of Islay. The mountains are associated with magic and witchcraft, according to traditional island stories

along with his son and two friends, while they were exploring the whirlpool in a small boat.

COLONSAY

The island of Colonsay lies in the Inner Hebrides, 12 miles (20km) south of the Ross of Mull and 9 miles (15km) west of the island of Jura. It is just over 8 miles (13.5km) in length from north to south, with a maximum breadth of 3 miles (5km). Aligned NE–SW, Colonsay was called descriptively in Gaelic 'Eilean Tarsuing' – the cross-lying island. Kiloran Bay is one of the finest unspoilt beaches in the Hebrides.

From May to September there are two ways of approaching Colonsay. The normal, year-round Calmac ferry makes a round trip from Oban three times a week. But on Wednesdays during the summer season, the Islay ferry from Kennacraig to Port Askaig continues on to Colonsay and Oban, returning to Colonsay and Kennacraig on Wednesday night. So, for the first time, it is possible to come to Colonsay as a day-tripper, spending six hours ashore and drastically increasing the effects, and possibilities, of tourism. An influx of 300 extra visitors has become normal, adding to the 'resident' visitor population of up to 250 and the long-suffering locals, who number under 120.

The declining population lives in the three small villages of Scalasaig and Upper and Lower Kilchattan, or are scattered around the island in 16 farms and crofts, which are stocked with 500

cattle and 7,000 sheep. In 1841, Colonsay and the neighbouring island of Oronsay to the south had a population of 979.

Accommodation on Colonsay is limited and often fully booked. The Isle of Colonsay Hotel is open from March to November, with additional chalets nearby. Kiloran Estates provide self-catering accommodation and there is a little B & B accommodation available. Caravans are not allowed.

Colonsay has some interesting geological features. The northern tip of the island is Lewisian gneiss, an ancient rock found also in the Rinns of Islay, Coll, Tiree and Iona, as well as in most of the Outer Isles. The rest of the island is made up of uninteresting Torridonian beds, but with remarkable igneous intrusions at Kiloran Bay and around Scalasaig. At the north end of the beach at Kiloran is a fine example of a volcanic breccia, which was pierced by a lamprophyre dyke. The intrusion around Scalasaig is diorite, a coarse-grained igneous rock with clearly defined crystals of feldspar, mica, horn-blende and augite. Contact with the Torridonian rocks can be seen on the slopes of the hill under Lord Colonsay's monument, overlooking Scalasaig pier. The low wooded ridge that runs westwards from the pier, parallel to the road, is composed of diorite.

The natural history is typical of the Inner Hebrides, with the bonus of a breeding population of about forty choughs, one of the rarest British breeding birds. Buzzards are common, but all the Highland birds of prey are represented. In two to three days it is possible to see peregrine falcon, merlin, sparrowhawk, kestrel, hen harrier and buzzard. Golden eagles and sea eagles pass by from time to time, but do not at present breed on Colonsay.

Colonsay is rich in archaeological and historical remains, from the standing stones at Kilchattan known as 'Fingal's Limpet Hammers' to the deserted township of Riasg Buidhe, which was abandoned in the 1920s. A kerb cairn incorporating a standing stone, behind the hotel at Scalasaig, is a fine example of its kind. Dun Eibhinn, also behind

Scalasaig, Colonsay, the main settlement of a small island in the Inner Hebrides, looking south-east to Jura and Islay

COLONSAY

Getting there

Calmac ferry Oban–
Colonsay; passage time:
2½ hours. Wednesdays,
summer only:
Kennacraig (Kintyre)–Port
Askaig (Islay)–Colonsay;
passage time: 4 hours
from Kennacraig.
Ferry information
Booking is essential for
vehicles. For
reservations, contact
Caledonian MacBrayne,
The South Pier, Oban,
Argyll. Tel: (0631)
62285; fax: (0631)
66588. If you are
coming from
Kennacraig, contact
Kennacraig Ferry
Terminal; tel: (088 073)
253. NB: caravans and
camper vans are not
permitted on Colonsay.

Railhead Oban: 2–3
trains a day to Glasgow.

**Tourist Information
Centre** Oban & Mull
Tourist Board, Bothwell
House, Argyll Square,
Oban, Argyll. Tel: (0631)
63122.

Scalasaig, is an Iron Age fort which in the Middle Ages was occupied by the MacDuffies or MacFies of Colonsay. They were replaced as the ruling family by MacNeills, in 1701.

Much local history and folklore surrounds the MacDuffies, particularly Malcolm, the last chief, who was killed at Baleruminmore in 1623. Ownership of the island was disputed between Malcolm MacDuffie and Colkitto (Coll Ciotach, 'left-handed Coll'). After hiding out for several years and avoiding capture, Malcolm was finally cornered hiding under seaweed on a skerry off the south shore of Oronsay, his position betrayed by a distracted sea-bird. He was tied to the cross-marked standing stone at Baleruminmore and shot, along with four other men. This has become a place of pilgrimage for the many people surnamed McPhee, Duffy, MacFie, MacDuffie and endless variations, who claim descent from the MacDuffies of Colonsay. The stone where Malcolm met his fate has been damaged several times over the centuries, but has now been repaired and re-erected in a protected plot.

Colkitto's son Alasdair, who was fourteenth in descent from Somerled, made a great name for himself in the religious wars of the 1640s as a general in the army of James Graham, the Marquis of Montrose, who was trying to win Scotland for Charles I and the Royalist cause. Sir Alasdair MacDonald was eventually defeated in Kintyre in 1647 and fled to Ireland, while his followers were massacred at Dunaverty. The lands of Colonsay and Oronsay eventually came under the control of the Campbells: the 10th Earl of Argyll sold them to Malcolm McNeill, eldest son of Donald McNeill of Crear, in Knapdale, in 1701.

Colonsay House sits in a pocket of mature woodland in the centre of the island. Built in 1722 by Malcolm McNeill, it was enlarged in the nineteenth century. In 1904 the estate was sold to Donald Smith, who left the small town of Forres on the Moray Firth in 1836 and made his fortune in Canada with the Hudson's Bay Company. A founding director of the Canadian Pacific Railway and eventually High Commissioner for Canada in London, he was raised to the peerage in 1897 by Queen Victoria, taking the title Lord Strathcona and Mount Royal from his Scottish estate in Glencoe and from Montreal, headquarters of the Hudson's Bay Company.

Church of Scotland, Scalasaig, on the island of Colonsay, which was built in the late eighteenth century

ORONSAY

The island of Oronsay (Norse *orfiris-ey*, 'ebb-tide island'), lies immediately to the south of Colonsay, in the Inner Hebrides. Islay is 5½ miles (9km) to the south, while the west coast of Jura is 9 miles (15km) to the east. There are only six permanent inhabitants.

Because of salt spray, it is not recommended to take a motor vehicle over to Oronsay. Access is restricted to 1½ hours each side of low tide. In some tidal and wind conditions, the tide never goes all the way out and wading becomes necessary. From the south end of Colonsay it takes about an hour to walk to the ruins of the priory on Oronsay, so there is little time to explore the island, unless you are prepared to wait for the next tide. It is sometimes possible, in good weather, to arrange in Scalasaig to be dropped off on Oronsay by boat. The Isle of Colonsay Hotel will have details.

Oronsay has Mesolithic shell mounds dating from before 4000BC, providing one of the earliest records of human settlement in Scotland, while the Iron Age fort of Dun Domhnuill is a fine example of its type, sitting on top of a classic *roche moutonnée*, a glacial feature that combines good natural defence with easily defended access.

Oronsay was once the site of a thriving Augustinian priory, of which the impressive ruins of the church and cloisters still survive. Founded under the patronage of the Lords of the Isles between 1330 and 1350, it was the location of one of the workshops in the West Highlands which produced intricately carved grave-slabs and stone crosses until 1500. The Oronsay Cross is a fine example.

GIGHA

The island of Gigha (Norse: *gia-ey*, 'cleft-island') lies 3 miles (5km) west of the Kintyre peninsula (ferry from Tayinloan). The name is pronounced 'gee-ah', with a hard 'g'. The locals prefer to say that it is derived from *Gudey*, meaning 'God's island'. Only 6½ miles (10.4km) long and under 2 miles (3km) wide. Gigha is fertile and productive, supporting a population of about 180, many of whom speak Gaelic. The only village, with the pier, post office and island shop, is Ardminish. The parish church here has a stained-glass window commemorating Kenneth MacLeod of Eigg, who wrote *The Road to the Isles* and many other songs. The old medieval parish church is at Kilchattan; in the burial ground are intricately carved late-medieval grave-slabs. Nearby is the 'ogham stone', with an indecipherable inscription in a script that was brought from Ireland in pre-Christian times.

Following the road past Kilchattan Church towards Ardlamey Farm and the cottage named Tigh nan Cudainnean, it is possible to reach the south-west shore of Gigha, which has safe sandy beaches that are ideal for a picnic. Offshore is the small island of Craro. The 'Bull of Craro', a rock formation which is only visible from the seaward side, features in an island story of a local boy who was taken prisoner by pirates. Further around the coast, at Port a'Gharaidh, is a quarry where quernstones (for grinding grain) were made from the epidiorite rock which outcrops all over the island.

South of Kilchattan is Achamore House, which is in private ownership, with surrounding gardens in the care of the National Trust for Scotland since 1962. The gardens and adjoining woodland, which has many exotic azalea and rhododendron species, were developed by Sir James Horlick (of beverage fame), who bought the island in 1944. The whole island, which includes a fish farm that was developed in the 1980s, was sold in 1989, amid some controversy and local apprehension. There are plans to develop a private airfield and to turn Achamore House into up-market

(Above) Colonsay House, built for the MacNeills of Colonsay and extended in the nineteenth century. The exotic plants and shrubs and surrounding woodland come as a surprise to most visitors

Visitors about to leave the post office, Gigha, to explore this small but beautiful Hebridean island (*Highlands & Islands Enterprise*)

accommodation suitable for conference retreats.

The Achamore creamery, which produced a fine cheese, is now closed, and the milk produced by the island's dairy herds is transported daily to Campbeltown. The estate, fish farm and small-scale commercial fishing provide a little employment.

Despite its small size, there are many archaeological sites on Gigha: cairns, standing stones, forts and duns. There is a fine cairn at the north end (Carn Ban) and an impressive standing stone beside the road overlooking East Tarbert Bay. South-west of Tarbert farm are interesting rock outcrops carved with early Christian symbols. The finest fort is Dun Chibhich in the middle of the island, which can be reached (with permission) from Druimyeonbeg Farm. The road to Ardailly, on the west coast of Gigha, passes close to a small Iron Age fort, Dunan an t Seasgain. Just past

THE WESTERN ISLES: THE INNER HEBRIDES

(Left) Kiloran Bay, Colonsay, regarded by many as the finest beach in the Hebrides.

Summer visitors awaiting the arrival of the ferry at Ardminish, Gigha, connecting the island with the mainland ferry terminal at Tayinloan (*Highlands & Islands Enterprise*)

GIGHA

Getting there

Calmac ferry Tayinloan (Kintyre)–Gigha; passage time: 20 minutes.
Ferry information For vehicle reservations, contact Caledonian MacBrayne Ltd, The Ferry Terminal, Kennacraig, Argyll. Tel: (088 073) 253; fax: (088 073) 202.

Railhead Glasgow: bus connections via Glasgow–Campbeltown bus (three daily), which also calls at the Kennacraig ferry terminal (Islay ferry).

Airport Private airfield for use of landowner and his guests.

Tourist Information Centre Kintyre, Mid-Argyll and Islay Tourist Board, The Pier, Campbeltown, Argyll. Tel: (0586) 52056.

Ardailly is another fort, Dun an Trinnse. Two stones near Leim, known as the Bodach and the Cailleach – the old man and the old woman – are likely to be several centuries old, but not prehistoric.

Gigha must have been visited by Norse raiders and settlers during their domination of the Hebrides. A Viking grave found by chance in 1849 at East Tarbert Bay produced an ornate portable balance, with decorative pans and weights; it is now in the Hunterian Museum at the University of Glasgow. It probably belonged to an itinerant Norse metalworker, dealing in gold and silver, during the eleventh century AD. The Norse King Haakon held court in Gigha in 1263, on his way to the Battle of Largs. According to a Norse saga, his court chaplain died on Gigha and was buried at the Cistercian abbey of Saddell, on the east side of Kintyre. Until the nineteenth century the island lairds were a branch of the MacNeill clan.

Gigha takes time to explore properly. In summer the day-trippers come for a few hours and can see a lot, but it is best to stay on the island for a few days and search out some of the nooks and crannies of the island's history. Unfortunately, some sites are almost inaccessible in summer due to the excessive growth of the bracken. The view from Creag Bhan, the highest hill (329ft/100m) takes in Kintyre, Knapdale, Islay, Jura, Arran, Rathlin Island and the coastline of Northern Ireland.

This is one island which is best explored by bicycle or on foot. The island's roads are all single track and are not suitable to deal with tourist traffic, especially in the summer months. No part of Gigha is more than 3 miles (5km) from the post office at Ardminish and it is often possible to arrange a lift with one of the locals. The local shopkeeper, Mr Seumas MacSporran, has achieved fame due to his many jobs, with hats to match.

There are four piers on Gigha, one at each end and two in the middle. At one time the ferry from West Loch Tarbert called at Gigha on its way to Islay, but now the new roll-on, roll-off pier at Ardminish is the only one served by Calmac. The pier at the south end is used by some of the island's fishermen.

Off the south end of Gigha are the small islands of Gigalum and Cara. The former farmhouse on Cara has been renovated recently as a holiday house. It is sometimes possible to arrange boat-trips to Cara to view the medieval chapel and the 'Brownie's Chair'.

FIRTH OF LORN

At the entrance to the Firth of Lorn there are several small islands, some of them inhabited, all in a beautiful scenic setting. The easiest one to get to is Seil, which is reached by road over 'the bridge over the Atlantic'. Tour buses from Oban come in their dozens during the summer, allowing visitors time to explore the craft shops and tea-rooms of Easdale and the old, abandoned slate quarries.

From the south tip of Seil a car ferry makes the short crossing to Luing, which is famous for its black cattle. From its village of Cullipool there are boat-trips to some of the smaller, unpopulated offshore islands, including the Garvellachs, where there is an important early Christian monastic settlement associated with St Columba, whose mother is reputedly buried there. It is a popular place for visiting yachts, but all the Garvellachs are uninhabited and there are no facilities or accommodation.

Guarding the entrance to Oban Bay is the island of Kerrera, with a small working population and some commuters who cross to Oban every day on the small passenger ferry. A day-trip to Gylen Castle at the south end of Kerrera makes a fine outing on a sunny day.

11
The Clyde Islands

ARRAN

THE island of Arran (Gaelic: 'peaked island') lies in the Firth of Clyde, 14 miles (22km) from the mainland coast to the east and 4 miles (6km) from the Kintyre peninsula to the west, from which it is separated by Kilbrannan sound. It is one of the most accessible of Scotland's islands, with five sailings daily (four on Sundays) from the mainland ferry terminal at Ardrossan on the Ayrshire coast. Especially in the summer months, booking is essential for vehicles and even for foot passengers on some sailings. The seasonal service from Lochranza at the north tip of Arran to Claonaig in Kintyre is a welcome and, in the height of the tourist season, a less hectic, alternative. Booking is not possible, but with up to ten sailings daily, including Sundays, delays are unusual. With a little forward planning it is possible to drive from Claonaig over the spine of Kintyre to connect with ferry services at Kennacraig for Islay, Jura and Colonsay, and at Tayinloan for Gigha. Kennacraig is 63 miles (100km) from Oban, the major ferry terminal for the Western Isles.

Occasionally, when there are south-westerly gale-force winds, the Brodick–Ardrossan ferry diverts to the more sheltered waters of Gourock. Buses connect the two ferry terminals.

Arran's population of just over 4,000 trebles in summer. The island is 20 miles (32km) long and 10 miles (16km) wide; it is encircled by 56 miles (90km) of coast road, much of it on the 25ft (7.6m) raised beach. Only two roads cross the island: the 'String Road' across the middle from Brodick to Blackwaterfoot and another road across the south-east corner from Lamlash to Lagg. An excellent island bus service makes Arran ideal for walkers and climbers, and independent travellers.

Often described as a microcosm of the Scottish landscape, Arran is divided in two by the Highland Boundary Fault. The northern half is rough and mountainous. The highest hill is the granitic Goat Fell (2,868ft/875m; Norse: *geit-fjall*, 'goat-mountain'), an igneous intrusion into surrounding Devonian sandstones and schists. There was an active volcano here 'only' sixty million years ago. The rugged peaks of Beinn Bhreac (2,332ft/711m) and Beinn

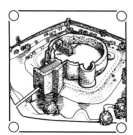

ARRAN

Getting there

Calmac ferry
Ardrossan-Brodick (all year); passage time: 55 minutes. Claonaig (Kintyre)-Lochranza (summer only, no vehicle reservations); passage time: 35 minutes.

Ferry information
Booking essential for Ardrossan-Brodick ferry; contact Caledonian MacBrayne Ltd, The Ferry Terminal, Gourock, Renfrewshire, PA19 1QP. Tel: (0475) 34531; fax: (0475) 37607.

Local ferry office The Pier, Brodick. Tel: (0770) 2166.
NB: in adverse weather the ferry sometimes diverts to Gourock.

Railhead Ardrossan: regular connections to Glasgow Central (50 minutes). From Glasgow Airport, catch the ferry train at nearby Paisley.

Tourist Information Centre Brodick, Isle of Arran, KA27 8AU. Tel: (0770) 2140/2401. Open all year.

Tarsuinn (2,706ft/825m) are visible over a wide area of the west of Scotland. From Islay and Jura they are seen over the top of Kintyre, while they can also be seen from tall buildings in Glasgow. The profile of the 'Sleeping Warrior' of Arran as seen from the Clyde coast is unforgettable.

The southern half of the island has a gentler landscape, reflecting the underlying geology, which is mostly New Red Sandstone, cut by igneous dykes. Glacial erratics brought from the northern mountains during the last Ice Age dot the landscape in the south.

Geologically, Arran is of great interest because of its complexity and is a popular destination for university field-trips. Recently, some landowners have let it be known that they intend to levy a charge on visiting groups and some universities have announced that they intend to take their business elsewhere. Sir Archibald Geikie, the eminent Scottish geologist, worked out the history of Arran's rocks in the late nineteenth century, while James Hutton had confirmed his theories of igneous geology there a hundred years earlier. One of the most famous sites in the history of geological science, Hutton's 'Unconformity', is on the coast north of Lochranza. Here, layers of schist inclined in one direction are overlain by a layer of sandstone with a different inclination.

Much of the coastline, especially on the west side, consists of raised beaches, showing how sea level has fallen since the end of the last Ice Age. Not until after about 8000BC did the shoreline begin to assume its current shape.

Arran's climate is often wet and frequently windy. It is advisable to come suitably prepared. Those who are bothered unduly by the likelihood of at least some rain during their holiday could think about coming in either May or September, when there are often (though not always) long spells of crisp, clear, magical weather.

The natural history of Arran is interesting and varied. Of particular note are the seals which can be seen all around the coasts, having fortunately survived the viruses of the 1980s, and the 2,000 red deer, which roam freely, mainly in the northern half of the island. There are no foxes, grey squirrels, stoats, weasels or moles. Walkers should be careful of adders, especially in rocky, bracken-covered ground. Bracken should itself be avoided in hot, dry conditions, as the spores have been shown to be carcinogenic.

The birdlife is abundant, with good seasonal variation. Most of the birds of prey which are distressingly rare now on the adjacent mainland are found, including golden eagles. Herons are common along the coasts and rivers. The basking shark, which reaches the frightening length of 50ft (15m) and is seen fairly commonly in coastal waters, only eats plankton.

Arran has had a long and often turbulent history. In prehistoric times, it was settled by Neolithic farmers, who have left their traces in the fine chambered cairns at Torrylin, Clachaig, East Bennan, Monamore and the Giants' Graves (two together, near Whiting Bay). In the Bronze Age, many stone circles and standing stones were erected, notably at Machrie Moor, which must have been an important ritual centre; some of the stones may have been used as primitive astronomical observatories to track the movements of the sun, moon and stars.

Arran is one of the most important prehistoric landscapes in Scotland: underneath the moorland peat, all of which has grown since the climate deteriorated at the end of the second millennium BC, archaeologists have found traces of huts, field boundaries and ritual sites. Some of the surviving standing stones at Machrie are truly massive, incredibly photogenic and well worth the easy half-hour walk from the main road. There are at least six stone circles in the area, all signposted.

There is another stone circle close to the Brodick–Lamlash road and other standing stones around Brodick and Dippen. Dun Fionn, on the headland between Brodick and Lamlash, is a fine example of an Iron Age dun. There are others at Corriecreavie and on King's Cross Point, at the south end of Lamlash Bay. Larger forts are also present – for example, on the high ridge on the north side of North Glen Sannox. There is a 'vitrified' fort, with burnt stone in the rampart, on the north side of Sannox Bay. The D-shaped enclosure at Drumadoon, the headland on the north side of the bay at Blackwaterfoot, is likely to have been the *oppidum*, or tribal 'capital', of Iron Age Arran.

As far as we know, the Romans never visited Arran, although their naval commanders and traders must have been familiar with it as they passed up and down the Clyde to their base at Old Kilpatrick. If the Picts ever occupied Arran, they have left no trace in either archaeology or place-names, so the first inhabitants whose identity we are completely sure about were the Gaelic-speaking Scots who moved into the area soon after AD300, as part of the territory of the kingdom of Dalriada. Probably the first Christians to come to the island were Irish monks, in the sixth century, at the same time that Columba was establishing his monastery on Iona. As both St Ninian and St Brendan are thought to have visited the neighbouring island of Bute, it is likely that they visited Arran too, or at least the Holy Isle in Lamlash Bay.

Arran was sacked by Vikings in 797 and was one of the islands claimed by Magnus Barelegs in 1098. Several Viking graves have been found and there are some Norse place-names. Arran did not become part of the Kingdom of Scotland until the Treaty of Perth in 1266. In 1503 it was granted by royal charter to the Hamiltons. Successive earls of Arran played major roles on the stage of Scottish politics. During Cromwellian times the island was

Standing stones on Machrie Moor, Arran, an important centre of ritual and ceremony in the Bronze Age

occupied, although the garrison was attacked and massacred at Corrie. Widespread clearances in the nineteenth century to make way for large-scale, enclosed sheep-farms led to the emigration of one-third of the population and effectively killed off Gaelic culture on the island.

The main town and principal ferry terminal is Brodick (population: 1,000; Norse: *breidr vik*, 'broad bay'), with many hotels and guest-houses, shops, a Tourist Information Centre and an interesting and informative museum. The Isle of Arran Heritage Museum, which is located at the north edge of Brodick, is a model of its type, and deserves a visit. The museum is open from mid-May to mid-September. The collections and exhibitions depict the island's geology and history from earliest times up to the 1920s, including a fully equipped smiddy, a typical island cottage, agricultural implements of all kinds, lots of old photographs and a small research library and archive, as well as a friendly tea-room. There are poignant descriptions of the devastating effects of the Highland clearances which affected Arran in the nineteenth century, as large-scale sheep-farming replaced traditional farming communities which had existed for centuries. Gaelic life and culture on Arran was effectively destroyed and large numbers of people moved first to the newly built coastal villages, then to North America and the colonies. Between 1821 and 1881 the population fell from 6,600 to 4,750, reaching a worrying low of 3,300 in 1967. Fortunately, numbers increased during the 1970s as a result of incomers who were in retreat from the urban rat race; the number stabilised in the 1980s at just over 4,000.

Another essential place to visit is the Tourist Information Centre, at The Pier, Brodick. Here can be found all manner of leaflets, maps, guides and brochures.

Brodick is a bustling, busy place in the summer season and can become overwhelming. Calmac sells over 225,000 return tickets to Brodick in the tourist season, so it is hardly surprising if it sometimes gives the impression of bursting at the seams. Yet, as on so many islands, few of this multitude seem to stray far from their hotels and guest-houses, and fewer still venture more than a few yards from the nearest road. There is still plenty of empty space for the visitor to explore and even at the busiest time of the year, it is not hard to find beaches which are, by mainland standards, deserted.

At the north end of Brodick Bay is Brodick Castle with its gardens, formerly a residence of the dukes of Hamilton but now owned by the National Trust for Scotland (NTS), which also owns the spectacular backdrop of Glen Rosa and Goat Fell. The gardens are famous for their rhododendrons, which are seen at their best in the month of June. A ranger service with guided walks operates during the summer season. The central round tower of the castle dates from the fifteenth century, but the building has been added to many times over the years, notably in the 1840s. The interior is lavishly furnished and decorated, and is open to the public. Over sixty thousand visitors take advantage of this opportunity each year, making it one of the top ten most popular NTS properties in Scotland.

The island's other ferry terminal is at the north end, in the village of Lochranza, from where a landing-craft type vessel plies to Claonaig, near Skipness, during the summer season. In the sea loch is a sixteenth-century castle, overlying an earlier fortification which, together with Skipness castle, guarded the approaches to Kilbrannan Sound for the Lords of the Isles.

There are a number of settlements on the west side of Arran, of which the largest is Blackwaterfoot, which is close to the archaeologically rich area of Machrie Moor. Near Drumadoon Point

Brodick Bay, Arran,
and Goat Fell, the
highest mountain on
the island (*Highlands
& Islands Enterprise*)

is the King's Cave, one of the many caves where the future King Robert the Bruce is supposed to have gained encouragement from a spider in 1307. Just south of Lochranza is the small village of Catacol, with an oft-photographed row of small houses known locally as the Twelve Apostles. Their picturesque appearance disguises the fact that they were built in the nineteenth century to accommodate folk who had been cleared from the farms in Glen Catacol to make room for sheep. A little further on is Pirnmill, where once the Glasgow steamer called on its way to Carradale and Campbeltown.

The north end of the island is attractive to climbers and hillwalkers throughout the year. There is a youth hostel in Lochranza. The climb to the summit of Goat Fell, from Brodick up Glen Rosa, is undemanding (although steep enough in places), but ultimately very rewarding for the fine view. On a crystal-clear day it is said that the spire of Glasgow cathedral can be seen. The

tougher breed will try the jagged ridges in the north-west of the island. Detailed guides to climbs and walks on Arran are available locally.

From the south end of the island there are fine views down the Firth of Clyde over Pladda Island, with a lighthouse, to Ailsa Craig, Galloway, Northern Ireland and Kintyre. Ailsa Craig, which is 10 miles (16km) out to sea from Girvan in Ayrshire, has been known to generations of Glaswegians as 'Paddy's Milestone' due to its position about half-way between Glasgow and Belfast. It is an elliptical volcanic lump of granite 1,114ft (340m) high, and 2 miles (3km) in circumference, inhabited by lighthouse-keepers and by about 9,500 breeding pairs of gannets – 5 per cent of the world's population, in the world's second-largest gannetry (after St Kilda). The rounded grassy top is surrounded by vertical cliffs up to 500ft (152m) in height, of columnar basalt. The granite has a speckled bluish-grey colouring which is very distinctive; it

Brodick Castle, Arran, formerly the home of the dukes of Hamilton, but now owned by the National Trust for Scotland (*Highlands & Islands Enterprise*)

was formerly quarried for curling stones. Glacial erratics from Ailsa Craig have been found on the coasts of Cumbria and Wales. It is a prominent landmark from most of the southern and south-eastern parts of Arran.

On the east side of Arran are the villages of Whiting Bay, a centre for arts and crafts of all kinds, and Lamlash. Details of all Arran's craft industries can be found in a special booklet, which is available at the Tourist Information Centre in Brodick. Lamlash is the island's administrative centre, containing the main health centre and hospital, the police station and Arran High School, which stands on the land where

Donald McKelvie produced his famous seed potatoes, from 1908 to 1947. The High School was upgraded in the 1970s and now provides secondary education to university entrance level – perhaps another factor in the population recovery in recent years. A helicopter landing-pad beside the hospital is used for medical emergencies.

A monument in Lamlash, consciously evoking the standing stones of Machrie, commemorates the inhabitants of North Glen Sannox who sailed from Lamlash for Canada in 1829. The poet Robert Browning stayed at Blairbeg, Lamlash, in 1862. The sheltered waters of Lamlash Bay were a naval base during

World War II, but in recent times have become a centre for water-sports; a large fish-farm is a modern and controversial intrusion, providing much-needed employment at the expense of scenic amenity beloved by tourists. Holy Island, a mile offshore, shelters Lamlash Bay. It was an early Christian and medieval monastery. The cave of St Molaise, at the base of Mullach Mor (1,030ft/ 314m), has Viking inscriptions. There are excursions to Holy Island from Lamlash and Whiting Bay in the summer season. In 1263, King Haakon of Norway anchored his fleet in Lamlash Bay before the Battle of Largs.

The pretty village of Corrie, with its tiny harbour, lies on the east coast, north of Brodick. It is notable for its sandstone quarries, which were active from the 1880s until their final closure in 1928. Some parts of Glasgow, Greenock and Clyde resort towns were built of Corrie red sandstone, as also were the harbour wall at Troon and Kinloch Castle on the island of Rum. There were smaller sandstone quarries at Brodick, Cordon and in Monamore Glen just west of Lamlash. Another former extraction industry was the mining of barytes in Glen Sannox, to the north of Corrie, from the 1840s until 1862, when it was closed by order of the 11th Duke of Hamilton on the grounds that it spoiled the scenery. It was re-opened in 1919, but closed finally in 1938, when the vein was worked out. In 1934, 8,554 tons (8,693 tonnes) of barytes were produced, for use in the manufacture of paint and in other industries. The spoil heaps of these operations, and the remains of the processing plant, still survive.

The main industries today are tourism, including many small-scale craft shops, farming, fish-farming, a luxury food-processing factory and a little commercial fishing. Outside of Brodick, the island is uncrowded and unspoiled, and ideal for all manner of outdoor pursuits.

Arran is not without its problems, but is working hard to overcome them. Tourism has become the mainstay of the island's economy, which makes life difficult in the winter months. Various 'packages' can be arranged, especially for those who are interested in the pursuits of golf (seven courses), pony trekking, sea angling, hillwalking, sub-aqua diving, wildlife, water-sports and painting. Many small craft-based enterprises are trying hard to broaden their markets, with varying degrees of success. All hope one day to emulate the success of Arran Provisions, makers of the famous Arran mustard, which is now the largest employer on the island, marketing numerous jams, jellies and preserves throughout the UK, Europe and North America. Their factory shop at The Old Mill, Lamlash, is hard to resist. Impossible to resist are the excellent cream teas which seem to be a feature of Arran craft shops – perhaps it is their aim to encourage visitors to take long walks in the countryside as the only effective antidote?

In recent years the extraction of sand and gravel deposits from Brodick Bay has proved to be, like the fish-farm in Lamlash Bay, a controversial and potentially divisive issue. However, Arran is one place where public meetings seem always to be well attended and they at least foster an exchange of views and, it is thought, occasionally promote mutual understanding. As in similar communities, the island has, in the end, to solve its own problems and to sort out these matters among the people who live there.

The influence of incomers, and Calmac's freight charges, are other topics that are regularly aired in the columns of the *Arran Banner*, the island's weekly newspaper. 'White Settlers' are a problem which is likely to get worse, but the locals, and incomers who have become permanent, hard-working residents, are fighting back. All islanders have the usual love/hate relationship with Caledonian MacBrayne, the ferry

company, which is apparent in all of the twenty-three islands it serves. Many advocate the Norwegian system of Road Equivalent Tariff as an alternative transport policy.

However, it is striking that in recent years islanders have become more aware of the constraints of government policy within which Calmac must work. They are appreciative of the investment in modern, roll-on, roll-off ferries, and often say so, and they are rapturous in their praise for the officers and crews of the ferries – when they are not condemning them for putting their lifeline at risk through occasional industrial action! When Calmac was threatened with privatisation in 1988, and in particular with the 'hiving off' of the profitable Clyde routes (including Arran) from the rest of the company's Western Isles services, it was gratifying to notice that Arran residents were to the fore in registering their objection to the proposed changes, which were subsequently put 'on ice'.

From the jagged mountain peaks of the north to the gentle farming landscape of the south, Arran has a much more varied landscape than most of Scotland's islands and in many ways justifies the local Tourist Board's slogan – 'Scotland in Miniature'. Administratively, Arran (along with the Cumbraes) sits somewhat uneasily as part of Cunninghame District in the enormity of Strathclyde Region. Before local government reorganisation in 1975, it was rather ridiculously part of the county of Bute. Its Highland heritage, landscape and residual culture are recognised by virtue of the fact that it is part of the area of Highlands and Islands Enterprise (HIE), formerly the Highlands and Islands Development Board (HIDB). Arran was recently described as 'a picturesque pastoral retreat on the fringe of an English-speaking industrial society'. But, although it is not as wild and as untamed as some Hebridean islands, it can maintain itself as a viable

and unique island community, provided it is given the appropriate support from sympathetic government policies.

BUTE

The island of Bute lies in the Firth of Clyde, nestled between Arran and the Cowal district of Argyll, from which it is separated by the Kyles of Bute. Together with Arran, the tiny island of Inchmarnock and the Cumbraes, it made up the former county of Bute, but since 1975 it has been part of the district of Argyll and Bute, in Strathclyde Region.

Bute is 15 miles (24km) long and 1½–5½ miles (2.4–8.8km) wide. It has a population of 7,525 (1981 census), which is concentrated in the main town of Rothesay. The island has a land area of 31,000 acres (12,555ha), which are worked by no fewer than eighty-four farms, most of them rented from the principal landowner, the Marquess of Bute. A frequent vehicle ferry links Rothesay by a thirty-minute crossing to Wemyss Bay, on the Clyde coast, from where a rail link allows residents to commute to Glasgow. The modern pier at Rothesay replaces an elegant Edwardian structure which burned down in 1962.

A smaller car ferry runs from Rhubodach at the north end of Bute to Colintraive in Cowal (a five-minute crossing). At one time cattle swam across the narrows of the Kyles of Bute.

Geologically, Bute is interesting, as it sits astride the Highland Boundary Fault, marked by Loch Fad, which almost cuts the island in two. To its north are Dalradian schists, to the south Old Red Sandstone and lava flows. Bute is a low-lying island, but its northern end is more hilly, rising to 913ft (279m) on Windy Hill.

The climate of Bute is far drier and milder, and less windy, than most of Scotland's islands. Most of the rain that comes Bute's way falls on the high mountains of Arran, to the south-west.

Bute has several important archaeological and historical sites. The chambered cairn at Glenvoidean, on the north-west coast, was excavated during the 1960s; the pottery is in the fine museum in Rothesay. There are several standing stones on the island and stone circles at Ettrick Bay and Kingarth. The Iron Age vitrified fort of Dunagoil, on a promontory at the south end of the island, was excavated at the end of the last century and produced many interesting finds. Nearby is St Blane's Chapel, which is dedicated to the early Christian saint and missionary who was born on Bute in the sixth century. The surviving ruins date from the twelfth century. The locals call themselves Brandanes, after the island's association with St Brendan.

The main settlement and administrative centre of Bute is Rothesay, which had a population of 6,025 in 1981. It is situated on the east coast of the island, facing Toward Point in Cowal and the Clyde coast. Rothesay has shops of all kinds, banks, a post office, local authority offices, Rothesay Academy, a police station, hospital, health centre, swimming pool, public library and the Bute Museum, which is an essential stop for the interested visitor. The museum was built in 1926 by the 4th Marquess of Bute to house the archaeological and natural history collections in the care of the Buteshire Natural History Society. It was reorganised in 1950 and subsequently modernised. It is an outstanding example of a small independent museum.

Rothesay is well provided with hotels and guest-houses, from the refurbished 'hydropathic' Glenburn Hotel, with 137 rooms, to more humble, but no less friendly, bed and breakfast houses. The Duke of Rothesay is Prince Charles, the heir to the British throne. In 1398, King Robert III of Scotland bestowed the title on his eldest son and it remains the premier Scottish title of the heir apparent. A royal charter was granted to the burgh of Rothesay in 1401.

In 1990 the refurbished Winter Garden was reopened after a ten-year closure, at a cost of £850,000. As well as housing a ninety-three seat theatre cum cinema, there is an exhibition of photographs, and a Funtime Maritime Heritage Centre, which tells the story of seaside leisure on the Clyde coast. Threatened with demolition by the local council in 1982, the necessary funds to preserve it were raised by a charitable trust, under the patronage of the marchioness of Bute and Magnus Magnusson. The money was raised by numerous local fund-raising ideas, coupled with grants from various public bodies, including the Historic Buildings Council, the Scottish Development Agency, the Highlands and Islands Development Board and the Scottish Tourist Board. This iron and glass building was once one of the most famous music halls in Scotland and is a welcome addition to Bute's leisure facilities. Its successful restoration is a tribute to what a small island community can accomplish and also to the immense reservoir of goodwill which exists where islands are concerned.

Rothesay Pavilion, in Argyle Street, is a modern multi-purpose entertainment and conference centre, seating up to 1,200, with a wide range of facilities. It is frequently used for Scottish political and trade union conferences. St Mary's Chapel, in the High Street between the hospital and the creamery, on the south edge of the town, dates from the thirteenth-century and contains two medieval canopied wall tombs of a lady and a knight, possibly Robert II or his father, Walter the Steward. The churchyard also contains the mausoleum of the marquesses of Bute.

Until 1957 the 3rd Submarine Flotilla, RN, was stationed in Rothesay Bay. Its departure was the main cause of the decline in the population of Bute from 9,793 in 1961 to 7,733 in 1981.

Rothesay Castle is one of the finest

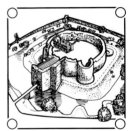

BUTE

Getting there

Calmac ferry Wemyss Bay-Rothesay; passage time: 30 minutes. Colintraive-Rhubodach; passage time: 5 minutes.

Ferry information For bookings, contact Caledonian MacBrayne Ltd, The Ferry Terminal, Gourock, Renfrewshire, PA19 1QP. Tel: (0475) 34531; fax: (0475) 37607.

Local ferry offices Rothesay, tel: (0700) 2707; Colintraive, tel: (070 084) 235. Occasional summer cruises by the paddle steamer (PS) *Waverley*, MV *Keppel* and other local pleasure boats.

Railhead Wemyss Bay – regular connections to Glasgow Central. From Glasgow Airport, catch the ferry train at nearby Paisley.

Tourist Information Centre The Pier, Rothesay, Isle of Bute, PA20 9AQ. Tel: (0700) 2151; fax: (0700) 5156. Open all year.

(Above) An aerial view of Rothesay Castle, a Stewart stronghold on Bute built in the twelfth century, with the addition of an impressive sixteenth-century gateway
(*Highlands & Islands Enterprise*)

Calmac ferry *Jupiter* leaving Rothesay on the Isle of Bute for the short trip across the Firth of Clyde to Wemyss Bay
(*Highlands & Islands Enterprise*)

(Above) A view across the fertile fields of Cumbrae to the jagged mountains at the north end of Arran (*Highlands & Islands Enterprise*)

The beach at Millport, the picturesque capital of the Great Cumbrae (*Highlands & Islands Enterprise*)

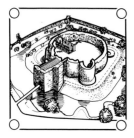

surviving medieval castles in Scotland, dating from the late twelfth century. It has a great circular enclosing wall, surrounded by a moat. In 1230 it was besieged and captured by Norsemen, who had to withstand the molten lead and pitch that was poured from the battlements, and occupied again by Haakon in 1263 before the Battle of Largs. The four drum towers were added around 1300. The impressive gatehouse was completed in 1541. The castle was restored in the nineteenth century by the 3rd Marquess of Bute and placed in the guardianship of the state in 1951, although the Stuart family remain hereditary keepers. The Great Hall of the castle was refurbished in 1970. Mount Stuart, on the east coast, south of Rothesay, is now the family seat.

Kames Castle is a sixteenth-century tower-house that was built on foundations as old as the fourteenth century. It housed the Bannatynes of Kames, chamberlains to the Stewart kings when Bute was a royal demesne. The last of the line died in 1780. His nephew was the advocate who became Lord Kames in 1799, a founder member of the Bannatyne Club, which published a series of books dealing with Scottish history and literature.

Outside Rothesay, Bute is a quiet and peaceful island, with much of interest for the antiquarian or naturalist. Many interesting and informative guidebooks can be obtained from the Tourist Information Centre in Rothesay or from Bute Museum. There is plenty of outdoor entertainment on Bute. Rothesay Golf Club has an eighteen-hole golf course; there are two other smaller courses on the island, at Port Bannatyne (thirteen holes) and Kingarth (nine holes). There are two pony-trekking centres, at Rothesay and at Kingarth, good fishing in Loch Fad and Loch Ascog, and two cycle-hiring companies in Rothesay. Several leaflets are available locally for walkers, amateur geologists and archaeologists, and car tourists. There is a good island bus service, and also regular coach tours from Rothesay of the main features of interest. There are plenty of taxis. The north end of the island, overlooking the Kyles of Bute, is an area of outstanding natural beauty.

The island of Inchmarnock, a mile (1.6km) offshore from St Ninian's Bay in the south-west of the island, is owned by Ian Branson, cousin of Richard Branson of Virgin Atlantic fame. Its two farms are now unoccupied, although they are still worked. A rare Bronze Age crescentic jet necklace from Inchmarnock is on show in the Bute Museum. St Ninian's Chapel, on Bute, is likely to be one of the earliest Christian sites in Scotland. Ninian, who died in AD422, operated from headquarters at Whithorn, in Wigtownshire. This corner of Bute is one of its most attractive and most peaceful locations.

After many years in the doldrums, Rothesay is rejuvenating itself as a tourist resort. The annual Bute Jazz Festival in May is attracting new visitors. The Marquess of Bute supports small-scale industrial development on the island. Both Bute Fabrics, which exports 80 per cent of its high quality furnishing textiles, and Rothesay Seafoods, which produces and processes rainbow trout on fresh-water Loch Fad and sea-water Loch Ridden, are subsidiaries of companies that belong to the marquess. Flexible Technology Ltd, which provides 150 jobs making printed circuits in a factory purpose-built by the Highlands and Islands Development Board (now the Highlands and Islands Enterprise), is an example of what is possible on an island, given reasonable infrastructure, good transport links to the mainland and initiative. Farming is still an important industry – the island is extremely fertile.

There are plans to establish yachting facilities and in 1990 three government agencies – Argyll and Bute District Council, the Scottish Development Agency and the Highlands and Islands

Development Board – came together to form the Bute Partnership to promote worthwhile projects on the islands for a period of three years. Tourism in Bute grew up to serve the Glasgow working classes from late Victorian times until the 1960s. Now the market is different, but the island is adapting to changing circumstances. It deserves to be more widely known.

THE CUMBRAES

The Great Cumbrae and the Little Cumbrae are two small islands in the Firth of Clyde, between Bute and Largs, from where a small car ferry provides a service to the new ferry terminal at Cumbrae Slip at the north end of the Great Cumbrae. There is a frequent bus service to Millport, the only village. The main shipping channel into the Clyde passes to the west of the 'Wee Cumbrae', where there was an important lighthouse. The 'Big Cumbrae', with a population of 1,600, is encircled by 12 miles (19km) of road. Once a popular resort teeming with day-trippers from Glasgow enjoying a day out 'doon the watter', it is now a quieter place.

There is a good network of footpaths around the southern half of the island, which is popular with walkers and cyclists. From the Glaid Stone at the highest point of the island (417ft/127m), there are extensive views over the Clyde Estuary and beyond, including Ben Lomond to the north and the Paps of Jura to the west. The National Water Sports Centre is near the ferry terminal, just around Clashfarland Point from Ballochmartin Bay, where King Haakon of Norway anchored his fleet before the Battle of Largs in 1263. Other leisure facilities include a golf course, bowling club and tennis courts.

The Episcopal Collegiate Church in Millport, which was consecrated in 1876 as the 'Cathedral of The Isles' – the smallest cathedral in Britain – was designed by William Butterfield in a Victorian Gothic style. Its founder was George Frederick Boyle, later the Earl of Glasgow, who was involved in the Oxford Movement in the 1840s. The Millport cathedral was his attempt to rejuvenate the Episcopal Church in Scotland. It has been described as one of the most moving expressions of Victorian architecture and Victorian piety anywhere. The Theology College closed in 1885; the buildings are now used as retreat and holiday accommodation. But it was in the local parish kirk that, in the early nineteenth century, the Reverend James Adam offered up regular prayers 'for the Great and Little Cumbrae and the adjacent islands of Great Britain and Ireland'.

Another architectural feature of Millport is 'The Wedge', reputedly the narrowest house in Britain, with a frontage of only 47in (1.2m). There is a small museum and library in Garrison House.

From 1876 Keppel was the headquarters of the Scottish Marine Biological Association, which moved to Dunstaffnage, near Oban, in 1970. The buildings are now used by the universities of Glasgow and London. There is an interesting aquarium and museum.

The island of Little Cumbrae, which is separated from its larger neighbour by a half-mile channel known as 'The Tan', is uninhabited, barren and private.

THE CUMBRAES
Getting there

Calmac ferry Largs–Cumbrae Slip; passage time: 10 minutes.
Ferry information No vehicle reservations. Frequent service: for timings, contact Caledonian MacBrayne Ltd, The Ferry Terminal, Gourock, Renfrewshire, PA19 1QP. Tel: (0475) 34531; fax: (0475) 37607.
Local ferry office Largs. Tel: (0475) 674134.

Railhead Largs – frequent connections to Glasgow Central. From Glasgow Airport, catch the Largs train at nearby Paisley.

Tourist Information Centre Isle of Cumbrae Tourist Association, 28 Stuart Street, Millport, Isle of Cumbrae, KA28 0AJ. Tel: (0475) 530753.

12
The Irish Sea Islands

RATHLIN

Getting there

Boat from Ballycastle
(50 minutes)
Information Tourist
Office, 7 Mary Street,
Ballycastle, County
Antrim. Tel: Ballycastle
(026 57) 62024/62225.

**Accommodation and
local information**
Rathlin Guesthouse.
Tel: (026 57) 63917.

ALTHOUGH the Irish Sea is now seen as a barrier that separates Great Britain from Ireland, students of archaeology and early history speak of it as a 'culture province' in order to emphasise the fact that in ancient times transport by sea was much easier than travel overland. There was a constant coming and going of people and trade up and down the coasts of both sides of the Irish Sea, and much interaction back and forth between Ireland and Wales, Cornwall, south-west Scotland and Argyll. The folk of all these territories spoke various versions of the same language, which in written form eventually diverged rather dramatically, but in their spoken form were mutually understandable. Culturally, all of the peoples surrounding the Irish Sea have always had a lot in common. Today, they are separated by national boundaries, some relatively recent, and to understand the interconnections they have to make the effort to travel.

RATHLIN

Just outside the northern boundary of the Irish Sea, situated in the North

Channel that separates Antrim from Argyll, is the tiny island of Rathlin, which justifies its inclusion in this book because it is such a wonderful place. Culturally and historically, it could be regarded as part of Argyll and until fairly recently there was regular contact with, for example, the island of Islay to the north.

Rathlin lies 6 miles (9.6km) off the coast of Antrim and is 14 miles (22.5km) from the Mull of Kintyre. It is L-shaped, with one leg 4 miles (6.4km) and the other 3 miles (5km) long; nowhere is it more than 1 mile (1.6km) across, with a land area of just over 5sq miles (13sq km). Its human population of about 100 shares the space with 20,000 birds. The sea-birds – guillemots, razorbills, shearwaters, fulmars, kittiwakes and puffins – breed on the cliffs, some up to 200ft (61m) high, which more or less surround the island.

Access to Rathlin is by motorboat from Ballycastle, a trip that takes about 50 minutes. No cars are carried on the boat, so it is definitely an island to enjoy a walking (or cycling) holiday. The landscape is bare, but beautiful. The underlying geology is chalk and columnar basalt, similar to the Giant's Causeway on the neighbouring Antrim coast. The highest point of the island is Slieveacarn (447ft/136m).

The East Lighthouse on Altacorry Head is visible over a wide area of south-west Scotland. Nearby is Bruce's Cave, one of the places where, during the Scottish Wars of Independence at the beginning of the fourteenth century, Robert the Bruce took inspiration from a web-spinning arachnid and went on to trounce the English at Bannockburn in 1314. It is certainly true that Bruce visited Rathlin in 1306, after his defeat by the English at Perth.

In prehistoric times Rathlin was important for its axe factory. Neolithic farmers were as fussy as farmers are today about buying the best tools for the job, and Rathlin porcellanite could be shaped by skilled craftsmen into sharp-bladed axe heads that were ideal for cutting down virgin forest. The axes were traded all over southern Scotland and northern England, and even further afield. The site of this prehistoric industry was at Brockley, near the middle of Rathlin's longer leg.

There are traces of later peoples on Rathlin: there is a standing stone east of the harbour and an Iron Age fort at Doonmore, north of the axe factory. The remains of a monastery founded by early Christian visitors can be seen at Knockans. However the Vikings plundered it in the ninth century.

From Easter to September there are daily boat crossings from Ballycastle, which allow five hours ashore. A minibus is usually available to transport visitors to the western point of the island. A guest-house and restaurant are situated near the harbour, and sometimes bed and breakfast accommodation can be arranged with some of the forty families who inhabit this lonely island. Apart from looking after visiting birdwatchers, the locals work at farming and lobster-fishing – often both. There is an RSPB warden on the island during the summer season.

THE IRISH SEA ISLANDS

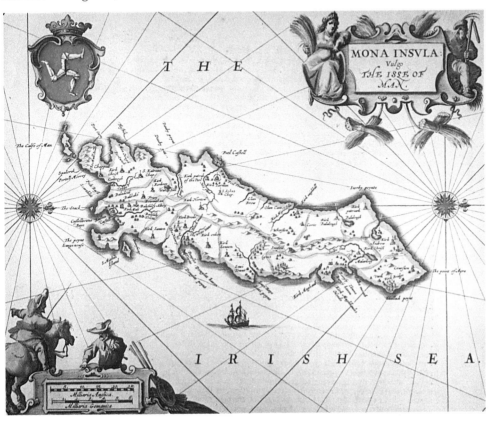

Jansson's map of the Isle of Man, 1646, one of a collection of historic maps in the Manx Museum, Douglas

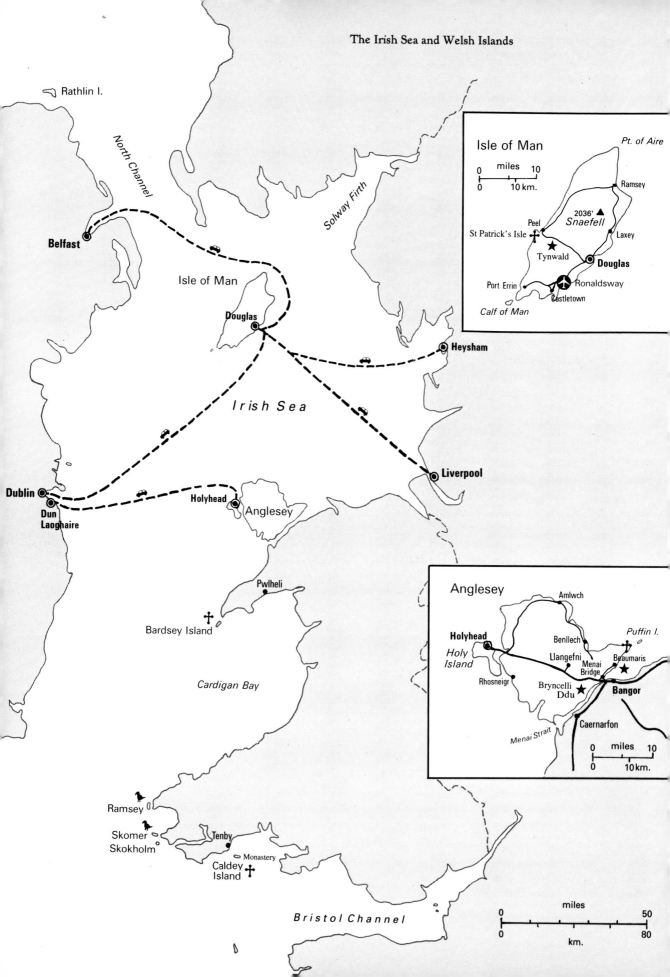

The Irish Sea and Welsh Islands

Rathlin I.

North Channel

Belfast

Solway Firth

Isle of Man

Douglas

Heysham

Irish Sea

Liverpool

Dublin

Dun Laoghaire

Holyhead

Anglesey

Pwlheli

Bardsey Island

Cardigan Bay

Ramsey

Skomer
Skokholm

Tenby

Monastery

Caldey
Island

Bristol Channel

Isle of Man (inset)

Isle of Man

miles 10

10 km.

Pt. of Aire

Ramsey

Peel

St Patrick's Isle

2036' ▲ Snaefell

Laxey

Tynwald

Douglas

Port Errin

Ronaldsway

Castletown

Calf of Man

Anglesey (inset)

Anglesey

Amlwch

Holyhead

Holy
Island

Benllech

Puffin I.

Llangefni

Menai
Bridge

Beaumaris

Rhosneigr

Bryncelli
Ddu

Bangor

Menai Strait

Caernarfon

miles 10

10km.

THE ISLE OF MAN

The ancient Kingdom of Mann lies at the hub of the Irish Sea. Inclined north-east/south-west, it is 32½ miles (52km) long and up to 13½ miles (21.7km) wide, with a land area of about 221sq miles (572sq km). The island is easily accessible by sea and air from all directions, although most passenger traffic is from Heysham, Liverpool, Belfast and Dublin. The Point of Aire, at the north-east tip of the island, is only 16 miles (25.7km) from Burrow Head in Wigtownshire, the site of St Ninian's early Christian monastery at Whithorn.

Getting to the Isle of Man is easy enough, if a little on the expensive side. Manx Airlines fly from Glasgow, Dublin, Belfast, Cardiff, London Heathrow and six regional English airports, including Blackpool, which is only a short half-hour flight from Ronaldsway, the island's airport. In the summer there are additional flights from Newcastle and from Jersey, in the Channel Islands. It is truly, as the Tourist Board says, 'conveniently located in the centre of the British Isles'.

The Isle of Man is an island of contrasts, for here elements of traditional Manx culture survive alongside the modern financial services industry, with all its associated technological and computer wizardry.

The island's history is one of its most attractive features and there is no better place to start learning about 'The Story of Mann' than in the Manx Museum, Douglas. Here a video presentation and an imaginatively designed series of displays give a superb introduction to the Manx heritage and landscape. The geology and natural history of the island are both exceptionally diverse and interesting, and these attributes are attracting increasing numbers of specialist tourists, especially outside the main summer season.

The island's population, which is rising slowly, now stands at about 70,000, making it the third most populous island, after the Isle of Wight and Jersey, in the British Isles. About 40 per cent are native islanders – ie, they were born on the Isle of Man. Manxmen are fiercely independent and there is a small but vociferous Manx nationalist movement. Unfortunately, the last native speaker of Manx Gaelic died in the early 1970s, although a few hundred learners strive to keep it alive.

Nearly half of the population live in and around the main town and ferryport of Douglas, which in recent years has become a major 'offshore' financial centre, offering attractive incentives to both companies and individuals. Offices and banks offering 'international tax consultancy' advice occupy whole streets in Douglas. The town centre has thriving shopping areas and pedestrian precincts, while facing the sea along the promenade are the massed ranks of late-Victorian and Edwardian hotels and guest-houses, looking like rows of wedding cakes in the early morning light. Perhaps the town's cultural and architectural gem is the Gaiety Theatre.

Another feature of the Isle of Man is that there are several smaller centres of population, each with its own attractions. Ramsey, on the north-east coastline, has a population of nearly 6,000, while Peel in the west, with its castle and thirteenth-century cathedral on St Patrick's Isle, has over 3,500. Castletown, on the south coast near the airport, has over 3,000 inhabitants, a fine castle and harbour, and some interesting architecture. The twin villages of Port Errin and Port St Mary, on the south-west corner of the island, have another 4,500 people between them. Nearby is the Cregneash Folk Museum, with restored cottages and a re-creation of farming life in the last century. From Port St Mary there are boat-trips in summer to the Calf of Man, a bird sanctuary that lies off the south-west tip of the island.

The village of Laxey, between Doug-

THE IRISH SEA ISLANDS

THE ISLE OF MAN
Getting there

By boat from Heysham, Lancashire-Douglas, all year; passage time: 3¾ hours; seasonal services from Fleetwood, Liverpool, Dublin and Belfast.

For information, contact the Isle of Man Steam Packet Company, PO Box 5, Douglas, Isle of Man. Tel: Douglas (0624) 661661; fax: (0624) 661065.

By air to Ronaldsway Airport from most UK airports, Dublin and Jersey. For information, contact Manx Airlines Ltd, Isle of Man (Ronaldsway) Airport, Ballasalla, Isle of Man. Tel: (0624) 824111; for reservations, tel: (0624) 824313; fax: (0624) 824578.

Tourist Information Centre Department of Tourism, 13 Victoria Street, Douglas, Isle of Man. Tel: (0624) 674323; fax: (0624) 672872.

(Right) The west coast town of Peel, Isle of Man, showing the beach and harbour (*Isle of Man Tourism*)

Holidaymakers enjoying themselves on the beach at Peel, Isle of Man (*Isle of Man Tourism*)

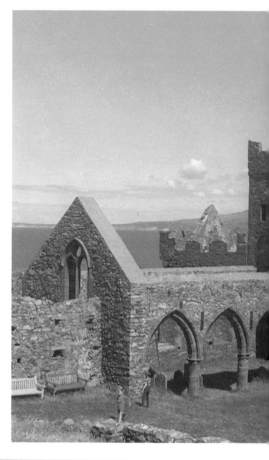

las and Ramsey, has another 1,200 inhabitants and one of the finest industrial museums anywhere in the British Isles – most of it either outdoors or underground. The highlight of the preserved remains is an immense waterwheel, with a diameter of 72½ft (22m). Dating from 1854, it operated various pumps and other bits of machinery in connection with mines in the Laxey Valley. The ore was rich in zinc – 11,000 tons (11,176 tonnes) was produced in 1875 alone – while there was also galena, a lead ore with a rich silver content. On the mainland the problems of flooding in the mines and a power source for associated machinery would have been solved by the latest coal-fired steam engines. But, because of the expense of importing coal into the Isle of Man, the engineers devised the ingenious but technologically obsolete alternative of the Laxey Wheel, which was christened 'Lady Isabella' in honour of

the wife of the island's governor, Charles Hope. The mine closed in 1929.

The Isle of Man has many places of exceptional archaeological and historical interest to visit. There is the usual quota of prehistoric cairns, tombs and standing stones, but several sites are of special interest either for their preservation or because of their evocative surroundings. The Neolithic chambered tomb at Cashtel yn Ard, not far from Ramsey, is well worth a visit, and there are other similar sites in the area. The island is particularly well off for booklets, guides, maps, leaflets of all kinds, and also for some fine monographs on different aspects of the island's history.

Laxey Wheel, the largest waterwheel in the world, christened 'Lady Isabella', forms the focal point of an outdoor museum of industrial archaeology on the east coast of the Isle of Man (*Isle of Man Tourism*)

(Left) The monastic buildings inside Peel Castle, on St Patrick's Island: the buildings are edged and decorated with red sandstone

THE IRISH SEA ISLANDS

This replica Viking longship, *Odin's Raven*, sailed from Norway to the Isle of Man in 1979, to celebrate the millennium of the Manx parliament

A typical Manx milestone, near Castletown

Manx cat, a genetic mutation – miaowtation? – which has made the Isle of Man a household word all over the world (*Isle of Man Tourism*)

One rather disappointing monument is 'King Orry's Grave', which is surrounded by buildings and a road, near Laxey. This is the remains of a Neolithic chambered cairn which is probably over four thousand years old, while 'King Orry' is, in fact, a historical figure, Godred Crovan, King of Mann from 1079 to 1095. In Manx his name was Gorree; in English he was King Gorree – the words became misdivided as 'King Orree'. He is an important figure in Manx tradition.

It was King Orry who defeated the Manx Celtic population in 1079 and brought the island under the jurisdiction of Norway, as described in Chapter 6. The Norse era came to an end in 1266, when all Norse territories in the Hebrides, including the Isle of Man, were ceded by Norway to the Scottish crown. Many place-names reflect the centuries of Norse occupation, and many of the island's institutions, notably the House of Keys (the Manx parliament) and the annual Tynwald ceremony at St John's recall this side of Manx heritage. The very word 'Manx' comes from the Norse *manskr*, meaning 'of Mann'.

Visitors who are interested in churches and abbeys will find many beautiful places to visit, most notably Rushen Abbey, at the south end of the island. The story of the early Christian period is perhaps best understood by visiting the Manx Museum, which has a fine collection of Christian stone crosses, including some from the medieval period. Another collection of early crosses can be seen in a shelter in Maughold churchyard.

The island has an excellent bus service, but the visitor has other, more unusual, alternatives for transport around the island. The Isle of Man Steam Railway operates a steam train from Douglas to Port Erin; branch lines to Peel and Ramsey closed in 1968. But the Manx Electric Railway, which dates from 1893 and still uses its original electric trams, still runs from Douglas to Ramsey and is much used by local people as their normal means of transport. And, the Snaefell Mountain Railway, the first and only electric mountain railway in the British Isles, still runs from Laxey to the summit of Snaefell – a fine tourist attraction, leading to a fine view from the 2,036ft (620m) mountain.

As already discussed in Chapter 6, the Isle of Man is a crown territory that owes allegiance to the British monarch, but constitutionally it is not part of the United Kingdom of Great Britain and

Victorian horse-drawn
trams still ply the
two-mile length of
Douglas Promenade
(*Isle of Man Tourism*)

The Victorian steam
railway is popular
with tourists on the
Isle of Man. The palm
trees grow tall in the
island's mild climate
(*Isle of Man Tourism*)

THE IRISH SEA ISLANDS

The gateway to Anglesey – the Menai Suspension Bridge, looking towards the mountains of North Wales (*MAGMA, Anglesey*)

Bangor Pier and the Welsh mountain, viewed from Anglesey (*MAGMA, Anglesey*)

Northern Ireland. Most visitors come with at least some idea that the Isle of Man is 'different'. We have all heard of tail-less Manx cats, the TT motorcycle races and the three-legged symbol of the island, but there are many other aspects of island life that make it different from the rest of the British Isles.

After the financial services industry, tourism contributes most to the island's economy – in recent years about 11 per cent, with over 3,000 people employed in tourism and tourist-related enterprises. In 1990 320,000 visitors came to the Isle of Man between May and September, which sounds a lot until it is compared with the heyday of mass tourism on the island before World War I – 640,000, mainly from the industrial towns of Lancashire, came in 1913. The reduction in numbers has meant some changes, notably a reduction in the number of 'accommodation providers' from about 1,000 in 1980 to only 420 in 1990. The type of visitor is changing and so are their expectations – for example, while over 120,000 day-trippers visited in 1980, there were only 35,000 in 1990. This is still, of course, a considerable influx. However, although the numbers

Newborough Forest and Snowdonia, looking south-east across the Malltraeth estuary from Bodorgan, Anglesey (*MAGMA, Anglesey*)

191

A view through the
trees at Ramsey golf
course, on the
sheltered north-east
coast of the Isle of
Man (*Isle of Man
Tourism*)

of visitors may be shrinking, the people who still come are spending more money and are expecting higher standards of accommodation and entertainment, so the future for tourism on the island looks bright.

Agriculture is still the mainstay for most of the island, although not for most of its population – probably over 50,000 of the 70,000 islanders live in its towns. Fishing, once a major island industry, especially in Peel and Douglas, is sadly a shadow of its former self. Manx kippers are still produced in the traditional way; for promotional purposes, the island's imaginative Department of Tourism sent a kipper to one thousand travel agents with the message 'This is not a red herring'! Since a kipper is, in fact, a red herring (its traditional name), this was particularly cunning marketing.

One final word: don't forget to try the local brew – Glen Kella Manx Whiskey. If you should by any chance happen to encounter some cold, windy, wet and miserable weather, it helps. The locally brewed beer is also worth trying.

ANGLESEY

Anglesey measures 21 miles (33.7km) from north to south by 23 miles (37km) from east to west at its maximum extent, with a land area of 276 sq miles (715 sq km). It is an undulating, fertile island, formerly the granary of Wales, from which it is often called *Môn mam Cymru*, 'Anglesey, the mother of Wales'. Its highest point, near Amlwch on the north coast, is only 580ft (177m), although on Holy Island, Holyhead Mountain soars to a height of 722ft (220m). Yet the scenery often includes views of high rugged mountains, for Snowdon and its surrounding peaks are only 10 miles (16km) to the south-east.

Ynys Môn, to give it its Welsh name, lies off the north-west coast of Wales, separated from the mainland by the narrow Menai Strait, which is bridged in two places, by the Menai Suspension Bridge and the Britannia Bridge. The Britannia Bridge was opened in 1850 and consisted of twin metal tubes carrying the railway to Holyhead for the Irish ferry. These were destroyed by fire in 1970 and the replacement is a double-decker bridge carrying both the railway and the main trunk road into Anglesey, the A5(T). The Menai Suspension Bridge was designed by Thomas Telford and opened in 1826. Still popular with visitors, it can get very congested.

The Menai Strait is more like a river than a stretch of ocean, but has dangerous tidal currents. Its western end is guarded by Caernarfon Castle. At the eastern end of the strait is the cathedral city of Bangor, a prosperous university town, and the main shopping centre for most islanders. The eastern entrance to Menai Strait is dominated by the medieval castle of Beaumaris, a World Heritage Site. The castle was founded by Edward I in 1295. The town has many interesting nooks and crannies and is perhaps the most anglicised of the island's settlements, with streets of Victorian and Edwardian terraced houses. But, without doubt, it is Anglesey's treasure. The delightful Museum of Childhood is on Castle Street.

The island of Anglesey has a population of about 72,000. This figure includes the 14,000 inhabitants of Holyhead, which, although technically on the separate Ynys Gybi (Holy Island), is firmly joined to Anglesey by road and rail. The main settlements are Llangefni (4,250), Amlwch (3,750), Menai Bridge town (3,000), Benllech (3,000), Llanfairpwll (3,000), Valley (2,400), Beaumaris (2,100), Llandegfan (2,000) and Rhosneigr (1,600). In addition there are many smaller villages, with populations ranging from a few hundred to just under one thousand. It seems churlish to pick out one place from among so many, but the old market town of Llanerchymedd, 'the glade of the mead', lies only 6 miles (9.6km) north of Llangefni and should be accessible to most visitors.

Locally produced guidebooks to the islands so far described have not been mentioned as they tend to be ephemeral, go out of print and date quickly, but one of the guides to Anglesey is an exception – *Môn, mam Cymru: the Anglesey Guide*, edited by Robert Williams with text by Philip Steele, is a model of its kind. Attractively designed and produced, with lots of colour photographs, it is an essential and inexpensive purchase for any visitor. Of particular value are the pages of 'Anglesey Listings', that give concise information on everything from bank cashpoints to medical emergencies. If every island produced a guide like this, it would greatly enhance the 'island experience' for both residents and tourists.

On the north coast of Anglesey, near Cemaes Bay, is one of the more bizarre tourist attractions on any of Britain's islands – the Wylfa Nuclear Power Station. There is an Information Centre and guided tours of the complex. Almost as unlikely is the aluminium processing plant on Holy Island, run by Anglesey Aluminium Metal Ltd, which produces 118,000 tons (120,000 tonnes) of primary aluminium annually. To illustrate the company's policy of inflicting the minimum impact on the environment there is an adjacent nature reserve and a farm with an award-winning herd of Holstein pedigree cattle. The employment which these enterprises bring to the island is crucial, but visitors will shudder at the thought of similar developments on some of the other islands around Britain's coasts.

Perhaps the most attractive feature of Anglesey is its coastline: bay after bay of sheltered, safe, sandy beaches. Most of the 125 miles (201km) of coastline is designated as 'areas of outstanding natural beauty' and the Anglesey Coastal Heritage project co-ordinates conservation efforts. There are miles and miles of coastal walks, and a Heritage Centre at Aberffraw.

ANGLESEY
Getting there

There are long-distance buses and trains from London to Bangor and Holyhead (4 hours by train); if you are coming by train from elsewhere in the UK, change at Chester or Crewe. Ferries sail from Holyhead to Dublin (Dun Laoghaire); passage time: 3½ hours.

Tourist Information Centres Salt Island, Holyhead; tel: (0407) 762622; Llanfairpwll Railway Station, tel: (0248) 713177.

A souvenir platform ticket from the railway station in Anglesey with the longest name in the world

Aerial view of
Beaumaris, whose
castle guards the
northern entrance to
the Menai Strait
(*MAGMA, Anglesey*)

The chambered cairn
at Bryncelli Ddu, near
Brynsiencyn,
Anglesey (*MAGMA,
Anglesey*)

CALDEY

Caldey is the only other island off the coast of Wales with a resident working population; most of the other islands, like Skoholm, Skomer, Ramsey and Bardsey are nature reserves with limited access. The island of Caldey is home to a small monastery of Cistercian monks and their support staff. Their church has been in use for fifteen centuries. It lies only 3 miles (5km) from the Welsh town of Tenby, so is not desperately isolated, but anybody who goes there comments on the peace and tranquillity of the place. It is indeed a haven of peace in a restless world.

One of the early abbots of the early Christian monastery on Caldey was St Samson, who is also known in the Channel Islands. An ogham stone with its strange script is a memorial to that period. The early monastery was destroyed in a Viking raid, but it was reconstituted in the Middle Ages as a Benedictine foundation. It was sold to the Cistercians in 1928. St Margaret's Island is connected to Caldey at low water. Now a nature reserve, it has been eaten away by limestone quarries.

Part of the Anglesey coastal footpath, north of Moelfre, which is well maintained and popular with visitors (*MAGMA, Anglesey*)

13
The English Islands

ALTHOUGH the English flock in hordes to other people's islands, especially in the sunnier parts of the world, they have some marvellous examples of their own to visit.

ISLES OF SCILLY

The Isles of Scilly are just a few scraps of land, amounting only to 6sq miles (15.5 sq km) in all, lying 25 miles (40km) off the south-west coast of Cornwall. Native Scillonians would perhaps claim that to be described as 'English' is a slur on their Celtic cultural background, but here we use the term geographically.

Like the Shetland Islands at the opposite extreme of the British Isles, the Scillies are a flooded landscape and are slowly sinking beneath the waves like the legendary Atlantis which tradition places somewhere to their south-west. If the sea level fell by 30ft (9m), all the Isles of Scilly would be connected again; but if the sea level rises, more of the islands will disappear beneath the waves. As some of the islands were still joined together in the first century AD, there are several places where prehistoric buildings can be seen at low tide.

Some may date to the Bronze Age – 1500BC or thereabouts.

There are about two hundred islands and substantial rocks in this archipelago, but only the five largest are inhabited: St Mary's, St Martin's, Bryher, Tresco and St Agnes. The total population is just over 2,000, of whom 1,600 live on St Mary's. The islands are all tiny; the largest, St Mary's, is less than 2½sq miles (6.4sq km). They are part of the Duchy of Cornwall, which owns the freehold of all the islands except for parts of St Mary's, including most of Hugh Town, which was sold to the sitting tenants in 1949. In 1985 the duchy handed over the management of the untenanted land in Scilly to the Isles of Scilly Environmental Trust on a 99-year lease, to protect and enhance the natural environment of the islands.

In 1990 conservationists lost a battle to prevent the expansion of the island's airport; the runway was extended to accommodate larger aircraft and to provide a greater margin of safety. As the accommodation resources of the Scillies are fully stretched in the summer season, there is no real danger of the islands being overwhelmed by tourists (any

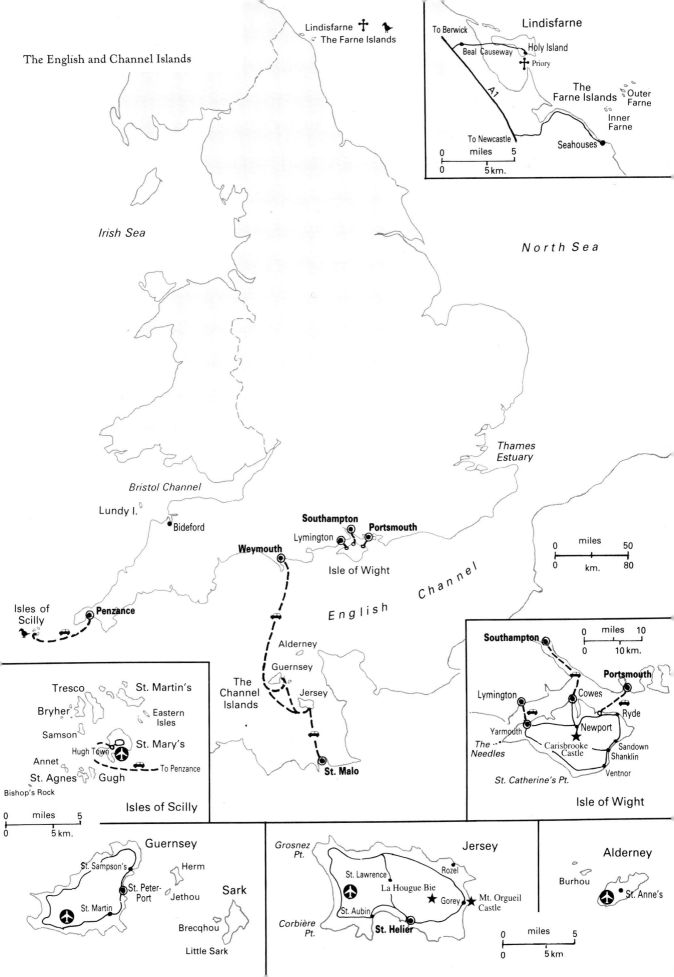

The English and Channel Islands

Lindisfarne
The Farne Islands

Irish Sea

North Sea

Lindisfarne
To Berwick
Beal Causeway
Holy Island
Priory
A1
The Farne Islands
Outer Farne
Inner Farne
To Newcastle
miles
0   5
0   5 km.
Seahouses

Thames Estuary

Bristol Channel

Lundy I.
Bideford

Southampton   **Portsmouth**
Lymington
Weymouth
Isle of Wight

English   Channel

Penzance

Isles of Scilly

Alderney
Guernsey
Jersey

The Channel Islands

miles
0   50
0   80
km.

Southampton
miles
0   10
0   10 km.

Lymington
Cowes
Portsmouth
Ryde
Yarmouth
Newport
The Needles
Carisbrooke Castle
Sandown
Shanklin
St. Catherine's Pt.
Ventnor

Isle of Wight

Tresco   St. Martin's
Bryher
Eastern Isles
Samson
Hugh Town   St. Mary's
Annet
St. Agnes   Gugh
Bishop's Rock
To Penzance

St. Malo

Isles of Scilly

miles
0   5
0   5 km.

St. Sampson's
St. Peter-Port
St. Martin
Herm
Jethou
Sark
Brecqhou
Little Sark

Guernsey

Grosnez Pt.
St. Lawrence
Rozel
La Hougue Bie
St. Aubin
Gorey
Mt. Orgueil Castle
Corbière Pt.
St. Helier

Jersey

miles
0   5
0   5 km

Burhou
St. Anne's

Alderney

The garrison on the
Isles of Scilly

more than they are already), but it is certainly possible that the number of day-trippers could continue to grow.

All the islands are places to explore at a leisurely pace and to appreciate the joys of nature. Vehicles are unnecessary, as the islands are all so small. During the summer season a generous choice of boat-trips is available to the outlying islands, with seals, puffins and shearwaters perennial favourites with the visitors.

The settlement of Hugh Town on St Mary's is well endowed with facilities: shops, banks, restaurants, cafés and hotels. The Isles of Scilly Museum in Church Street is a good place to learn about the history and environment of the islands. A favourite pastime with all visitors is collecting sea-shells, of which

The town of St Mary's on the Isles of Scilly

St Mary's Harbour, Scilly, on a peaceful summer's afternoon

there is a great variety; an exhibition in the museum identifies many different types. Built on a narrow isthmus joining the two higher parts of the island, Hugh Town seems very precarious and liable to be washed away in winter storms, but it has been there since the sixteenth century. All the islands have interesting archaeological and historical sites. Guided walks are easy to follow and good guide-books for all the islands are available from the Tourist Information Centre. The climate of the Scillies is extremely mild by mainland standards and many sub-tropical and semi-tropical plants, trees and shrubs can be found in the islands' gardens. The growing of flowers (and bulbs) for the UK market is one of the local industries, together with fishing and a little farming – and, of course, tourism.

The history of the Isles of Scilly can be seen in the coastal defences of various periods which are preserved all around the islands. Star Castle, which overlooks St Mary's Harbour, and Cromwell's Castle on Tresco are two fine examples of surviving fortifications. During the English Civil War the islands were held for the king and heavily defended. In modern times, the islands were occupied and fortified by hundreds of servicemen in 1914 and in 1939–45. In recent times, the islands have been patronised as holiday places by some senior UK politicians, and this, coupled with the personal interest of the Prince of Wales who counts the Duchy of Cornwall among his titles, has brought added publicity and added interest to the islands.

LUNDY

The island of Lundy, which means 'puffin island' in Norse, stands in the middle of the Bristol Channel, 11 miles (17.7km) north of Hartland Point, although the nearest harbours are at Bideford and Ilfracombe, both about 24 miles (38.6km) distant. The island is 3 miles (5km) long and ½ mile (800m) wide, and at its highest the sea cliffs are 400ft (122m) above the Atlantic Ocean. It commands fine views of the Welsh and English coasts. It is administered on behalf of the National Trust by the Landmark Trust, which restores historic dwellings for use as self-catering holiday homes.

Throughout the year, weather permitting, there are day-trips to Lundy from Bideford in North Devon – a two-hour trip gives ample time ashore to explore the island. Exact timings depend on the tide. No pets are permitted and landing is not absolutely guaranteed if weather conditions are unsuitable. For information and bookings contact the Lundy Office on Bideford Quay; tel: (02372) 70422. There is a mid-thirteenth century castle built by Henry III and an early chapel dating possibly to the fourth century AD. The Old Light, which was built in massive granite blocks in 1820, stands on the highest point of the island. There is another lighthouse at the north end.

ISLE OF WIGHT

The Isle of Wight has the largest and densest population of any of the islands around the British coasts and has probably been visited by a larger proportion of the population of southern England than any other island in this book. The Isle of Wight Tourist Board reckons that over one and a half million British and foreign visitors make the trip each year. The shortest crossing is by Hovercraft from Southsea to Ryde, which takes only eight minutes.

Once you are on the island, it is easy to get around. The island bus company is Southern Vectis, which blankets the island with its routes. It operates bus tours as well as scheduled services, and sells Rover tickets. There is a railway from Ryde to Shanklin, operated by British Rail, and also a steam railway from Havenstreet to Wootton.

Shaped like a diamond, the Isle of Wight is divided from the coastline of the south of England by the sheltered waters of the Solent, which is 3 miles (5km) wide. Spithead, where naval reviews take place, is the area between Ryde and Portsmouth, where there is a large naval base. The island is 23 miles (37km) from east to west and 13 miles (21km) from north to south, with a population of over 110,000 in 147sq miles (380sq km). Some older readers may recall being told at school that the Isle of Wight could accommodate the entire population of the world, standing bunched up together. If it was ever true, surely it is no longer possible!

The Isle of Wight has a long history. The landscape has been farmed since the Beaker people arrived in 2000BC

and many traces of their activities remain. It is thought that the Solent became flooded as late as the Bronze Age – how the Isles of Scilly were inundated and much reduced in land area at this time has already been discussed. The present name of the island is thought to have come with the continental tribe known as the Belgae, who arrived in the first century BC and called the island *wiht*, meaning 'raised' (from the sea), perhaps preserving a folk memory of Bronze Age floods. The Romans called it *Vectis* – a version preserved by the local bus company.

During the English Civil War, Charles I fled to the Isle of Wight, to Carisbrooke Castle. Eventually, he was imprisoned in Carisbrooke, from where he was taken to London and beheaded

Carisbrooke Castle, fortress centre of the island from earliest times, first appears in the historical record a *Wihtgaraburgh* (*IWTO*)

THE ENGLISH
ISLANDS

(Right) At the west
tip of the island are
the chalky pinnacles
of The Needles, and
Alum Bay (*IWTO*)

Snow-white chalk
cliffs rise from the
salty waters of
Freshwater Bay, near
the western end of the
Isle of Wight. The
Victorian Poet
Laureate Tennyson
had a home here
(*IWTO*)

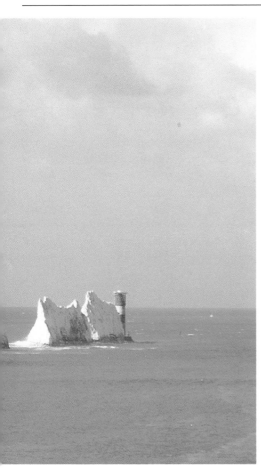

(Above) Every August Cowes hosts the premier events in the world's yachting calendar in the waters of the Solent (*IWTO/ Peter Titmuss*)

Ventnor, with its famous landslip Undercliff, was once the smuggling capital of the Isle of Wight (*IWTO*)

ISLE OF WIGHT

Getting there

By sea several companies run ferries from the English mainland: from Lymington to Yarmouth, from Southampton to Cowes, and from Portsmouth and Southsea to Fishbourne and Ryde.

British Rail has stations adjoining the ferry terminals at Portsmouth and Lymington, and there are connecting buses from the stations at Southampton and Southsea.

Airport Bembridge-Southampton by Air Sarnia. Tel: (0481) 822283.

Tourist Information Centre Isle of Wight Tourist Office, Quay Store, Town Quay, Newport, Isle of Wight, PO30 2EF. Tel: (0983) 524343; fax: (0983) 521606.

in 1649. Queen Victoria used Osborne near Cowes as a winter residence for many years. This really put the island on the tourist map and it became a popular resort. When Queen Victoria died in 1901, Edward VII presented Osborne House to the nation. Her apartments and personal possessions are preserved as a museum and are visited each year by thousands of tourists.

The Isle of Wight is one island where visitors can never complain that there is nothing to do. There are dozens of tourist attractions: theme parks, fun parks, craft centres, country parks, historic buildings, sporting and leisure facilities, and five vineyards. The Tourist Information Office provides comprehensive information on local attractions. Its accommodation brochures are bulging with information on hotels, guesthouses, caravan parks, camping sites, self-catering units and holiday camps – there is something for everybody and in generous quantities.

There is only one week in the year when accommodation is hard to find and that is during 'Cowes Week', a yachting extravaganza which fills the waters of the Solent with boats of all descriptions and the pubs of the Isle of Wight with their crews. It is a spectacular week and is a premier yachting event not just of the UK or Europe, but worldwide. Nine separate yachting clubs hold races, foremost of which is the Royal Yacht Squadron, the ultimate in exclusivity.

Near the western tip of the island, on the coast, is the town of Freshwater. A feature of the Isle of Wight is the perversity of the place-names. Newport is in the middle of the island (although it is on the River Medina); Newtown is one of the oldest villages on the island, and so on with Ryde, Blackwater and others. The perversity of the island's place-names is a godsend for the manufacturers of picture postcards, but the locals are a little weary of it, especially of the 'Cowes' joke – yes, the Isle of Wight

ferry really is brown in colour and comes out of Cowes – or maybe it was once, for the ferries there today are red!

Tennyson, the Victorian poet laureate, lived just outside Freshwater for thirty years. Here he wrote 'The Charge of the Light Brigade' and entertained Lewis Carroll and Charles Kingsley. The island seems to have had an attraction for Victorian literary figures: Keats, Longfellow, Swinburne, Dickens and Charles and Mary Lamb all worked here. West of Freshwater, at the western extremity of the island, are The Needles – dramatic, sharp pinnacles of chalk, which are separated by sea erosion from the cliffs. Three of these rock stacks survive; a fourth, known as 'Lot's Wife', crashed into the sea in a storm in 1764. At Alum Bay, just north-east of The Needles, the sandstone cliffs are famous for the extraordinary coloured stripes – twenty-one in all – which are the result of varying amounts of iron salts and clay in the sandstone. The colours range from white to brick-red to brown, and souvenirs of all kinds are sold, exploiting this unusual natural resource. Examples of Victorian art incorporating these sands in all sorts of ways can be seen in the museum at Carisbrook Castle, just outside Newport.

Although the Isle of Wight is sometimes too crowded for connoisseurs of islands, there is no denying its attractions. It is a great place to spend a holiday, especially with children. As the tourist market changes, the island will have to work hard to keep up the numbers – perhaps the trends seen in other places will take place here, too. But judging from the numbers of new attractions opening up every year, the marketing strategies used by the local Tourist Office are proving successful.

The Isle of Wight provides a gentle introduction to what islands are all about, giving some of its visitors the confidence to tackle somewhere more demanding and remote.

LINDISFARNE

The Holy Island of Lindisfarne and the other Farne Islands all lie off the coast of Northumbria, between Bamburgh and Berwick. Lindisfarne is connected to the mainland by a causeway which is covered at high tide. It is L-shaped, covering less than 2sq miles (5sq km) with a resident population of about 200. A Celtic monastery was founded on the island by Aidan from Iona in AD635. Nothing material remains from this period – only the emptiness, tranquillity and solitude which attracted Aidan to Lindisfarne in the first place.

The Lindisfarne Gospels, which are beautifully illuminated manuscripts dating to around 700, represent (with the Iona *Book of Kells*) the finest work of the Celtic period. The original is preserved and exhibited in the British Library in London (formerly the British Museum). This important Christian settlement was first attacked by Danish Vikings in 793 and was finally obliterated in 875. Its most famous abbot was St Cuthbert, who died in 687 and was buried on the island. When the Vikings threatened, the monks took Cuthbert's body to Durham for safe keeping. In 1083 a Benedictine priory was founded and the Christian presence was re-established. In architecture, it is very like its mother church at Durham. The medieval parish church dates mainly from the twelfth and thirteenth centuries. A facsimile of the Lindisfarne Gospels is kept in the church. Lindisfarne Castle was built about 1550.

FARNE ISLANDS

Of this group of twenty-eight uninhabited islands and rocks, only fifteen are visible at high tide. St Cuthbert picked Farne Island, which is also known as Inner Farne, as his retreat from the hustle and bustle of the monastery at Lindisfarne. From 676 he spent eight years there and was visited by hundreds of pilgrims. He was made Bishop of Lindisfarne in 684 and was forced to leave his lonely cell.

The Farne Islands have become part of the folklore of the British Isles due to the heroism of Grace Darling, who, with her aged father, the lighthouse keeper, rescued the survivors of the *Forfarshire*, which was wrecked at Longstone Lighthouse in 1838. In appalling conditions they were only able to save nine people, but they became national celebrities. Grace died four years later at the age of 27 and is buried at Bamburgh church. Her boat is preserved in the Memorial Museum opposite the church.

FARNE ISLANDS

For information on accommodation and guided tours in the area, contact the Northumbria Tourist Board, Aykley Heads, Durham, DH1 5UX. Tel: (091) 384 6905; fax: (091) 386 0899.

(Above) Lindisfarne Castle, a stronghold built in 1549 on Aidan's Holy Island, off the coast of Northumbria (*Berwick Borough Council*)

Herring boat sheds on the Holy Island of Lindisfarne (*Berwick Borough Council*)

14
The Channel Islands

VICTOR HUGO, who had a house in Guernsey, once described the Channel Islands as '. . . fragments of France chopped into the sea and picked up by England'. The people of the bailiwicks of Guernsey and Jersey are proudly independent and bring a different perspective to their history and culture, compared to that of the British mainland. The Channel Islands are not part of the United Kingdom, but owe allegiance directly to the British Crown.

GUERNSEY

Guernsey is triangular in shape, measuring about 7 miles (11km) from north to south and 7 miles (11km) across the southern coast, with a land area of 25sq miles (65sq km), into which are squeezed about 59,000 inhabitants. Some green fields survive on which the famous Guernsey cows graze, but many acres are covered by glasshouses, filled with tomatoes and other fruits.

Guernsey coastline north of St Sampsons, near Vale Castle

A nineteenth-century
view of St Peter Port,
Guernsey

Geologically, most of Guernsey is made up of bluish-grey granite, which looks at its best in sunshine after a shower, but can look rather drab on a cloudy day. It is, however, excellent building stone. A large chunk of the northern part of the island is made up of much younger igneous rocks, the result of volcanic activity. And, strangely to one who is used to the rocks of the Hebrides, there are outcrops of gneiss in the south-west and west of the island. Before the last Ice Age, all of the Channel Islands were connected by dry land to the south of England; the inundation occurred about eight thousand years ago.

The main settlement and ferry port is St Peter Port, on the sheltered east coast. It is a gem of a town, very French looking and very photogenic. As the morning sunshine streams over the smaller islands of Herm and Sark onto the houses, hotels and public buildings of St Peter Port, it is truly a beautiful place. The harbour contains commercial quays, the car ferry terminal and an enormous yachting marina, all guarded by Castle Cornet, of which the earliest parts date from the thirteenth century.

Unlike the Isle of Man, Guernsey is most definitely not 'an island caught in time'. The last twenty years have seen tremendous changes – whether for the better is a matter of great debate. As always, there are gains and losses. The growth of St Peter Port as an international financial services town has not caused serious physical damage to the beautiful townscape, but it has brought a changing outlook and caused social changes.

Foremost among these changes is the erosion of the local patois, a dialect of Normandy French, which is of great interest to linguists. There are less than two thousand speakers of patois left, and the number is declining almost daily. For long enough it was thought to be a social stigma to speak it and one native speaker described how his mouth was washed out with carbolic soap by his French-speaking mother for calling a cow *vacqe* rather than the Parisian *vache*.

Much of Guernsey is covered by

glass, but the fruit industry is in serious decline now. Tourism is an important industry, worth over £120 million annually to the island's economy. Many visitors bring their own cars, but in recent years the car-hire firms have built up that alternative. Unfortunately, there are far too many cars on Guernsey, but car tourists are mainly confined to the coast road and the few two-lane roads joining the main villages. Most of the interior of Guernsey is effectively out of bounds to car tourists, partly because of the pitiful signposting, but mainly because the narrow, twisty, high-sided lanes mean that even when you know where you are going, you can only proceed at a snail's pace. It is far better to explore these areas by bicycle, or better still, on foot. The local car-hire firms, anticipating some of these problems, have branded all their cars with an 'H' on the front and back – a warning to residents to steer clear and be prepared for sudden stops. Continental visitors must find driving especially horrendous, as traffic keeps to the left; in the lanes this is rather academic, as there is only room for one car anyway.

Many people have commented on the 'Frenchness' of Guernsey in both its rural and town environments, in its place-names and food, and in what is left of its language. While all this is certainly noticeable, above all Guernsey is distinguished from all other islands in this book by its fortifications: castles, martello towers, and German concrete bunkers and towers. All of the Channel Islands were occupied by the German army after the fall of France in the summer of 1940. The story of the German occupation is told in the Museum of Occupation which has an interesting collection of paraphernalia of the time, including a period tea-room. It was a difficult time, especially after the D-Day invasion in June 1944 cut off the eleven thousand strong German garrison from supplies. They finally surrendered on 9 May 1945, amid scenes of celebration.

The story of the earlier history of the island of Guernsey and the other islands that make up the bailiwick of Guernsey is told in the fine Museum and Art Gallery in the Candie Gardens, St Peter Port. A Victorian bandstand has been incorporated into a purpose-built museum, which opened in 1979 and promptly won an award as Museum of the Year. The museum bookshop sells a good selection of material about the history and archaeology of the island. The bandstand is used as a tea-room.

Fort Grey, on the west coast of Guernsey in Rocquaine Bay, opened as a museum of shipwrecks in 1975. The Fort itself was erected in 1804 as part of the island's defences against Napoleon. Guernsey's new Maritime Museum in Castle Cornet, guarding the entrance to St Peter Port Harbour since the thirteenth century, opened in 1991. It traces the maritime history of the island from the famous Roman wreck, through medieval sea-trade to the age of sail, when Guernsey-built merchant ships travelled to the far corners of the globe, and on to the early days of steamships and the railway steamers. The exhibits include a re-creation of a quayside scene in 1900, a restored fishing boat and a scale model of St Peter Port Harbour.

The National Trust of Guernsey, which was founded in 1960, runs a small folk museum in the old stable buildings at Saumarez Park. Here the daily life of the country people of the island before the modern electric age can be seen, including a typical farmhouse kitchen, parlour, nursery, bedroom, dairy, washhouse and cider barn complete with cider press. Until the end of the eighteenth century, stone from island quarries was exported, mainly to England – the stone for the steps of St Paul's Cathedral in London is said to have come from Guernsey. Some tools from this industry, and some examples of stone working, are also exhibited. There are also tools and photographs of an important domestic industry – seaweed

GUERNSEY
Getting there

By sea from St Malo and Cherbourg in France, or from the southern English ports of Portsmouth, Poole, Weymouth and Torquay.

By air from twenty-three UK and many continental airports.

Tourist Information Centre Guernsey Tourist Board, PO Box 23, St Peter Port, Guernsey. Tel: (0481) 723552; fax: (0481) 721246.

St Peter Port,
Guernsey, the island's
capital and ferry
terminal

The harbour at St
Peter Port, viewed
from Castle Cornet
which guards its
entrance

(Above) St Martin's parish church, Guernsey; La Gran'mère, a prehistoric Earth Mother statue, guards the entrance to the churchyard

The medieval parish church in St Peter Port, Guernsey. Nearby is a fascinating covered market, part of the very 'French' character of this island

gathering. Known as 'vraic' on Guernsey and as 'wrack' in the Scottish islands, seaweed was cut off the rocks with a special sickle, dried near the foreshore on drying grounds and burned when dry for use as a fertiliser. 'Vraicing' was an important social occasion involving family and neighbours, and was highly regulated. Today, hundreds of tons of vraic are still gathered, although now by tractor-driven mechanical fork-lifts. It is still the custom to put two stones on top of your heap of seaweed on the beach as a sign of ownership.

Cider was made in Guernsey from the sixteenth century, but became a major industry in the nineteenth century

Talbot Valley, Guernsey, in the fertile and sheltered interior of the island (*Guernsey Tourist Board*)

when metal machinery that had been introduced from France replaced the old presses and made small-scale production possible. Cider-making was a skilled and laborious process. In a day's crushing, about half a ton of apples would make 100 gal (450 litres) of juice.

There are some fine archaeological sites on the island, including several chambered tombs, of which the mounds or cairns covering them have been completely robbed away, leaving only the massive slabs and cap-stones of the burial chambers. A feature of Guernsey archaeology is the presence of several pre-Christian 'Earth Mother' stones which have been incorporated into Christian sites. The most famous is La Gran'Mère, standing at the entrance to St Martin's churchyard, just 2 miles (3km) south of St Peter Port, but there are others. Newly married couples put coins and flowers on the grandmother's head for good luck.

Probably the most impressive and most important prehistoric site on Guernsey lies near the fifth tee of the L'Ancresse Common golf course, in the north-east of the island. It was only discovered in 1977 and excavations were completed in 1981. The dig revealed a complex series of stone structures, trapezoidal in shape, dating from around 4600BC. It is principally a burial site, with chambers and a ceremonial courtyard, and may well be the oldest man-made structure in Europe. It produced over thirty-five thousand finds, a selection of which are in the museum in St Peter Port.

There are smaller islands to the east of Guernsey which are administratively part of the bailiwick of Guernsey. Herm is an island of outstanding natural beauty, 5 miles (8km) east of Guernsey and only twenty minutes by catamaran from St Peter Port. It is only 1½ miles (2.4km) long and ½ mile (800m) wide, but is packed with interesting features, including a medieval chapel. The residential population is about 50, but

thousands of day-trippers make the pilgrimage in the summer months to Herm, but on the even smaller neighbouring island of Jethou, which is privately owned, landing is not permitted. Both islands were once the home of the Scottish writer Sir Compton Mackenzie who died on the Hebridean island of Barra.

To the south-east of Herm and 8 miles (13km) east of Guernsey, is the fief of Sark, which is still run more or less on feudal lines by its seigneur. The population is about 550. No cars are permitted. There are day trips from St Peter Port to Sark, although at 3 miles (5km) long by 1½ miles (2.4km) wide, it is too big to see comfortably in a day. There are several hotels and guest-houses.

Alderney, which is even more heavily fortified than Guernsey, is the closest of the Channel Islands to France, being only 8 miles (13km) from Cap de la Hague. It is 21 miles (34km) north-east of Guernsey and has about 2,000 people, although it is only 3½ miles (5.6km) long and 1 mile (1.6km) wide. The Norman-French name for the island is Aurigny, which visitors will recognise as the name of the inter-island airline. There are also connecting flights to England and France.

JERSEY

The largest of the Channel Islands is Jersey, with a population of 80,000 in an island 10 miles (16km) long and 6 miles (9.6km) wide. It is only 12 miles (19km) from the Normandy coast. The island slopes gently to the south from a high point of 450ft (137m) on the north coast, making it ideal for early potatoes and tomato crops. The Jersey 'Royal' is an early potato that first appeared in the 1880s, like the Manx cat an accidental genetic mutation which is now identified with one particular island.

Whereas Guernsey granite is mostly grey or slaty blue in colour, the granite rocks of Jersey are pinker, and therefore

**JERSEY
Getting there**

By sea from St Malo and five other Normandy ports; from Poole, Torquay and Weymouth on the south coast of England. Contact Jersey Tourism for details.

By air from all London airports and thirty regional UK airports and from many continental cities. Contact Jersey Tourism for details.

Tourist Information Centre Jersey Tourism, Liberation Square, St Helier, Jersey, Channel Islands, JE1 1BB. Tel: (0534) 78000; fax: (0534) 35569. Also Information Centre at Weighbridge, St Helier.

warmer, especially in evening light. This gives the whole island a rosy glow, which seems to be enhanced in winter rain, as if the warm summer sun was somehow trapped in the building stone.

The main town and ferry terminal is St Helier, which is dominated by the futuristic buildings of the entertainment and leisure complex of Fort Regent, which stands on the site of a Napoleonic fortress. There are some delightful public buildings, but St Helier does not stand comparison with St Peter Port in Guernsey as an architectural gem, being much more of a mixture of industrial, commercial and tourism-related enterprises.

The story of Jersey's history is told by the Jersey Museums Service at several locations on the island. The geological and archaeological collections are at La Hougue Bie Museum, beside a 40ft (12m) high burial mound dating to before 3000BC. This chambered tomb is very reminiscent of Maes Howe, in the Orkney Islands, and is another reminder of the wide geographical spread of prehistoric cultures, which functioned without the relatively modern complication of national boundaries.

The main island museum is in St Helier, where an early nineteenth-century merchant's house, with modern additions, houses fascinating collections that illustrate the island's history. A favourite with the tourists is Mont Orgueil Castle, a fairy tale medieval complex at Gorey, overlooking a picturesque harbour. The harbour is floodlit at night and looks almost as if it was designed by Disneyworld for the local tourist board. There is a stunning view from the battlements, beautifully kept gardens and picnic areas, and interesting tableaux throughout the castle apartments, with commentaries in both French and English bringing to life some incidents in the history of Jersey since the castle was built in the thirteenth century.

Jersey Heritage, which is the 'trading name' of the museums service that is operated jointly by the Société Jersiaise and the Jersey Heritage Trust, also operates a military museum at Elizabeth Castle, in St Aubin's Bay. It is reached by a causeway at low tide and by ferry at other times. Other attractions are a restored water-mill in St Peter's Valley and a martello tower at St Ouen's Bay, which has been converted into an interpretation centre. Jersey Heritage also

La Hougue Bie, Jersey: an ancient burial tomb with medieval chapels on top

Castle Cornet, Guernsey, viewed from the coast south of St Peter Port

Some typical features of Guernsey island life: blue postal box, German fortifications, and yellow 'give-way' stripe on the road

(Below) Two of the features that assert Guernsey's differences from the UK: yellow telephone boxes and blue post boxes

THE CHANNEL ISLANDS

The southern coastal town of St Aubin's, Jersey, a picturesque and beautiful place

No problems with carbon monoxide here, on the island of Sark, part of the bailiwick of Guernsey – motor vehicles are banned (*Guernsey Tourist Board*)

A picturesque country scene in the sheltered interior of Jersey (*Jersey Tourism*)

hosts a series of special exhibitions, usually at the Sir Francis Cook Gallery, 2 miles (3km) north of St Helier on the Route de la Trinité.

Jersey is definitely an island which needs time to explore. British visitors will already be familiar with many features of its landscape from the BBC television detective series *Bergerac*, in which the hero has pursued villains all over the island, from La Corbière lighthouse to the back streets of St Helier. Unlike Guernsey, a car is a definite advantage. The roads are better, with reasonable signposting, and the distances are greater. There are supposed to be 500 miles (805km) of roads on the island, although many are narrow lanes. There are 70,000 motor vehicles on Jersey, which is too many, including 11,000 hire cars, which, as in Guernsey, are 'branded' with the letter 'H'.

Jersey Tourism produces a generous amount of leaflets and brochures to help the visitor to explore the island, and

there are also many commercial publications. A good map is essential. The twelve parish churches are all well worth visiting and this would make a good way to explore the terrain and achieve an introduction to the lay-out of the island. Arguably the most photogenic is at St Brelade, where the medieval parish church and its Fishermen's Chapel sit on the coast overlooking a sandy bay. The core of the church is twelfth century, and the chapel, which has medieval wall paintings, is thought to stand on the site of an early Christian chapel which would have been at the heart of an early monastic settlement.

One aspect of Jersey life which the visitor is likely to encounter is the presence during the main tourist season of about five thousand Portuguese waiters, barmen, porters and chambermaids. Most come from Madeira and so are islanders themselves. They have been coming to Jersey (and Guernsey) for generations, to provide seasonal labour originally as agricultural workers, but nowadays mainly in the accommodation sector of the tourist industry. Some have settled permanently in the Channel Islands.

Many special events are held each year, some of them important markers in the island's calendar. Most important to the locals is the annual 'Battle of Flowers', a colourful floral carnival with a spectacular parade of floats. It also attracts thousands of tourists and is the high point of the summer season. Other annual events include a Spring Festival, an International Air Rally, a Good Food Festival, and various folk festivals and sporting events, culminating in the Jersey Half Marathon in November.

As on the other Channel Islands, the occupation by German forces during World War II was a very difficult period in island life. A massive underground hospital in St Peter's Valley, which was built by slave labour, was never used and is now a tourist attraction. There are several excellent books on the occupation. This was the last piece of Europe to be liberated, on 9 May 1945. The island surrendered on 1 July 1940, the British garrison having been withdrawn after the fall of France. It was judged that the island could not be defended without a terrible toll of civilian life. No doubt it was viewed as an idyllic posting by the German garrison. The most difficult time was from the invasion of France by Allied forces in June 1944, after which the Channel Islands were cut off from supply and were bypassed by the invading armies. On three occasions the Red Cross ship *Vega* arrived just in time when food supplies were perilously low. In 1942 over one thousand non-Jersey people were deported to Germany.

THE CHANNEL ISLANDS

La Corbière lighthouse, Jersey – a long way from Muckle Flugga!

THE CHANNEL ISLANDS

Mont Orgeuil, Jersey, which was built to defend the island from invaders from the French coast

St Brelade's Parish Church, Jersey, in a picturesque setting overlooking the sea. The building to the right of the church is the Fishermen's Chapel, with restored medieval wall paintings

The castle of Mont Orgeuil, Jersey, above the town of Gorey, seen at night. It has played an important role in the island's history for many centuries (*Jersey Tourism*)

15
Concluding thoughts

THE English writer D. H. Lawrence wrote a short story about a man who is obsessed by islands which came to dominate his life and eventually overwhelm him completely. Bearing in mind Lawrence's interest in sexual symbolism, this story is something to think about both for people who like to visit islands and for those who like to read about them – not to mention people who like to write about them. In several places in this book something of the almost atavistic power of the island experience for residents and visitors alike has been indicated – what the Tourist Boards call 'island magic'. That some powerful force exists is undeniable.

Angus Martin has written about islands in a short but powerful poem:

> Islands are bits of the land
> that prefer their own company,
> recluses that sea and wind
> address in peculiar accents.

Sometimes the 'peculiar accents' of islanders are 'foreign' enough to be incomprehensible to mainlanders, even when they are dialects of standard English. The dialects of Shetland and Orkney, the Gaelic of the Hebrides, the Welsh of Anglesey, the patois of the Channel Islands – these are all barriers to understanding, but are essential elements of the islands described in this book. Already Manx Gaelic has disappeared and the Cornish of the Isles of Scilly, while Scots Gaelic has gone from too many islands already and the Norman dialects of the Channel Islands are declining. Artificial attempts to hold the line are laudable, but of limited value. What is needed most of all is for islanders to stay and to have the self-confidence to use their languages, and for that to happen the rest of us will have to support the island communities to keep them alive.

It is hoped that readers of this book will support their local islands and, where possible, lobby the authorities on their behalf. Hopefully, too, visitors will always act sympathetically without being patronising and will help wherever possible to support island economies. But most of all, it is hoped that readers will go and see the islands for themselves and enjoy their special island magic.

Fertile grazing in the flat landscape of Tiree, once the granary of the Hebrides

Island House, Tiree, once fortified by a castle; now a holiday home for the Duke of Argyll

Acknowledgements

I would like to thank all the many people who helped in the preparation of this book, but especially the following: Murdo Macdonald, archivist of Argyll and Bute District Council, for many leads and good ideas; Alison Todd, Branch Librarian, Campbeltown Public Library, for getting me lots of books; the many island Tourist Officers and their staffs, for their hospitality, for lending me photographs and for answering all my questions; Angus Martin, poet, of Dalintober, Campbeltown, for permission to use the poem on the title page; my editors at David & Charles, especially Faith Glasgow and Alison Elks, for their encouragement and forbearance; Caledonian MacBrayne Limited, Loganair, and Manx Airlines, who helped with travel arrangements; but most of all, the islanders, without whose many kindnesses this book would have not been so much fun.

Photographs, where not credited, are by the author.

Index

Page numbers in **bold** indicate illustrations.

Access, 15
Alderney, 212
Anglesey, **22**, 75, **190-1**, 192-3, **194-5**
Archaeology, 20-31
Arran, **12**, **35**, 169-76

Barra, **7**, **68**, **71**, **86**, 124-8, **127**
Bee-hive huts, 36
Benbecula, 120
Bersu, Gerhard, 21
Book of Kells, 37, 41
Breachacha Castle, Coll, **143**
British Airways, 101
Brodick, Arran, 172
Brodick Castle, **174**
Brown, George Mackay, 101
Bute, 176-81
Buying and island, 10

Caldey, 195
Caledonian MacBrayne, **7**, 10, 57, **62**, 88-9, 108-9, 149, 175-6
Callanish, **30**
Campbell, John Francis, 43-6, **44**
Canna, 80, 141
Carrisbrooke Castle, **201**
Castlebay, Barra, **7**, **86**
Castle Cornet, Guernsey, **210**, **214**
Channel Islands, 75-6, 207-18
Climate, 82
Coll, **31**, **67**, **87**, 141-4
Colonsay, **47**, **71**, **72**, 80, **84-5**, 162-4, **163**
Colonsay House, **166**
Conference tourism, 61
Cumbraes, **179**, 181

Druids, 32-3
Dunvegan Castle, 133

Eigg, 140
Equipment, 13
Eriskay, 124, **126**

Fair Isle, **102-3**

Farne Islands, 205
Finlaggan, Islay, 157, **158**
Finlaggan Trust, 157
Folk museums, 28
Folklore, 43-51

Garvellachs, **36**, **38**, **39**, **59**, 168
Gates, 15
Gigha, 80, 165-8
Goat Fell, Arran, **173**
Guernsey, **27**, **46-7**, **54**, 76, 207-12, **210-11**, **214**

Harris, **34**, 114-17, **115**
Herm, 212
Highland clearances, 64-5

Iona, **38**, 150-3
Iona Abbey, **38**, **152**
Island government, 9, 74-81
Island living, 9-11
Island newspapers, 13
Island passport, 9
Islay, 13, **17**, **34-5**, **50-1**, 81, 154-61, **155**, **160**
Isle of Man, 20-1, **56**, **57**, **58**, **61**, **63**, **77-9**, 77-80, 185-92, **186**, **189**
Isle of Wight, 200-4, **201-3**
Isles of Scilly, 196-200, **198-9**

Jersey, **15**, 21, **22**, **51**, **59**, **75**, 76, 212-19, **216**
Johnson, Dr Samuel, 53, 67, 87, 137, 152-3
Jura, **30**, 44-8, 161-2

Kildalton cross, 35, 157
Kirkwall, **99**

La Corbière lighthouse, **217**
Lawrence, D. H., 220
Laxey Wheel, 187
Lewis, **27**, **30**, **88**, **93**, **110**, 111-14
Lindisfarne, 37, 205, **206**
Lismore, 153-4
Loganair, 101, **127**
Lords of the Isles, 41, 157-8
Lundy, 200

MacCulloch, Sir Charles, 48
MacDonald, Flora, 121, 130
Maes Howe, **24**, 100
Manx cat, **188**
Manx language, 49, 220
Maps, 8, 12, 97, 109, 132, **183**, 184, 197
Martin, Angus, 220
Martin, Martin, 49–50, 52–3
Medical advice, 14–15
Millport, **179**
Mont Orgueil Castle, Jersey, 213, **218–19**
Muck, **139**, 140
Muckle Flugga lighthouse, 105, **106**
Mull, **16**, 146–50, **147**
Mull Little Theatre, 149
Munro, Neil, 43
Murray, Mrs Frances, 55–6
Museums, 29, **79**, 98, 101, 104, 113, 114, 125, 133,
    144, 151, 157, 159–60, 172, 177, 181, 185, 187,
    188, 193, 198, 204, 205, 209, 212, 213

North Uist, **66**, 83, 117–20, **118**, **123**

Oban, **10**, **62**
Orkney, 20, **24**, **31**, 96–101, **98–9**
Oronsay, **25**, **37**, 41–2, 60, **92**, 165

Paps of Jura, **30**, **48**, **162**
Peel Castle, **187**
Populations, 6, 64–73
Population statistics, 68, 73
Portree, Skye, 136

Raasay, **54**, **66**, **67**, **91**, 137–8
Raised beaches, 24
Rathlin, 182–3
Rhum, see Rum
Ring of Brodgar, **31**
Road Equivalent Tariff, 88
Rothesay, Bute, 177, **178**
Rothesay Castle, **178**, 180
Rum, 80, **95**, **139**, 140–1

Sabbatarianism, 15
Sark, 212, **215**
Scalasaig, Colonsay, **163**
Scalpay, 117
Scilly Isles, see Isles of Scilly

St Brendan, 40
St Clement's, Rodel, 34
St Columba, 36–7, 151
St Cuthbert, 36
St Kilda, **19**
St Magnus Cathedral, Kirkwall, 41
St Molaise, 35
St Ninian, 33, 36, 105, 180
St Patrick, 33
St Peter Port, Guernsey, **208–11**
Sark, 212
Self-catering, 16
Shetland, 102–7, **108–9**
Shops, 16
Single-track roads, 14
Skara Brae, **21**, 98, 100
Skye, **55**, **62**, **66**, **86**, 129–37, **134–6**
Small Isles, 138–41
Smith, W. A., 57–60
South Uist, **26**, **42**, **65**, 70, **90**, 121–4, **122–3**
Stornoway, **88–9**, **110**, 111, **112**
Stromness, **98**
Synod of Whitby, 40

Tacitus, 32
Teleworking, 92, 105
Tiree, **23**, **33**, **39**, **83**, 144–6
Tobermory, **16**, **147**, **150**
Tourism, 60–1
Treasure Trove, 29
Tourist Information Centres, 12–13, 21, 49, 100, 104,
    110, 113, 116, 117, 119, 121, 125, 128, 130, 138,
    140, 142, 144, 148, 151, 153, 156, 159, 164, 168,
    170, 172, 177, 181, 182, 185, 193, 196, 204, 209,
    212
Tynwald, 49, 79

Uig, Skye, **133**
Unst, **105**

Vatersay, **128**
Vikings, 41

Weather, 13–14
Western Isles, 108–68
Westray, **99**
Whalsay, **90**